Both Art and Craft

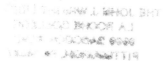

Both Art and Craft

Teaching Ideas That Spark Learning

Diana Mitchell
Sexton High School

Leila Christenbury
Virginia Commonwealth University

National Council of Teachers of English
1111 W. Kenyon Road, Urbana, Illinois 61801-1096

Staff Editor: Bonny Graham

Interior Design: Doug Burnett

Cover Art: Arielle Greenleaf

Cover Design: Jenny Jensen Greenleaf

NCTE Stock Number: 03804-3050

Library of Congress Cataloging-in-Publication Data

Mitchell, Diana.
    Both art and craft: teaching ideas that spark learning/Diana Mitchell,
Leila Christenbury.
        p. cm.
    Collection of columns by Diana Mitchell that originally appeared in the
English journal.
    Includes bibliographical references and index.
    "NCTE stock number: 03804-3050"—T.p. verso.
    ISBN 0-8141-0380-4 (pbk.)
    1. Language arts (Secondary) 2. Activity programs in education. I. Title:
Teaching ideas that spark learning. II. Christenbury, Leila. III. English
journal. IV. Title.

    LB1631 .M49 2000
    428'.0071'2—dc21

                                                            00-055033

To Marilyn Wilson, friend and mentor

To my teachers who, early on, showed the way: Miss Carney (second grade), Mrs. Pendleton (seventh grade), Miss Fountain (Latin), Mrs. Duke (music), Mr. Campbell (mathematics), Mr. Duncan (English), Sister Marita Denise, IHM (French)

Contents

Preface

I was editor of *English Journal (EJ)* for five years (1994–1998), and during that time it was my job to solicit and publish the best articles on all aspects of secondary English teaching. *EJ*, published since 1912 by the National Council of Teachers of English (NCTE), is a well-established, widely read journal, and it was a privilege to be its editor. During my editorship, one of my most important tasks was providing *EJ* readers a balanced magazine containing both theory and practice. As a teacher, I knew well the frustration of picking up an education journal only to find mostly academic discussions and theoretical arguments with precious few practicalities. Under my editorship, *EJ* needed to remain a place where classroom teachers could indeed find suggestions for something to do on Monday morning. While that *something* needed to be sound, based on theory, and workable with real students, it nevertheless should also be practical, clear, and geared to the reality of today's classroom. And it needed to be in every issue of *EJ*.

The only solution was a monthly Teaching Ideas column. And, as far as I was concerned, the only person to write it was Diana Mitchell.

Diana and I have known each other for almost twenty years. We met at NCTE meetings and conferences, and over the years I came to know and value the kind of teaching genius Diana represents. Through conversations, her writing, her presentations at NCTE conferences, her discussions of her classroom and her students, I became familiar with Diana's work and ideas. What has always impressed me about her is her great devotion to the practicality of teaching and her firm grasp of the realities of the classroom. In addition, for Diana there are never just one or two ways to help students grasp a concept or learn a skill; she can come up with a dozen. There are never just a handful of project ideas; she can provide a basketful. And, in Diana's hands, they all ring true: the cornucopia of concepts that Diana Mitchell presents is uniformly solid, sound, and directly related to either an idea or a text. Further, it comes from her long experience in the classroom with real students in real schools.

For me, Diana is a teacher's teacher who, throughout her career in the classroom and in her work with NCTE and *English Journal*, has been a virtual showcase of best practice. When she invited me to Michigan a few years ago to speak to her state teaching organization, I expressed interest in visiting not just her home and her town but also her school. Walking into her classroom at Sexton High School, I saw what I expected to see: a colorful, lively room, packed with books and posters and plants, where her students were as engaged and busy and noisy and funny and smart and irrepressible as I knew they would be. That visit reinforced for me the fact that the *EJ* columns Diana had crafted for five years had come, front and center, from her work with these students and from her experience in the classroom over her long and eventful teaching career.

When I had completed my editorship with *English Journal,* I thought of the wonderful Teaching Ideas columns Diana had written and for which she had received much reader praise and notice. My own students—preservice teachers—had always turned first to her section of *EJ* for advice, direction, and help, and I had used many of her ideas in my own classroom. I decided I should make sure that Diana's columns from *English Journal* didn't stay buried in past issues but that they be collected as a book. Diana has been willing to cooperate in this venture, and for me it has been a labor of love and respect.

Diana Mitchell is the kind of classroom teacher I am still working on becoming. I continue to learn from her and continue to be stimulated by her inventive, joyful approach to teaching. Her columns represent imagination, energy, and all the worthwhile things that we and our students can accomplish in the English classroom. She views a book, a skill, an issue, an idea with fresh eyes and also with appreciation for her multitalented students. Further, like all teachers from whom I have learned, her work stimulates new connections, variations, and interpretations. Diana also insists on the importance of using student interest in her planning because she knows that students who are engaged can perform at superior levels and with a real sense of personal satisfaction.

Teaching is an exciting but often arduous journey. We need companions along the way, master teachers who can inspire and guide. It is my hope that *Both Art and Craft: Teaching Ideas That Spark Learning* will accompany you on your journey and give you help and resources. In this collection of Diana Mitchell's work, may you find, as I have, fresh connections, resources for your teaching life, and advice on using your own teaching as a wellspring of inspiration and imagination.

Leila Christenbury

Permissions

Slightly different versions of the following sections by Diana Mitchell were originally published in the Teaching Ideas column of NCTE's *English Journal:*

"Approaching Race and Gender Issues in the Context of the Language Arts Classroom" 85.8 (1996): 77–81.

"Connecting Short Stories" 83.7 (1994): 87–91.

"Creating Thematic Units" 86.5 (1997): 80–85.

"Fifty Alternatives to the Book Report" 87.1 (1998): 92–95.

"Ghostly Themes in the Classroom" (originally published as "Halloween Is Coming: Ghostly Themes in the English Classroom") 86.6 (1997): 94–99.

"Heroes Bring Literature to Life" 83.8 (1994): 90–93.

"A New Look at Nonfiction in the Classroom" 85.2 (1996): 74–79.

"Projects That Promote Authentic Learning" (originally published as "Four Projects That Promote Authentic Learning") 86.4 (1997): 68–72.

"Putting Poetry in Its Place" 83.5 (1994): 78–80.

"Scripting for Involvement and Understanding" 83.6 (1994): 82–85.

"Springtime Sanity Savers" 85.4 (1996): 67–72.

"Tapping into Family Stories and Themes to Heighten End-of-Year Engagement" 87.4 (1998): 65–69.

"Using Children's Literature to Spark Learning" 87.2 (1998): 94–97.

"Using New Novels without Being Overwhelmed" 85.3 (1996): 85–90.

"Using Newspapers and Magazines—the Multipurpose Teaching Tools" 86.7 (1997): 109–13.

"Using Short Story Collections to Enrich the English Classroom" 86.8 (1997): 73–77.

"Using Student Work as the Basis for Classroom Activities" 84.6 (1995): 110–14.

"Ways into Literature" 84.5 (1995): 106–10.

"Writing to Learn Across the Curriculum and the English Teacher" 85.5 (1996): 93–97.

1 Both Art and Craft in the World of Teaching Ideas

Leila Christenbury

When I first began teaching English, I was literally desperate for ideas. I hadn't planned on being a teacher and thus had little preparation for my first teaching job. While it was no one's fault but my own, I had taken no courses in educational psychology or human development or teaching methods, and I had had no student teaching. Other than two degrees in English and a lot of optimism and enthusiasm, I was really not ready for 120 teenagers and three class preparations. The principal who hired me was encouraging about my potential, but it became evident early on that I needed a whole lot of instructional ideas and a whole lot of help.

And when neither were immediately forthcoming, I found myself struggling on a daily basis. Confronted with the typical high school teacher's schedule—five periods a day, five days a week—there never seemed to be the time to come up with creative and workable or even appropriate ideas. I used the questions in the literature textbook; I recycled activities dimly remembered from my own experience as a student; I concocted some impossible assignments and found myself revising and altering them every day, occasionally in the middle of class. Used to academic success as a student, I was more than mildly shocked at the difficulties I was having as a beginning teacher and, truth be told, embarrassed at what was going on—and not going on—in my classroom.

When I got up the courage, I tried to talk with other teachers in my school, but no one had enough time to help me—at least to the extent I needed it that first semester of teaching. Even the professional reading I attempted early on seemed abstract and unconnected to what I saw sitting in the desks in front of me. My despair deepened.

Early one morning, I threw myself on the mercy of the English teacher next door. Although a generally aloof colleague, she was very popular with her students and also had an enviable two years of teaching under her belt, exactly twice my classroom experience. As usual, she was not particularly interested in my teaching struggles, but, in this one (and not repeated) instance of collegial generosity, she did offer an idea.

As we stood in the hall at 7:45 A.M. before classes began for the day, she suggested that I have my students participate in a "trust game." She had seen this activity in a workshop, and it involved dividing the entire class into pairs. One student would blindfold the other and, using verbal cues only, would guide him or her around the room, down rows, under desks, and even out into the hall. Then the students would exchange roles. The activity was fun, she observed, and she had done it yesterday in her afternoon classes with great success.

I was immediately grateful for the suggestion, happy for the unusual gesture of camaraderie. No wonder my colleague was enduringly popular with her students. After a moment, though, I asked her what had precipitated the use of the game, how it connected to what she was doing in class, what she did afterward as a follow-up. My colleague just smiled. Those two years of experience quickly reasserted themselves as an unbridgeable gulf between us. Once again I, the novice, appeared to be missing the point. My colleague patiently explained that the game idea had been spontaneous, the students had enjoyed it, and it took up the whole period. That was that, she said, and she went back into her classroom.

Yes, the activity seemed like fun—but when I returned to my classroom for first period, although I was tempted I knew I wouldn't be doing any trust games that day. Even at that point in my career, even as desperate as I was for teaching ideas, I realized that this activity bore no conceivable relation to what I was trying to do in my classes. Frankly, I suspected the same was true of my colleague next door, but, in her case, a game which students enjoyed for the entire class period appeared to be justification enough. Well, for me, it wasn't. Inspirationless, I trudged through another difficult teaching day.

Looking back on that early incident in my career, I can draw some conclusions. I was not a well-prepared teacher, but despite my very real and daily struggles, I did understand the general concept of curriculum and how it should shape and govern teaching activities and truly spark learning. I was trying, I think, to set up experiences in which students could connect the ideas in our work to their own lives and to their other readings. I wanted students to explore and argue and experiment and bring to whatever we were doing in class—from the "The Scarlet Ibis" we read in eighth-grade English to the argument essay we were writing in honors eleventh—some kind of personal and intellectual connection. I think even then I knew that teaching activities had to be intimately related to classroom goals and to student needs. And a disembodied, disconnected activity, even the fun trust game, did not come near fulfilling that criterion.

As I stumbled through my first years of teaching, I of course got more experience in the classroom. I encountered other teachers who were more willing to share and teach me. I began to read widely in professional journals and books about what others did in their classes and, unlike my early reading, it began to make sense. I went to English and education conferences and picked up materials there and elsewhere. I became a scavenger of teaching ideas and practices and, slowly but steadily, I improved as a teacher.

Over the years, I took my nascent intuitive sense and some of my natural presentation skills—my classroom art, as it were—and combined them with my developing craft. The craft, which was emerging through repeated practice and skill, involved my ability to create and pace activities for a large group and to adjust those activities when needed. The combination, the balance, of art and craft has sustained me through my years in the classroom.

Teaching as Both Art and Craft

We titled this book *Both Art and Craft* because certainly the heart of teaching involves both. A successful teacher uses art and is often a bit of a magician, a person who can motivate and inspire a group and get the members, at times almost despite themselves, to work and achieve and also feel a sense of satisfaction in the process. A successful teacher is also a craftsperson, an artisan, someone who can deliberately select from a solid repertoire of intellectual and curricular components and then combine, rearrange, and refine to fit the needs of the classroom curriculum and the needs of the students.

Teaching as Art

Discussing the art of teaching is a bit dangerous because many otherwise sensible people wax mystical when they consider the topic of teaching as art. For some, teaching is essentially an alchemy which is accessible only to certain types of charismatic or otherwise gifted individuals. They believe that teachers are indeed born, not made, and that these individuals' personal magnetism, and most likely their strong ability to inspire others, are the sole sources of classroom success. Carried to an extreme, this belief in teaching as art can lead to the conclusion that success in the classroom can be achieved without much study or preparation or even practice and that, indeed, one's fitness for a career in teaching can be determined early on, mostly by personality traits. Fed in many ways by media images of brave and charismatic teachers—who are not only talented but also photogenic—many people believe such gifted individuals can conquer (usually in one or two dramatic confrontations) the ennui and disaffection of not only their own students but often of the entire school, if not the whole educational system.

There *is* art in teaching, but it is my opinion that this art is not related to an inherent gift for teaching, and those who have been in the classroom for some time know that this image of teachers is unfaithful to the reality. Successful teaching requires a more arduous process than those represented by most popular movies about and images of teaching, and it is filled, as veteran teachers know only too well, with countless instances of failure and stasis. Even the most charismatic, the most artful teacher can often fail, and fail repeatedly, to engage certain students and certain classes and to ignite that spark of learning.

Yet, while there is more than likely less art in teaching than many outside the classroom assume, the art is there. It involves the ability to capture imagination and to create infectious enthusiasm. It takes the form of being able to motivate a group. It consists of being able, often in a fairly quick manner and at times apparently subliminally, to predict and "read" an instructional situation and intervene. It also extends to the ability to create an often palpable feeling of comfort and success for students in the classroom, an environment that is not just supportive but also stimulating and, when appropriate, challenging. Often this teacher art is born of years of watching students and thinking about and experimenting with instruction. Conversely, sometimes it comes in the form of relatively instantaneous inspiration in the classroom. Regardless, there is in teaching a certain element of art.

Teaching as Craft

The craft of teaching is in some ways easier to discuss than the art of teaching. Craft is a more concrete concept: it involves study; it takes some years of practice. Teachers who have mastered craft have acquired a repertoire of skills that has expanded far beyond the things they would "naturally" be able to—or even want to—do or plan. Craft is largely independent of what most would call *inspiration* and comes from knowledge and experience.

Practically speaking, a teacher who practices craft can lead a large group discussion, structure a small group, or monitor individual work with equal skill and comfort. When craft is involved, a teacher can meet a curricular requirement through a number of equally appropriate strategies and approaches. Most tellingly, craft also involves the ability to anticipate what students will need for a specific lesson or unit of study and to provide it in a clear and understandable manner. Thus, having a repertoire of skills, knowing how to implement a variety of activities in a coherent and thoughtful manner, and understanding that those real and messy entities, our students, can—and will and should—change the shape of the most "perfect" lesson are part of the craft of teaching.

How Both Art and Craft Are Needed

A teacher who relies solely on art will not last long in the classroom. He or she will become discouraged and resentful, as the magic does not work reliably every period, every day, with every student. A teacher solely involved in craft—"I read it and considered it and therefore it can be replicated in my classroom with my students"—will become similarly disheartened because teaching is never like following a cookbook, never a series of steps which can be unfailingly followed to the letter with all students and all classes.

The most successful teachers are those who possess both craft, a solid repertoire of skills and an understanding of curriculum, and art, the ability to inspire, motivate, and understand student needs and interests. And the combination of art and craft sparks real student learning.

Characteristics of Good Teaching Activities

Beyond the major divisions of art and craft are other criteria to consider. Despite the varied circumstances of your students, classes, and needs, whatever you implement in your classroom needs to have the three characteristics of *simplicity, relevance,* and *workability.* You will find all three in the many activities in this book and, as you think of how to expand on these activities and use them in your classroom, you want to keep these three characteristics in mind.

Simplicity

A simple teaching idea is not a simpleminded one but one which has a major thrust and focus. Teaching ideas which rely on multiple, complex components—most of which necessarily would be interconnected—can fall apart due to their own elaborate nature. Both teachers and students can become hopelessly confused if a teaching activity has too many parts, too many concepts, too many grading rubrics, too many components. Keeping an idea and its attendant activities simple—and thus central—will make the idea more successful in almost any setting.

Look, for example, at the section "Scripting for Involvement and Understanding" in Chapter 5. The point of this exercise is to get students to evaluate others' scripts in small groups. This could involve many components and could even lend itself to a fairly involved ranking and rating rubric. Diana, however, presents students with only nine questions to discuss and answer. Further, the questions are central to scripting: summary, narration, dialogue, interest, and so forth, and the one question on ranking asks students to select the single script which, in their opinion, most effectively mirrors the one chapter on which it is based. In the best sense of the word, this evaluation activity is simple.

Relevance

Relevance is a highly complex topic and, in this context, does not relate to the contemporaneity of an activity. Relevance means that the activity is directly tied to the text or to the concept itself. The trust game discussed earlier in this chapter provides a good test of an activity's relevance: while such an activity may be otherwise admirable (in a psychology class, for instance?), it was not related to any sort of instructional point in English class.

As another example, look at the section "Fifty Alternatives to the Book Report" in Chapter 4. While the activities are intriguing, note how Diana encourages the use of the activity only if the piece of literature justifies it. Thus, creating a childhood for a character (item 3) is only relevant if the main character is an adult, and the social worker's report (item 5) should be used only if the literature contains events which might indeed be of interest to such a worker.

Workability

Workability is wholly context dependent and involves the chances of the activity being successful in your school setting and with your students. If, for instance, a completely relevant and simply designed activity calls for significant equipment to which you and your students have only partial or inadequate access, you might want to reconsider the activity. As an example, if students are to use the Internet extensively to complete an activity but you can only get into the computer lab infrequently, it may be a frustrating assignment for all involved. Likewise, putting students in groups to create a short video is a great idea, but if you and your students have access only to a few camcorders and if students have rarely done group work, you will not be happy trying to fulfill the project's expectations. Finally, if students need to obtain materials from outside sources—a university library, for instance, or a municipal office downtown—and they don't have ready transportation, the activity may fail before it begins.

Another concern with workability is attention to student skills. Take a look in Chapter 6 at the section "Creating Thematic Units." Before she even starts the unit, Diana brainstorms the skills students will need, lists them for herself and includes them in her planning, and makes sure they are attended to beforehand and also within the unit itself. In this way, students are not thrown into activities for which they have no real preparation. Anticipating what specific skills are necessary for the students to experience success in the unit is smart planning and ensures the workability of a teaching activity.

Teaching Principles to Guide You

Beyond the characteristics of the art and craft of teaching and beyond the characteristics of good teaching activities, you need to consider your students and your classroom and remember some essential teaching principles, principles which are the foundation of all good practice.

Student Engagement: Interest and Background. It is imperative that any activity you use in your classroom build on, or even emanate from, student interest and background. Only if students have some sort of prior knowledge or interest in acquiring new knowledge will they work and work well. The alternative is to present students with disconnected information for which they see no need and to which they can connect very little. If you want your students to work steadily and productively, you must account for and appeal to their interests and their background.

As an illustration, look at the section "Tapping into Family Stories and Themes to Heighten End-of-Year Engagement" in Chapter 6. In such a unit, students have an opportunity to research, write, compile art and dictionaries, and read relevant literature. The range of activities is broad, and the skills involved are considerable. Most students will attempt this unit willingly, however, because it explicitly capitalizes on their interest in themselves and their background. Further, they bring to the unit a certain undeniable expertise, i.e., knowledge of their own family. And the extensive section in Chapter 5 on "Using Student Work as the Basis for Classroom Activities" helps you see how student questions, student generalizations, and student responses can shape and guide literature study.

Explanations and Modeling. When we ask students to attempt new or unfamiliar activities, they can often appear reluctant, possibly even uncooperative. What many of us fail to remember is the fear almost all students have of trying something new—and failing. While part of our job as teachers is to extend student skill, to nudge them into new territory, we must be willing to give students clear explanations and, when appropriate, specific models of what we want.

Look at the section "Heroes Bring Literature to Life" in Chapter 6. One of the student activities suggested is a résumé. While many of us as adults have written and revised countless such documents, for most of our students the concept may be pretty hazy. Giving students a sample—such as the Superman résumé provided—will not only allay fears but also will help students fulfill expectations.

Collaboration. "None of us is as smart as all of us" is a popular phrase which has much good sense behind it. Collaboration can help students make connections they otherwise might miss. In addition, our students are generally social creatures, and the opportunity to work with others in the classroom is important for their psychological health as well as their intellectual ability. Negotiating with others' points of view and learning to compromise or ask helpful questions can be some of the most important skills students learn as they work with others in school. Also, many of the projects and ideas presented in this book are complicated; when more than one student has to list, define, explain, argue, or present, there is a greater chance that the resulting work will be multifaceted, complex, and important.

For instance, in the subsection on cutting up words and phrases from the section "Using Newspapers and Magazines—the Multipurpose Teaching Tools" in Chapter 5, students are asked to select fifteen to twenty interesting or intriguing phrases from advertisements and then connect these phrases to anything they have studied or read in the last marking period. As Diana notes, "this activity really pushes students to think and bring into play all they have learned or been exposed to in class." Certainly the depth of exploration will be far greater when students work with others in cooperation rather than trying to come up with a list of pertinent topics on their own. In this activity, as in many others offered in this book, collaboration is helpful to success.

Meaningful Work. Because it is in the curriculum guide, because we've always done it that way, because I told you to (and I am the teacher)—these are not sufficient rationales for students. When students suspect that what they are doing in class is not important, not significant, not connected to anything else, they will rarely work at a high level. Thus providing meaningful work for our students ensures interest and possibly a higher level of quality.

And what is *meaningful* work? When, as described in the section "Projects That Promote Authentic Learning" in Chapter 6, students must create handbooks or videos for incoming ninth graders, create poetry books for special persons, or compile research packets for next year's students, there is a need, an audience, and a reason for the project. From our teaching perspective, these projects use all sorts of skills which are important in English language arts. And, from our students' perspective, the projects themselves, creating guides or books which others can really use, will make this assignment important and useful.

Conclusion

You may never be as desperate for teaching ideas as I was my first year in the classroom, and you may never be as tempted as I was to use an unconnected, albeit lively activity like the trust game. But you will find in *Both Art and Craft* myriad useful ideas, and you will also find that these ideas can be significantly altered and adapted to fit more specifically your teaching context and your students' needs. With attention to the characteristics of good activities, with adherence to sound teaching principles, the ideas in this book can help you discover your own individual combination of teaching as both art and craft, teaching that sparks learning.

2 The Theory beneath the Practice

Diana Mitchell

Diana explores the relationship of theory and practice, outlining theories of learning that have influenced her and discussing how classroom teachers need theory in order to examine and revise their teaching. A best-practices checklist near the end of the chapter provides specific markers to look for as we create teaching ideas that spark learning.

I have learned that theory is at the root of all we do in the classroom and even at the root of all we do in our personal lives. My actions are informed by my theories about humans and about my purpose in the world. Accordingly, I may be kind to others because I believe we are all one and that to be kind to others is to be kind to myself. On the other hand, I may only be kind because I think I'll be doomed eternally if I'm not. When these theories are a core part of a value system, we usually call them beliefs. I have come to understand that whether or not we can name them, theories or beliefs undergird everything we do and every way we behave. This is also true of teaching. How we involve children in learning, how we view discipline, what we select for students to study or read, how we view young people as learners—all of these decisions we make grow out of theories lying beneath them.

Theories about Learning

As teachers, we all base what we do on a theory of how learning takes place. Some people believe children are empty vessels who come to us to be filled—their part in learning is to be passive and receive information, and our part is to give them that information. Others believe children come to us full of experiences, knowledge, and curiosity. Our job, then, is to find ways or structures that allow us to build on what they bring and to help them fit new information and ideas into the scaffold of what they already know.

Some believe learning is a no-nonsense proposition. Kids do as they're told, complete the required work, and learn. Still others believe motivation is important, that students have to feel connected to their education, that their imagination has to be tapped so they can see multiple possibilities, not the dead-end road of regurgitating teacher-processed information.

From my language, you can tell that I believe learning is constructive—the learner must be active to learn. This is both a philosophical and a psychological stance, which argues that the human mind does not simply take in the world but creates it in an active way. To use an image, I envision the mind as filled with little stacks of open files. The stacks represent our understanding of the world so far. When new information comes in, the mind looks through the stack for a place to file it. If there is no container or stack into which it will fit and no one helps the learner see how it connects to what he or she already knows, the new information simply makes no sense to the learner and is discarded. That is why I accept the constructive theory of learning as articulated by Gordon Wells and others. We have to help learners build the connections that will allow them to construct another stack or slot or file into which the new information can be filed.

I also believe that different people learn in different ways. Howard Gardner explains that we have multiple intelligences, multiple ways to grapple with and express our understandings. This belief or theory lies at the heart of the assignments I create that don't limit children to one way to respond, that encourage variation, that celebrate imagination.

Behaviorism: Extrinsic vs. Intrinsic Motivation

Other psychologists see learning as a behaviorist process. This view of learning dominated for the first half of the twentieth century, when mental processes were viewed as invisible and not subject to scientific observation. The concern was only with outward behavior, which could be measured by how an individual responded to a stimulus. Learning consisted of a stimulus followed by a response. Behavioral psychologists believed that if children's responses were sufficiently rewarded, they would continue to repeat the behavior. Rewards were seen as extrinsic to the children—outside of rather than part of them. Even in the early days of my teaching career when this type of thinking dominated, I didn't accept this theory of learning because I don't believe real learning takes place just for others, nor do I believe children learn for extrinsic rewards. In my thirty years of teaching at the secondary level, I have seen students dive into learning activities when they could see a connection to themselves or could see its intrinsic worth. Few children in my years of urban teaching even responded to the threat of failure; there had to be a more important reason to learn than grades. They had to feel that what they brought to the classroom was important, that their histories and cultures were important, and that the learning was worthwhile.

I think that taking a behaviorist approach to teaching drains the joy and raison d'être from education because it reinforces that learning is for others. Many of the children we teach are not intrinsically motivated, because they have been taught that education means jumping through hoops for others. Although it is not easy to turn around this attitude, I believe that when children have an element of control and choice over parts of the work they do in the classroom, they can begin to experience this intrinsic motivation and will complete work because they feel a pride or joy in what they can do.

In order to learn, students have to believe that the work is not just for the teacher; it's for them. Building on what students bring to the class is one way to validate who they are as learners, as is using material that is part of their lives. We can ask students to share the stories of how they were named, for example, or the stories of the games they played as a child. They are willing to analyze if we ask them to look at things familiar to them such as the values being taught through the games they played as a child. They are willing to think deeply about issues that are part of their lives.

When students are involved in material like this, it's easy to introduce new skills such as drawing inferences. We can ask them what inferences they can draw about power and about the order of things in our society by looking closely at the games they played as children. From there we can examine the values embedded in the games and speculate on what this means about what we are teaching children. But beginning with what the student knows or understands is the first step, and we have to be able to show students how what we teach connects to their lives. We have to help children understand that what we're doing in the classroom can be important to them. And we can do this by using their backgrounds and interests and building on them.

Constructivism

Involving students in the construction of knowledge also means that we have to value student talk and understand what it has to do with learning. (I do not mean here "stray" talk but rather the talk students engage in in small groups about the literature or writing they are studying.) In our daily lives, we solve most of our problems through talk—talk with a friend, a spouse, or a therapist. Yet we as teachers often forget the opportunities talk can provide in our classes to further understanding. Through talk we assimilate new knowledge, make sense of it, and integrate it into what we already know. When we can explain a concept or idea to another orally, we know that we have a clear grasp of it. Talk allows us to offer our ideas, hear others' ideas, discuss and grapple with differences in these ideas, and come away with a new or clearer understanding of the concept or idea. Through talk students show us they can think and solve problems. Curt Dudley-Marling and Dennis Searle help me see another dimension in the importance of talk:

> Talk is not only a medium for thinking, it is also an important means by which we learn how to think. From a Vygotskian perspective thinking is an internal dialogue, or internalization of dialogues we've had with others. Our ability to think depends upon the many previous dialogues we have taken part in—we learn to think by participating in dialogue. (60)

Because I understand the necessity for talk and collaboration, I make time for them in my class by structuring small-group discussions frequently.

Theories about Literature

One of my main passions in life—the teaching of literature—has changed and expanded as I have learned more about theory. Since many of us were not taught to examine our stances on teaching literature, I wasn't even aware when I began to teach that I based my literature teaching on a theory. Yet we all do. As Jeff Wilhelm explains, many teachers base what they do with literature in the classroom on the literary theory known as New Criticism. This theory views literature as a thing to be taken apart. Elements are looked at carefully and then put back together with a focus on how it all fits, how all the parts make a beautiful pattern. Inherent in this view is the belief that if examined "correctly," all analysts will come up with the same meaning in a text: there is only one meaning in a text, and the reader's job is to find it. Thus, since most students are not sophisticated enough to extract this meaning, we as teachers tell them the meaning or guide them to it through a carefully structured series of questions or worksheets. Wilhelm emphasizes that this view still regards reading "as a passive act of receiving someone else's meanings" (13).

I turned away from this view of literature as I became aware that it disregards the reader and what a reader brings to a piece of literature. Also, I wasn't comfortable with the elitist stance this theory assumes, that only the knowledgeable (read English teachers and critics) can truly know the meaning of a piece of literature. And like many teachers before me, I occasionally turned to CliffsNotes to find out what a novel is about so I could teach it "correctly." I now find this ironic since I learned that CliffsNotes are usually written by people trying to make a buck, not by literary scholars. I am now horrified that I was willing to put my trust in someone else's judgment!

The work of Louise Rosenblatt on reader-response theory made a great impact on me. Rosenblatt articulated the view that the meaning of a text lies in the interaction between the reader and the text. This now seems to me to be common sense. When we go to a movie, for instance, we each come out of it with different impressions and different views; some think the movie is brilliant, while others express disdain for it. Sharing our ideas on the same movie may help us see it in another way. Yet we don't assume that one perspective is wrong and the other is right. We know people take who they are to a movie and usually respond in terms of their own frame of reference. For instance, I loved Richard Dreyfuss in *Mr. Holland's Opus*. I responded mainly from my background as a teacher of thirty years. Here was a man who imparted a love of music to his students and helped them become more than they were. I loved the ending. I loved him as a teacher. I didn't notice if minor characters were well drawn or not; I wasn't very conscious of the set. I was involved in the main character's passion for teaching. I would like to sit down and discuss this movie with others because I know that in talking about a text (a movie, a book, a tape), meanings are made, altered, and remade. I love that process. So the meaning of the movie was only partly *in* the movie; the other part was within me.

Kathleen McCormick's work helped me understand that when I read a book I am situated in a context of my own history, of which I am not always aware. What I bring to a text comes from my social, religious, economic, and political background; my gender, age, race, sexual orientation, and even my urban origins all cause me to read in a certain way. Furthermore, different texts bring different parts of this repertoire of mine to the forefront. In my response to *Mr. Holland's Opus*, I viewed the movie mainly through the lens of a teacher. But other movies and books tap into other parts of my repertoire. Sometimes I respond from my role of mother, other times from my background as the daughter of a union worker for a big automobile company. Everything we are colors what we bring to a text and what we carry away from a text. Understanding McCormick's work reinforced my view that we have to respect what our students bring to a text and begin with their responses. Only in the discussion and projects in conjunction with a text do we negotiate, add to, and perhaps change our view of it. Thus, for teachers to impose their views of a text (or the view provided by CliffsNotes) is to truncate the process for the reader and to diminish the meaning students could come away with. In Gordon Pradl's *Literature for Democracy,* the importance of negotiating meaning through discussion is explained in full, rich ways.

Looking at Literature as a Reader

Judith Langer's work also informs my approach to literature. Langer has examined the reading process from the readers' point of view and found that readers experience four different stances or *envisionments* as they read. An envisionment is a reader's understanding of the text at any one moment and is always open to change and new information.

Stance 1: Being Out and Stepping into an Envisionment. In this stance, readers begin a book or story and look around for clues that will let them know what the story will be about. Readers work to get a sense of the story and figure out what it's going to be about (Langer 16). When students begin books, we can ask such questions as: What's the first image you see? Where were you in the story—behind the characters, above them? Were you one of the characters?

Stance 2: Being in and Moving through an Envisionment. In this stance, readers are firmly into the story and enjoying the experience (Langer 17). I consider this the stance in which we get to muck around and simply wallow in the experience of the book. This is my favorite stance, although sometimes I get trapped in it and don't want to put the book down. I just want to continue to savor the experience. In this stance, we as readers fill in the gaps and develop our understandings of the book. This stance—the most enjoyable one for readers—is the stance for which schools allow the least time. Most teachers are not skilled at knowing how to validate and expand on the readers' experiences. After digesting Langer's work on envisionments, I realized that I had to validate students' immersion in books by asking such questions as: Which characters can you relate to the most? What events or behaviors cause other things to happen? Whose point of view do you think you're most in tune with? What happens that is hard for you to understand?

Stance 3: Stepping Out and Rethinking What one Knows. Stance 3 is the one in which we step outside the book and think about it in terms of ourselves (Langer 17). We're not trying to make sense of the text world now; we're looking at how the text has added to our understanding of the world. Are we like that character? Could we ever do what he or she did?

Stance 4: Stepping Out and Objectifying the Experience. In this stance, we think about the book in terms of other books we've read (Langer 18). This stance is the analytic one in which we talk and think about what we liked about the book and how it compares to other books by the same author or different authors. Here too readers might be interested in looking at how the author created the effect she or he did. How did the figurative language add to the impact? Was the characterization realistic? Did the plot move well or did it just lumber along? Too often teachers move directly to this stance without giving readers time to be immersed in the story or to think about what they can learn about themselves from the story.

Using the Stances. These stances are not experienced in a linear manner, going from stance 1 straight through to stance 4. Instead, they are recursive. We may begin in stance 1, go to 2, then 4, then 2, then 3. We constantly move in and out of these stances as we read.

We have to understand the processes readers use so that we don't prevent students' involvement with a book by overlaying a structure that interferes with their reading or their willingness to become deeply involved in a piece of literature. For instance, if part way through a book we ask students analytic questions from stance 4 while they are deeply into stance 2, we may stop students' further engagement and thinking about the text by imposing our own meanings or views of the text on them. We are asking students to become involved in *our* agenda, *our* way of viewing the book, instead of encouraging them to dig deep and extract meanings we may not have thought of.

Implicit in this view of teaching literature is treating questions as part of the literary experience, because questions are a fundamental way through which students develop understandings. We help students learn that questions are a way to deepen their understandings. We spend class time developing these understandings rather than finding "right answers," and we welcome and use multiple perspectives to enrich an interpretation. Students are asked to become aware of all the perspectives they bring to a reading and to reflect on which part of their experiences leads them to the interpretation they put forward.

The Importance of Literature

To me, literature is the stuff of life. We take this "stuff" and look at it in terms of ourselves and our world. What do we learn from fictional characters and the decisions they make? What can we learn about the world and the author's view of the world? How does my vision of the world differ? And above all, how does literature connect to me, connect to the world, and connect to other texts? To teach literature as a piece of content in reference to which only remembering details is validated is to drain the life from the literature, rendering it meaningless. Thus it's important as a teacher to understand how you view literature. Is it a medium through which to teach skills? Is it only important as a piece of content about which students remember facts regarding the characters, plot, and setting? Or is it a medium through which we view the world and grapple with the great ideas and themes embedded within it?

I have never found it productive to treat literature like a piece of content in which we ask students to hunt for the elements of literature. That does not touch on what's important about the text. Literature isn't about identifying theme, plot, point of view, setting, and so on. We use those elements when we want to look more closely at a work and ask such questions as: Could the story have been written in anything other than this point of view? What effect would changing the narrator have on the story? Were there any limitations in using this particular point of view? Was the plot seamless or were you occasionally jolted by its bumpiness? Which parts puzzled you? Were there any parts you thought were superfluous? Anything you wish had been included? What themes did you notice in the story? What vision or view of the world underlies this work? Is this how you see the world? What would you like to have a conversation about with the author?

Literature gives us a chance to talk about life, to examine it, to meet characters and think about them as people we may or may not want to know. Literature gives us an occasion to interact with our ideas about life, the world, and even ourselves. To teach only skills through the study of literature, to use it only as an exercise in comprehension, is to diminish the possibilities that lie within each piece of literature to illuminate our thinking and our world.

Theories about Writing

James Britton, Peter Elbow, Donald Graves, Donald Murray, James Moffett, Janet Emig, and Nancie Atwell are some of the main influences on my teaching of writing. I was struck with the work of Britton and his matter-of-fact approach to writing: if something wasn't working, he looked for another approach. One of the things I most clearly remember about Britton's work is his use of the term "dummy runs." He could see absolutely no sense in having students do something just to show they could; an activity had to be embedded in a reason or purpose. In his work with young children, he found that when students wrote for real purposes, their writing was clear and interesting. When teachers had students write to see if they could construct a paragraph or made them write on a topic of no interest to them, however, the writing reflected the students' disinterest. Throughout my years of teaching writing, I certainly found this to be true, and I internalized the importance of a writer's interest in the topic. But I also found that if I did assign a topic, students would still produce excellent writing if I did not specify a writing form. So specifying either a form or a topic still produced good writing, but in general specifying both resulted in flat writing. Therefore, if I wanted students to write a persuasive essay, they could select any topic they wished. If I wanted them to write about the impact Thoreau's work had on them, they could choose to do it in the form of a poem, a play, an essay, or a story.

Understanding that writing is a process also helped me see that first drafts are not finished pieces and should not be graded as though they are. I learned that students learn to write by writing, not by engaging in practice activities such as worksheets on punctuation. The results of that kind of "practice" didn't find their way into student writing. I also came to see that students needed models of what good writing looks and sounds like and the many formats that can be used. So I began to bring in children's picture books to show the variety of formats, and I used students' work (without names) to explore what makes writing interesting, what "having a strong voice" means.

Attention to audience is of the utmost importance in order to elicit good student writing. If students know that only a teacher will read their work, it doesn't seem to be as important as writing generated for another audience. Students also produce better writing within a specific context and for a specific purpose. One of the things I learned later in my teaching life from educators such as Jane Hansen is the importance of reflection in the whole writing and learning process. We have to help students articulate what they have accomplished in their work so they can take pride in it and see how much they have grown.

Best Practice: A Checklist

As I construct units and generate ideas for writing assignments or projects, I try to keep the list of questions in Figure 2.1 before me to maintain my focus. These questions tell me whether I'm working toward the "best practice" based on solid theory and whether I'm putting what I believe into practice.

Am I providing opportunities in my language arts class

☐ for students to be involved in a classroom that integrates speaking, listening, reading, and writing and that practices all skills instruction in context?

☐ for students to actively construct meaning through their reading, writing, and viewing?

☐ for students to build on what they already know and have an interest in?

☐ for authentic, real-life learning that is valuable outside as well as in the context of the classroom?

☐ for students to work collaboratively in small groups?

☐ for students to have some choice in materials or formats of assignments?

☐ for student contributions to be viewed as an important part of the class?

☐ for students to read and work independently?

☐ for students' thinking to be expanded or challenged?

☐ for students to be involved in activities that ask them to synthesize and/or apply what they have read or viewed?

☐ for students to receive writing instruction that is embedded in authentic activities and assignments and that focuses on the content of the writing?

☐ for daily writing done in support of reading?

☐ for students to look closely at and reflect on their own written work?

☐ for students to develop rubrics and criteria to apply to their own and others' work?

☐ for students to read both contemporary and classic works across many genres?

☐ for students to read works by and about the diverse peoples who are part of this country?

☐ for students to think about how the classroom reading, writing, speaking, and viewing is connected to them and to their peers?

☐ for students to learn vocabulary, including literary terms, in the context of the reading they are doing in class?

Figure 2.1. Best Practice Checklist

Conclusion

When I read theoretical work, I think about it carefully in terms of what it says, but I also measure it by my own experiences as a reader, a writer, and a teacher. For instance, when I first read about Langer's stances, I was excited because I realized that I experienced the stances as I read. Then, when I thought about them in terms of my own teaching, I was able to understand why students seemed reluctant to jump into analytic activities without having time to grapple with the book and immerse themselves in it. Langer's research and theory became important to me because, by understanding how my students read, I became a better teacher.

Sometimes I have found, however, that no one has yet written about strategies I was using successfully in my classroom, works that would help me reflect on and expand those strategies. I could see they were working because students were engaged and producing good work. A case in point is my belief that reading aloud to students has merit. Although many teachers I worked with were disdainful of this approach, I knew that reading aloud, especially to my general ninth-grade classes, was magical. I saw students engage with characters. I saw them care about what happened. Much later, after reading research, I realized that many of my students didn't see pictures or images in their heads as they read. They didn't know they were supposed to. Without the ability to do this, they could not engage with and make sense of the text. But when I read aloud, students could use their imaginations and get involved. I also later figured out that students feel nurtured and taken care of when someone reads aloud to them. But the theories about why reading aloud can be a good strategy hadn't yet been articulated. Now that I understand what happens to many students when confronted with a text, I can shape teaching activities around encouraging students to see pictures and also helping them fill in the gaps the author left. Even though my instructional strategy was sound, reading others' research helped me see how I could help students become better readers on their own. It also introduced me to areas I didn't even know existed. I became aware that all students do not visualize as they read, do not fill in gaps left by the author, and do not connect stories to their own lives. Research and theory have helped me become a better teacher because they have taught me new things about processes that I can then apply to my own students and classrooms.

Works Cited

Britton, James. *Language and Learning.* 2nd ed. Portsmouth, NH: Heinemann, 1993.

Dudley-Marling, Curt, and Dennis Searle. *When Students Have Time to Talk: Creating Contexts for Learning Language.* Portsmouth, NH: Heinemann, 1991.

Hansen, Jane. *When Learners Evaluate.* Portsmouth, NH: Heinemann, 1998.

Gardner, Howard. *Frames of Mind: The Theory of Multiple Intelligences.* New York: Basic, 1983.

Langer, Judith A. *Envisioning Literature: Literary Understanding and Literature Instruction.* New York: Teachers College P, 1995.

McCormick, Kathleen. *The Culture of Reading and the Teaching of English.* Manchester, Eng.: Manchester UP, 1994.

Pradl, Gordon. *Literature for Democracy: Reading as a Social Act.* Portsmouth, NH: Boynton/Cook, 1996.

Rosenblatt, Louise M. *Literature as Exploration.* 3rd ed. New York: Noble, 1976.

Wells, C. Gordon. *Constructing Knowledge Together: Classrooms as Centers of Inquiry and Literacy.* Portsmouth, NH: Heinemann, 1992.

Wilhelm, Jeff. *"You Gotta BE the Book": Teaching Engaged and Reflective Reading with Adolescents.* New York: Teachers College P, 1997.

3 Creating and Adapting Ideas for and from Your Teaching

Diana Mitchell

Diana outlines what is important to her about teaching ideas and activities. One thing you will notice in this chapter is her emphasis on student interest. Effective teachers know that students who are engaged and care about their work not only are happier in the classroom, but they also learn more. Capitalizing on student interest and knowledge can be one of the most potent strategies we have in teaching. Diana starts with her beliefs and understandings about teaching the language arts and then moves into the world of students.

The field of language arts interpenetrates almost all aspects of the world. It includes reading, writing, talking, and drawing about any issue we want to grapple with and make sense of. Within that broad framework, I can plug in language arts skills to help students become better readers, willing to tackle more complex texts; better writers, whose work makes an impact on others; and better speakers, with the tools and structures to offer their ideas confidently and effectively.

When I think about creating teaching ideas and units, I never restrict myself to what sound like "English-class" subjects. I don't create units on short stories or poetry, because with those kinds of titles I don't know how to breathe life into them and transform them into topics I want to explore—or that my students will be interested in.

When I think imaginatively, my mind flies from one thing to another because I don't feel constrained; I am free to let my mind roam, to figure out how I can best involve students in reading and writing and language and thinking. I've never worried much about whether I'm "covering" the content of language arts, because I know how to connect almost every reading and writing and speaking experience to what I am doing. I can see the big picture, how things fit in and together. Thus, I don't have a narrow view of the language arts, nor do I feel I can teach little pieces of things unless they are in the context of a big question or unit that we—my students and I—are working on.

The Ideas behind the Ideas

I see myself as a pathfinder of sorts. I love to create teaching ideas and assignments because I like to deal with the excitement of possibilities. I love the thought of opening up something, of helping students find ways into material or ideas. As I see it, my job is to help students see the possibilities within an approach, or to see the excitement of that approach. I know that creativity and engagement cannot be forced; it can only be coaxed. So for me teaching isn't about frontal assaults, telling students what they must do and how they must do it. It's about gently uncovering ways for students to find their way into the learning by making connections within themselves. Then they will have places to put new ideas within the framework of their own thinking.

I also believe that my students come to my classroom full of experiences, thoughts, feelings, and ideas. I have to tap into those sources to help them discover what is within them and to help them be willing to go beyond what they already are or what they already know. I do not believe in a deficit model of education—that our job is to fill up those empty heads. I respect my students and know I am enriched by being with them—I too will learn from them. This is reflected in my teaching ideas and assignments. Too often we are asked only to find things outside of ourselves; we are rarely called on to look inward, to find the sources of our originality.

My job, then, is to raise questions within the classroom since questions are the place where the unknown becomes knowable in our lives. We give voice to thoughts; we dig deep inside ourselves to find ways to approach the questions. Of course, the characteristic of a good question is that it has no one answer but instead helps direct us in our quest to find answers.

I constantly ask myself: Is this topic or issue important to think about? Since we are educating both the minds and hearts of students, we want them to immerse themselves in significant ideas, not just get a dollop of this or that subject. What we do in class has to be part of this big picture called life; it can't be about trivia that would be considered unimportant outside the language arts classroom. Take the ideas on heroes (see Chapter 6), for instance. These ideas are not merely exercises in mental gymnastics; they help us look at what is important and what we value through a consideration of what we admire in others.

I also feel that to involve students in our classes, we have to show them that *we* are excited and interested in the unit of study. If it seems uninspired, boring, or ho-hum to us, think how students will feel. Almost anything can be made interesting if we find questions within the topic to which we—not just our students—can connect.

What an Effective Assignment Looks Like

I like assignments that:

- awaken and activate what is within me
- provide lots of possibilities and tap into my imagination
- are fun and interesting and make me want to think about them
- ask me to wake up and use the bits of life and living around me—I have to be reminded to open my eyes, my ears, my senses of smell, taste, and touch so that I can make use of all the ways I have of knowing
- allow new thoughts to flower, bring out the unexpected, help me discover what I think
- have a "nowness" about them; there is a reason for and importance to doing them at this point in time
- push me to know more while validating what I bring to them
- have an element of spontaneity in them; they are not plodding or predictable, leading only to someone else's answers
- let me create my own shapes and don't expect me to produce cookie-cutter-like thinking

In sum, I love assignments that place me squarely on the threshold of who I am and what I can become. This kind of assignment begins with me and what I know or perceive and gently pushes me to uncover new ways of seeing. At the end, I have a clearer vision of the question I am pursuing, and through these new thoughts or realizations I learn more about myself.

What an Ineffective Assignment Looks Like

I dislike assignments that:

- put boundaries on my thinking and tell me there is only one way to see or do something
- give me no choices about either format or content
- give me a model of perfection that is beyond my reach and makes me freeze up instead of igniting ideas within me (perfect models deaden—they do not inspire)
- ask me to memorize bits and pieces of subject matter so I can parrot them back on a test; this memorization creates dry pock-

- ets within my mind instead of producing fertile soil in which seedlings of new thought can grow

- assume I am deficient in some way

- assume learning is a step-by-step linear process and that learning does not depend on being embedded in a meaningful context

- have no connection to anything else nor any apparent reason for being required except that they are "good" for me and will benefit me in the future

Any of these characteristics of ineffective assignments will prevent students from achieving their best in your classroom.

Examples of Effective and Ineffective Assignments

One assignment that has always worked well is the yearbook assignment (see Chapter 4), in which students create yearbook pages with cutout magazine pictures representing characters from a novel they have just read. The students are part of a wonderful creation: they are giving face to the characters they have read about, taking what they know about them from the novel and thinking hard, digging deep to create words and ideas that will help them know these characters better. Students spent one of our most exciting days in class paging through heaps of magazines looking for pictures to capture the vision they held in their heads of the characters in *The Great Gatsby*. The talk was constant and exciting: "Doesn't this look like Daisy because she has that passive, spoiled look?" "How about this for Jordan—she looks like she isn't apt to tell the truth."

Then students had to think of book titles or create one that could be a character's favorite book. One student thought Jay Gatsby's favorite book would be Charles Dickens's *Great Expectations*. Students worked to capture the essence of fictional characters. They did this work to find out what they thought these characters would be like outside the confines of the book. Of course, the actions and descriptions of the characters had to be built from what students knew of them in the novel, and students added to what they knew by exploring the characters in new ways.

What about assignments that don't work? I had to learn the hard way that assignments that are unsuccessful smack of the do-it-for-practice-until-you-get-it-right mentality. One such assignment asks students to learn to write sentences. The assumption here is that students can learn to do something perfectly outside of any context or meaning and then transfer this skill to the "real" work. This sounds plausible, but it simply isn't successful.

Part of the reason this strategy doesn't work is rooted in learning theory and part in writing theory. Students don't learn if they don't see how the skill fits in with what they already know or if they feel there is no reason for them to practice. Can you imagine your feelings if I asked you to write ten examples of declarative sentences before I let you write anything of substance? Also, doesn't just hearing the assignment make your eyes glaze over? What would make you want to create beautiful, astonishing sentences? Those kinds of sentences are created only within the context of a writing assignment that the writer cares about.

Strategies for Creating Units

I see a unit as "the big picture" that acts as a framework into which the work students will be doing will fit. So, when I create teaching ideas and units, I try to *start with things that fascinate me and interest me.* For example, when I created a unit around what we were like as kindergartners or young children, I was genuinely interested in pursuing this topic, thinking about it, and discovering what I could learn from reflecting on myself as a child. I also knew that my students would find the idea equally fascinating. I knew that new ninth graders would not be able to talk about how awkward it is to begin high school, but that they were far enough away from their kindergarten years to feel safe talking, writing, and reading about them. Likewise, when I put together the unit of short stories about parents (see Chapter 4), I knew students would be interested in thinking about their parents and how they have been treated by them. But I also knew the stories could help us look at our parents more dispassionately. I suspected students would be engaged because almost everyone is still struggling through these issues. I "hooked" students by my series of true and false questions which got them to thinking about, among other things, whether they "owe" their parents anything.

So I start preparing a unit by considering what I might want to know more about, what issues it touches on, and whether students might be interested in those issues. That is why teaching is never boring, cannot ever be boring—it is a constant process of discovery. I get to learn and think and create along with my students. Through language arts, we study such things as our childhoods, what being a teen is like today, the nature of violence, what motivates people, what respect is and how to get it.

I always *create a reason or a context* in which to read the stories or do the writing or the speaking. We never read just to get through a story but to discover things, such as that "friends" may urge us to make a bad decision (as in Walter Dean Myers's *Monster*), or to talk about things, such as what it's like to be alone. I am not a plodder, working through an anthology having students answer the questions at the end and then moving on. Our purpose is not to answer chapter questions; our purpose is to answer life's questions. Students need to know that they are reading or writing stories for a reason.

I can't think of anything deadlier than announcing, "We're going to have a short story unit now." Somehow, we have to create excitement, find the questions students want to explore and answer. So what I do when I use some of the wonderful stories in an anthology is to *group them in meaningful ways and frame them in a way that interests students*. That is how I selected the stories in my American literature anthology for the unit I created on parents. I found stories in which parents were central, and those were the stories we read as a unit (see Chapter 4).

Teachers cannot be one-dimensional. We can't read a story with a single purpose in mind. Instead, we have to encourage responses from students and build on those responses. When I was working with the stories in the parents unit, other issues and ideas of course came up. This was completely acceptable: we should not be in the business of "allowing" discussion of a story only in the ways we have mapped out. Since the point of literature is to make an impact, we have to celebrate and encourage that impact by listening to other issues and ideas that students raise.

I also constantly think about how to *make connections*. How can this idea connect to students' lives? Will it generate issues or topics that will excite them or that they will want to grapple with? How can this idea connect to other genres? Will we be able to find poems, nonfiction, films, TV shows, children's literature, tall tales, short stories, and novels that will relate? Will we be able to connect this unit to the other literature we have already talked about or to stories students have read in literature circles? How can it connect to the larger world? Are the issues in the unit important ones that humans think about and wonder about?

Creating Options in Assignments

Once I have created the idea for the unit—the umbrella under which our work will be conducted—I think of specific assignments and projects that can help students accomplish the unit goals. When I create projects and assignments, I always work to provide options. There is nothing worse than being given a topic to write on that makes your mind go blank. I generate options by first thinking about what I or my students might want to know more about. I try to think of questions that go to the heart of human existence and living, questions that are not made-up or trivial. Essentially, no matter what grade I teach, I always try to tap into the heart of what is important to us as human beings, and I have been surprised by the commonalities of concerns we share throughout our lives.

When I create these options, I usually simply start with whatever occurs to me; then I use the following categories to extend my thinking as I try to generate more connections:

Can I change a point of view? Would students think it interesting to write as if they were another character and tell the world what he or she thought?

Can I bring someone else in? Can I think of someone who might have an interesting point of view on the characters or events? For *Maniac Magee*, I brought a social worker into the classroom so students could think about how someone from the outside with authority would look at the McNab house.

Can I encourage students to think about characters in new ways? When I created the hero unit (see Chapter 6), the seed came from reading about the idea of a hero, getting excited about the possibilities, and then realizing that the idea of heroes could be integrated into much of the discussion about literature we read by asking students who a character's hero might be. This pushes students to analyze what they already know about a character and to extend that knowledge by thinking about the kind of heroes that would appeal to that character.

Can I encourage students to extend what is in the story? Can students add to what they know about the characters by putting the characters in new situations and seeing how they would act, such as having them write about a character appearing at our school? Or can they develop or explain something that was only alluded to in the story, such as creating the scenes in *Maniac Magee* when Maniac first went to live with his aunt and uncle?

Can I identify new formats in which students can respond? I decided to use the format of answering machine messages to give students opportunities to show what they know or can infer about characters. Students could use the language and expressions of the characters to create answering machine messages that reflected the characters' attitudes and personalities. Other formats include character monologues for characters who haven't had a chance to say what is really on their minds, or a college application for a character in a novel.

Can I identify issues in stories that connect to the students' lives? Sometimes an idea is so powerful that students need to respond to it. Oftentimes, because the issues mean so much to students they are eager to explore them. For instance, when my students wrote in response to *Bud, Not Buddy* by Christopher Paul Curtis, they wrote with real feeling about such things as the racism they have witnessed or been subjected to, or the death of a loved one. Literature is full of rich issues that connect to the lives of our students.

Getting Ideas for Units and Making the Unit Blossom

First and foremost, I watch what students respond to and try to build on that response. For example, because of an offhand comment by a ninth grader indicating that he wouldn't date girls who didn't have breasts, I developed a unit around body image. The focus of the inquiry was on the values the students held about physical appearance.

I tried to think of ways to make visible the beliefs that undergird our thinking about appearances. We began by creating collages made from magazine pictures that we thought exemplified what girls "should" look like and what boys "should" look like. Each student worked on a collage for his or her gender. Then students made another collage of photographs of people they love, both male and female.

We discussed the first collages in terms of the media-generated standards of perfection for both males and females. We contrasted the first collages with the collages of people we loved, noting that appearance has very little to do with who we love. From there, we wrote and read stories that dealt with appearance and characters who felt they should change their appearance for someone else (even the last scenes of the movie *Grease* can be used). Students also hunted for poems in books I brought to class that spoke to this issue. These activities elicited strong feelings, most students believing they should be accepted the way they are.

I also create units around the strengths and knowledge of the students I teach. I notice what they like, what they're worried about, what concerns them. That's why I created a unit around being a teen in the 1990s. We read fiction, nonfiction, and poetry, and looked at these works in terms of our own experiences. Did this story seem to portray teen life accurately? How are our lives different? What isn't portrayed in the literature? Students were the experts, bringing knowledge of their lives to evaluate these stories.

Another way I get ideas for units is to go to the library and look mainly at children's books, both fiction and nonfiction. When I see books, I see possibilities. Picking up Jacob Lawrence's *The Great Migration,* I think about where our families came from, why they came here, and what drove them away (such as the Jim Crow laws in the South or lack of work), or about what draws us to places, such as geography or climate. I consider stories of moving I could ask students to write—what the hard parts or the joyous parts of moving were. The song "Moving Right Along" pops into my head. I wonder if I could use that to explore different takes on change and moving along. Is getting somewhere new half the fun? Then I wonder what stories, picture books, poems, nonfiction, novels, or movies I can find. And so I begin.

Or I might discover a book such as *Richard Wright and the Library Card* by William Miller or *Kids Still Having Kids* by Janet Bode. I brainstorm ways in which the subjects might interest or involve my students. Discrimination (a theme in the Richard Wright book) because of race, age, or gender would probably result in lots of student stories. We could find people in the community to talk about racial discrimination in our city. I know the woman who was the first black teacher hired in our school district in the 1950s. Potential projects jump into my mind—kids doing pamphlets or ad campaigns or public service campaigns about discrimination. What rights do *they* have as teens? What should they do when they're followed by security guards at the mall?

I create units around the material in the textbook. In my American Literature classes, I frame my units around questions students can get involved with. When we read Thoreau, I wanted to move students to their own frames of reference, so I framed the unit around the question: Can we learn about ourselves and the world through nature? Before we started the unit, students had to spend ten minutes alone under the stars and then write a reflection on the experience. We read *Walden* and the writings of Gary Paulsen and worked to articulate the impact that nature could have on us.

These larger questions give me points of entry into the topic. I ask myself which poems, short stories, novels, nonfiction, or films I can use. I think about how I might be able to work music into the unit. I try to bring things from student life—such as music—into the classroom as another lens through which to view our work. I might have students bring in songs or instrumental pieces they think Thoreau would like. We could play a piece, jot down the impact it made on us, and then talk about how Thoreau might react.

When I think about writing and project ideas, I start with the ones that interest me. What would I love to write about in response to a piece of writing or a unit? What would I learn from this experience? What would open up possibilities and not make me feel hemmed in? I ask myself how I can get kids fascinated and engaged with the question or the topic, how I can get them inside the learning and become more than passive bystanders. Can I start with a survey to pique their interest, create questions they can write or talk about, ask them what they know about something?

Integrating Ideas from This Book into Your Own Teaching

Each of us has a different teaching style, different way of approaching things, different way of being with students. But no matter how your approach differs from mine, if you understand the theory or philosophy at the heart of my teaching, then pieces of these ideas and approaches can be worked into whatever you are doing.

You can start by creating new frames or new ways to look at the material you are using. For instance, if you are using Ben Franklin's *Autobiography* in your American Literature textbook, instead of asking what the piece is about and what we learn about the times in which Franklin lived, come up with a new question or new way to think about this work. Consider what Ben Franklin thought he needed to change about himself. Are these things we are concerned about today? Or have students explore what they think Franklin would be writing about now if he were alive. Or have students draw up resolutions they would like to live by and compare them to Franklin's. What can they glean from setting their piece of writing next to Franklin's? Have values changed?

Or if students are reading "Sinners in the Hands of an Angry God" by Cotton Mather, they could think about which of his ideas still resonate today. They can discuss how effective Mather's fire-and-brimstone delivery would be today and why it would or would not be used. They can even talk about why humans have such differing views of what God is like. Some see God as a harsh, judgmental, ready-to-dump-us-into-hellfire Being, while others conceive of God as an all-loving, accepting Being. These kinds of questions work to create approaches to literature that will make it alive and current for students.

You also need to consider how to begin formulating your questions. Paying attention only to form and how and why something is written the way it is can be deadly. Consider instead the issues at the heart of literature. Think about what you would like to talk about or explore after the class has read a particular work of literature.

To begin, contemplate the piece of writing outside of the traditional framework in which you are used to thinking about it. Don't start with plot, character, setting, theme, point of view, or style. Trying to limit your thinking to these categories only blocks your thinking. Don't dwell on what you think you *should* be doing; dwell on what sounds interesting to you.

Another way these ideas can be worked into the framework of what you already do in class is to look at what you are asking students to do. Are you giving them options? Are you validating the worth of their contributions in class? Or do you assume that the most important talk in a class is your talk, teacher talk? Using students' ideas to build on what they bring to class in the way of knowledge and experience is one cornerstone of good teaching (see Chapter 5 on using students' ideas). Inviting and building on student talk is one way students grapple with the questions and content they are dealing with. Allowing only teacher talk deadens a class and gives students the message that there is only one way of knowing, only one way to view things. Further, it gives students the wrong idea—that language arts is not about being expansive and opening up the world but is instead a tightly prescribed body of content that students should master and be able to prove mastery of.

Providing writing and project options is another way to tell students that you value difference in their writing and that they are not writing only for you. Before they are willing to take risks in their work and try out new formats or genres, students need to feel safe from emotional ridicule, accepted by the teacher and their peers, and unafraid of not measuring up to harsh standards.

You might wonder how to begin creating options. After you read a piece of writing, several themes or issues usually surface quickly. Take one of those themes and issues, such as friendship or being accepted or being connected to nature, and structure options that allow students to apply that theme to their own lives. Do they have their own story of friendship? Has the same kind of incident as that described in the story ever happened to them?

Once I exhaust the possibilities of how I can relate the options to the lives of my students, I move on to other areas. What opportunities can I create for students to interact with the characters and with the characters' thinking? Can they find poems that the character would like? Can they write from the point of view of the character? Can they compose a letter from one character to another?

Other options can be created by connecting the literature to life. Do students agree with the beliefs demonstrated by a character? Can they dramatize issues in the novel or explore issues such as living with stepparents, perhaps in a talk show format? Also, when I create options I include some that push students to think critically. They can brainstorm the themes they believe were present in the story and write about which ones were most important; they can look at gender and race within the story by writing about which roles could most easily be played by a character of another race or gender, and why.

Other options give students the opportunity to create in response to the text. They might draw images or make a collage that captures the essence of the novel, or they might write a short story or create poems on the same theme. (Before I finish creating options, I also go over all the formats or "ways into literature" and/or my list of fifty alternatives to the book report to see if these pieces give me any more ideas. For specifics, see Chapter 4.)

Another way you can use these ideas to add to your own teaching is to use what students generate in class. Do you ask them to respond in writing with their own opinions or their own understandings about something? If so, then use their responses. This is a wonderful way to encourage student understanding and to build on what students bring to the class in the way of information and experience.

One simple way to get started using student work is to have students "inkshed," i.e., write on each others' papers with responselike comments. As an illustration, if all the students in your class are writing about their reading autobiography, put them in groups and have them pass the papers around, responding only to the content. They might say such things as "Me too!," or "How awful!," or "I had a teacher just like that." When students finish reading all four or five papers, they discuss the similarities and differences in their early reading experiences and work to draw conclusions. Each group then tells the whole group what they have learned, and often a whole class discussion will be sparked. Students can also generate themes or motifs from novels, create lists of questions for characters, and come up with myriad other responses on which to build the work of the class (see Chapter 6).

Conclusion

Student interest drives student learning. Keeping in mind that our major goal is to answer life's questions, analyze what you do in class in this light. We all have the ability to extend invitations to learning that will make our students imagine, wonder, and crave more learning. With some thought and preparation, with some attention to our students and their needs, we can all create and implement innovative, exciting teaching ideas.

Works Cited

Bode, Janet. *Kids Still Having Kids: People Talk about Teen Pregnancy.* New York: Watts, 1992.

Curtis, Christopher Paul. *Bud, Not Buddy.* New York: Delacorte, 1999.

Lawrence, Jacob. *The Great Migration: An American Story.* New York: HarperTrophy, 1995.

Miller, William. *Richard Wright and the Library Card.* New York: Lee, 1997.

Myers, Walter Dean. *Monster.* New York: HarperCollins, 1999.

Spinelli, Jerry. *Maniac Magee.* Boston: Little, 1990.

4 Literature

Diana Mitchell

Diana addresses not only literary genres (novel, short story, poetry, children's literature, nonfiction) but also, in the first two sections, practical ways to get "into" literature. Specifically, she offers multiple approaches to literature and fifty different activities appropriate for book reports. Literature is the staple of the English language arts classroom, and this chapter will provide many ideas for student investigation and exploration of text, as well as specific suggestions for pieces of literature you might want to use in your classroom. Presented with intriguing literature and given a choice in response activities, most students will thoroughly enjoy their reading— and, as an added benefit, learn along the way.

WAYS INTO LITERATURE

I hear and read about lots of great ideas I would like to use in my classroom, but if I don't write them down, I quickly forget about them. The problem now is that even though I have notebooks full of good ideas, I often don't have the time to skim through the notebooks! So, to be able to retrieve what I know and learn, I write down lists of the things I want to remember to use and then post them by my desk. This way the list is in sight, and I can use it whenever I want to implement an approach I haven't yet used that year.

This section is intended to be that sort of list—a catalog of ideas and ways into literature that will motivate students to think further about what they're reading by involving them and asking them to do something with the literature.

While Reading the Literature

1. Questions and Issues. I pass out 3" x 5" note cards and ask students to write down two or three questions or issues they want to discuss from their reading. I collect the cards as the students finish them, try to skim them to organize and categorize a bit, then either begin a whole class discussion on issues brought up or divide the class into groups and give them a few of the cards to respond to.

This technique usually guarantees student involvement since these are student- rather than teacher-generated questions. I have found that with this type of invitation students tend to focus on questions about the characters in the novel, why they act the way they do, and what motivates them.

Usually, after these kinds of questions are answered, students then turn their attention to clarification questions, which are aimed at figuring out why something happened or at getting more information on events they did not understand. Next, students seem to be concerned with societal issues, such as how families handle death. The questions and issues that students want to discuss are often ones that would not have occurred to me, a fact that supports the importance of having students generate their own questions.

2. Monologue about and to a Character. When the class gets to an especially upsetting or dismaying part of a book, students can write a monologue meant to be delivered to the character involved. Monologues could be based on student reactions to something the character did, advice to a character, or impressions of the character and where that character seems to be heading.

This activity works well at such points as the following: in *Romeo and Juliet* when Juliet decides to take the poison; in John Steinbeck's *Of Mice and Men* when George goes after Lennie; and in Rob Thomas's *Satellite Down* when Patrick decides to disappear into a small Irish town to escape the media whirlwind that surrounds him.

3. Protest Campaign. If students become upset about something that happens in a novel, let them organize a protest campaign. In *Don't Care High* by Gordon Korman, my students were upset that the principal would not let the student body have a president. In groups students spent two days writing a speech to rally other students, composing a letter that would be read to the fictional principal, and making posters and buttons in favor of the deposed president. On the third day, each group delivered a speech to the rest of the class to try to rally them to the cause, read a letter addressed to the principal in the novel, and shared other material created for the campaign.

This activity works at the point in a book when a person or group is being wronged--such as when Harry Potter is being treated unfairly in Mr. Snape's class in *Harry Potter and the Sorcerer's Stone* by J. K. Rowling.

4. Telegrams. When students get to a point in a story or novel at which a character might want or need to send a telegram asking for help, have students write the telegram from the character's point of view. I encourage students to keep to a fifteen-word limit. They then write the telegram on a form I created, and we talk about and then display the telegrams around the classroom.

5. Pick an Issue. When a major issue looms up in a novel, such as physical abuse in *Max the Mighty* by Rodman Philbrick, I ask students to write about it. I usually give them several suggestions. I might ask them how they would react to Worm's dilemma, what steps a person in her shoes could take, and what they would do if they had a friend in the same situation.

6. Editorials. After students understand how to write a persuasive editorial, have them write an editorial about an issue in a book. For instance, while reading Charles Dickens's *A Tale of Two Cities*, students might want to write an editorial beseeching people to stay out of Paris; while reading Walter Dean Myers's *Fallen Angels*, they might want to write about their view of war; while reading *When Zachary Beaver Came to Town* by Kimberly Willis Holt, they might want to express their opinions about the way the obese Zachary is treated. Is he being exploited?

7. Daily Journal. Students choose one major character from a novel and keep a daily journal for that character, reporting what happens to him or her as the story progresses. Students can record the feelings and motivations of their chosen character, as well as events in the lives of individuals near their character that affect him or her.

This idea works well with characters who are preoccupied or introspective, such as Hester Prynne or Arthur Dimmesdale in Nathaniel Hawthorne's *The Scarlet Letter*, Myrtle in F. Scott Fitzgerald's *The Great Gatsby*, Sura in *The Buffalo Tree* by Adam Rapp, and Finn in the novel *Finn* by Katherine Jay Bacon.

8. Letters. When the plot seems to merit it, students can write letters from one character to another. For example, in *The True Confessions of Charlotte Doyle* by Avi, Charlotte could write a letter to the crew explaining why they should trust her and give her another chance after she betrayed them. In *Bud, Not Buddy* by Christopher Paul Curtis, students could write the letter that Herman E. Calloway longs to write to his departed daughter.

9. Three Words. Have students write down three words which they feel best describe a character. In groups, students share their words and their reasons for selecting these words. Each group decides which three or more words best fit the character. They then share their conclusions with the class.

This simple activity stimulates valuable discussions as students justify their word choices. I've used this idea with short stories such as

Eudora Welty's "A Worn Path" and am often amazed at the wealth of ways in which students view the same character. Students have described Phoenix Jackson, the main character in the story, as old, humble, peaceful, stubborn, senile, buffoonish, sly, determined, dignified, angry, dishonest, fearless, selfish, and venerable. The discussions that followed were lively as students disputed or agreed with word choices.

After Reading the Literature

1. Characters' Quotations. Students dig back into the book to find ten quotations or sentences that reveal the character they've been assigned or have chosen and that show what the character is like. Students explain what these quotations tell or show about their character.

A variation of this idea is to divide the students into groups of three with specific chapters assigned to each group. They go through the chapters, locating what they consider to be important quotations from many characters. I compile all the groups' quotations, duplicate them, and hand them out the next day in class. The same groups get back together to try to identify as many of these quotations as they can, using the novel as needed, skipping the ones their group chose. This activity really gets students back into the book as they try to identify who said what and what it shows about the character. Spirited discussions result when students have to deal with the words of Curley's wife in *Of Mice and Men* when she says, "You can talk to people, but I can't talk to nobody but Curley" or when Crooks says, "You guys comin' in and settin' made me forget."

2. Awards. After reading a novel or group of short stories, students brainstorm categories for awards that could be given to characters such as "most caring," "most dedicated," "most selfish," "most troubled," "most courageous," "most pitiful," "most heartless," "most imaginative," "hardest role to play," "person who put up with the most," "worst parent," or "most dramatic." Students then decide which character should receive the award and write up a brief summary of why that character should get that award.

Some of my classes have really gotten into this activity, and we have even had several nominations for each award and then a vote. After deciding which students would speak about which award, students gave speeches explaining why the winner deserved this honor while the other nominees did not.

3. Comics. Students go through the comics for several weeks looking for comic strips that specific characters would like. They mount the comic strips on paper and write their explanation of why this comic would appeal to or speak to the character. Crowds of students will read these papers if they are displayed in the classroom.

4. Make a Newspaper. After students have read a novel, they write and design the front page or two of a newspaper that includes stories about the events and characters in the story. They can write news stories based on happenings in the story, interviews of the characters, news briefs about the main events in the story, a weather box, and a "What's Inside" box.

When my students read Ernest Hemingway's *For Whom the Bell Tolls*, one newspaper, "The Republic Weekly," contained a feature about Anselmo titled "A Freedom Fighter and His Cause," a news story titled "Fascist Air Raids Rake Spanish Cities," and another news story, "Peasants Blow Up Train." Found on the second page were a letter to the editor about death in the mountains, three obituaries, an opinion piece on why the peasants seemed to have lost their powerful religious faith, and weather reports, so that both sides could better plan their strategies. Another student paper included an ad for El Bango Munitions, which boasted, "We specialize in guerrilla services."

5. Pictures. After reading a novel, students bring in a picture that a specific character would like or appreciate, or that they feel would have a special meaning to that character. They can share these in groups, each student explaining what about the picture would appeal to the character. Students can also write up their reasons for choosing the picture.

6. Word Collage. Students cut out of magazines thirty to forty words or phrases that describe the novel or a character in the novel. They write the book title or the name of the character in the center of a blank sheet of paper and then glue on all the words, filling the entire sheet. Students then write about why they chose the words they did. Although this activity seems easy, and students do enjoy doing it, they often make connections that illustrate deep and sophisticated thinking about the novel.

7. Connecting Poetry to Stories. Bring in poems that relate to the novel or story and ask students to discuss and write about the way the poem speaks to the issues in the novel. For instance, after reading Robert Newton Peck's *A Day No Pigs Would Die*, we read Robert Frost's "The Mending Wall" and discussed it in terms of the two families in the book—the Tanners and the Pecks. Then students made lists of why good fences make good neighbors and lists of what fences keep in and what they keep out. Students can also write about which character in the novel would most agree with the sentiments in the poem.

8. Writing a Scene and Acting It Out. Students choose a scene that was alluded to but not completely developed in a novel and flesh it out in script form. For example, after reading *Monster* by Walter Dean Myers, a group of students could write and enact the robbery scene as they think it happened and then present it to the class. Also lending themselves to scripting are the events surrounding the murder scene in *The Crusader* by Edward Bloor.

9. Advertisements. After reading a novel, you can brainstorm the kind of products that characters in the novel could use, creating an assignment similar to the following:

> Miss Havisham from Charles Dickens's *Great Expectations* needs help! Her clothes are yellow, her stockings are tattered and ragged, her face is wrinkled, her body is withered and sagging, she is tired and worn out, she has no color in her face and skin, and she has a broken heart. In addition, the rooms in her house are smelly, dust and mold are everywhere, cobwebs fill the corners, spiders and mice abound, and all her furniture is on the verge of falling apart.

Create a product that could help Miss Havisham, her clothes, or her house by:

    a. making up a name for your product

    b. listing all the things it can do

    c. listing all the reasons someone should buy it (e.g., everybody's doing it; a famous person uses this product; you deserve the best; be the first to use this product)

Then "sell" your product by:

    a. writing up an advertisement for a newspaper about your product that includes a drawing or a picture cut out of a magazine illustrating your product

    b. writing an ad that could be used on the radio, trying to incorporate into it sound effects or a song

10. A School Visit. Students lift a character out of the book and drop him or her down in their school. They must decide if the character is a student, a teacher, a custodian, a secretary, a nurse, a principal, a cafeteria employee, and so forth. Students cannot change the character's personality, but must explain what might happen if he or she came to their school.

After my students read the play "The Night Thoreau Spent in Jail" by Jerome Lawrence and Robert E. Lee, they wrote about Henry David Thoreau appearing at our school as a student. They focused on such things as the unconventional way he would probably dress; how he would react to a football game; how he would react to the waste of food and the excess trash in the cafeteria; how he would react to classes that expected rote memorization; what he might want to share in a science class; other students' reactions to his lack of concern about fitting in; and which of his views might get him in trouble with the administration.

11. Pamphlet. With drawings or pictures and text, students create a brochure advertising or promoting something in the novel. In *The Crazy Horse Electric Game* by Chris Crutcher, students could create a brochure to advertise One More Last Chance High School, a private, alternative high school. After students have decided on a cover and how to describe the school to persuade students to want to attend, students can fold a plain white sheet of paper in thirds to create a trifold pamphlet. Students could cover aspects of the school such as class size and teacher-to-student ratio, who is eligible to attend, cost of tuition, and the kind of education a student could expect to receive. Students should remember that the major audience for this brochure is parents who are considering sending their children to this school.

12. Values. Create a list of values that characters in the book seem to have. For instance, in Chris Crutcher's short story "A Brief Moment in the Life of Angus Bethune," I listed values such as loyalty, self-acceptance, importance of physical appearance, and importance of having fun, and had students rank two characters in terms of these values. Students then wrote out an explanation of why they believed these characters held these values so highly.

13. Create a Childhood for a Character. Before asking students to do this, I pass out a sheet of sentence starters so students can begin to think about the kind of childhood their character might have had. I include starters such as the following:

    a. My earliest memory is of . . .

    b. One time I was really scared was when . . .

    c. I remember being very embarrassed when . . .

    d. My hero was . . . because . . .

    e. One of the happiest times of my life was when . . .

    f. One of the worst times of my life was . . .

    g. My biggest worry is . . .

    h. I dislike people who . . .

    i. One thing that really upsets me is . . .

    j. One thing I wish my parents realized about me is . . .

After this type of sheet has been filled out and students have thought deeply about the childhood experiences that made the character as he or she is presented in the novel, I ask them to write up the story of the character's childhood.

14. Gender/Violence Critique. When stories lend themselves to this assignment, I use it as an option. I ask students to imagine that they are members of either the National Organization of Women or the Coalition to Stop Violence and that they have been asked to write up a critique of this novel in terms of gender stereotypes or whether the story promotes violence. This idea works well with *Of Mice and Men, The Great Gatsby, The True Confessions of Charlotte Doyle,* and many other novels.

15. Interview a Character. Each student chooses a character to interview. In groups, students first construct a list of questions to ask characters in the novel. Then each person writes up the interview by having the character answer the questions. When we read *The Giver* by Lois Lowry, students wanted to ask Jonas's parents why they never questioned anything in society, how Jonas's father could justify killing infants, how Jonas's mother felt knowing that her job in the justice system often meant violators of minor "crimes" were put to death, and how they felt about being moved to housing for "Adults without Children" when their children grew up. Students generate the questions together, then individually write up the interviews, which reveal how they think the characters would answer.

16. Stamps. After class discussion about how stamps are issued to commemorate great people or important events, ask students to think about the book they have just finished in terms of what person or event or issue in the novel would merit a commemorative stamp. On a stamp form I created, students draw the stamp design or use magazine pictures to represent the person, event, or issue, and then write about why they think the person or event or issue is worthy of a stamp. After reading *Roll of Thunder, Hear My Cry* by Mildred Taylor, one of my students created a stamp to celebrate the courage of Mama in standing up to the school board member. Another did a stamp to commemorate brotherhood.

USING NEW NOVELS WITHOUT BEING OVERWHELMED

Introducing a novel in the language arts classroom that is new to you may seem like a daunting task. Without a teacher's guide, some teachers fear they will founder. They are uncertain whether they will focus on the issues and elements others see as important about that novel. They worry about having the time to prepare a whole unit on a novel on top of everything else they have to do. But we all get tired of the same old material we've been using. By interacting with new material, we stay more alert and interested. The other good news is this: it doesn't have to take as much time as you think.

From my experiences using novels new to me, I have developed some ideas and approaches that can help relieve the burden of preparation. But first, a few words of advice and encouragement:

1. *Don't try to do it all at once.* When you teach novels over a period of years, you gradually develop assignments and projects to go with them. This doesn't happen the first time through.

2. *Give yourself permission to just read and discuss the novel in your classroom.* Students do not have to respond to every chapter, note every detail, or identify every method of characterization. Read the book with the students just as you would read a book for pleasure.

3. *Look on this as a learning experience.* You will be experiencing the same things students do the first time they read a novel. You won't be the expert; you'll be working together to create a satisfying reading experience. Just as we like to talk about a book, figure out why people act the way they do, and discover what exactly happened, so do students.

4. *As you read the book the first time, try to jot down your own thoughts and reactions* so you will have concrete evidence of how you approach a book and what interests you about it. This will help you remember what it is like for students to approach a new book.

Getting Ready

After you have selected a possible novel, read it through quickly, writing reactions in the margins if you have time. The second reading will come when you're reading it with the class.

1. *Can you define issues or questions the novel raised for you?* You can use this information to develop introductory activities.

2. *Does any other material come to mind that you could link to issues in the book?* If so, perhaps you can use this material as a way to introduce the book or have students respond during the reading. For instance, since *Toning the Sweep* by Angela Johnson focuses on a grandmother, I brought in the book *Grand Mothers*, a collection of poems, reminiscences, and short stories edited by Nikki Giovanni. I read a few selections to the class, and we compared the qualities of the grandmothers in this collection to the grandmother in *Toning the Sweep*.

3. *Does this novel require that you provide background material on any aspect of the book?* To better understand *Toning the Sweep*, students needed information on the hostile and dangerous conditions that permeated parts of the South in the 1960s for African Americans. I asked students to talk to their parents or grandparents about the kinds of things that went on in the South at this time. They each brought back bits of information the next day that we talked about together.

4. *What would you like students to get out of the novel?* This is important to answer for yourself so that you don't lose your focus and so that you can work to deepen student involvement. Also, you can focus activities on these reasons.

Before-Reading Activities

After you have read the novel, the first step is to look back over the notes you've jotted down to help you create an introductory activity that will draw students into the novel. This activity might be as simple as answering questions, filling out surveys, reading related material from other sources, or developing a scenario for students to respond to. The important thing is to raise questions in the minds of students and increase anticipation so they will want to read the novel. The following sections discuss my approaches to three new novels.

Toning the Sweep

Most of the introductory activities I use are fairly easy to create. I started the discussion of *Toning the Sweep* with some questions based on the issues I had earlier determined were important or interesting. I first asked students to write down a few words or phrases that described what came to mind when they thought of a grandmother. They shared their answers in groups, and the groups shared with the whole class so we could all see how others viewed grandparents. I then had students write out answers to the following questions: How do you let go of the past? How do you forget painful things? In your experience, do teens relate better to their parents or their grandparents? Then to elicit their views of older people, I asked students to describe a hairdo that a sixty- or seventy-year-old woman would wear, describe their idea of how someone in their sixties or seventies drives a car, and describe the music they thought older people listened to. All of these questions and exercises were designed to involve students with the issues and characters in the novel.

The Giver

For Lois Lowry's *The Giver*, which is packed with thought-provoking issues such as whether we can ever have a truly peaceful society in which people have some measure of freedom and choice, I wanted to thrust students into the heart of these issues, so I made up twenty fairly serious questions or activities, such as:

1. Brainstorm a list of all the things wrong with society and with people.

2. Oftentimes when people are different, they get picked on or discriminated against. What kinds of differences bring out these responses or reactions in people? For example, in school, what differences cause people to get picked on or treated differently?

3. If you knew of a society that had full employment, no crime or violence, and no unwanted children, would you want to live there? What questions would you ask about that society before you moved there?

4. When someone says something is for the "good of the community," what does that mean to you? Who gets to decide this?

5. Every society defines which of its citizens it is acceptable to get rid of. In some countries many years ago, it was considered okay to put girl babies on mountains to die. In Hitler's Germany, it was considered okay to kill anyone Jewish or anyone who criticized Hitler. In this country, it is considered okay to execute some criminals. Do you believe society has the right to make these kinds of decisions? What kinds of people do you believe it *is* acceptable to get rid of?

After students wrote their answers (which took most of a class period), we spent at least the next day and a half discussing these provocative issues. I explained to students that the society we were to read about appeared perfect on the surface but that all the issues we had addressed were present in the book.

Monster

When we read *Monster* by Walter Dean Myers, a book about a teenage boy who is incarcerated when he's accused of being an accessory to a murder, I asked students to complete sentence starters that asked for fairly short answers. Starters included:

    a. Being really alone means_____.

    b. People cry when_____.

    c. People beat up on other people because _____.

    d. If I was ever in jail, I would _____.

By raising these issues before students read the novel, I helped them articulate their own views before they compared them to the perspectives played out in the book.

Scenarios

Scenarios are another strategy that can be used to involve students deeply in the concerns or attitudes expressed in a novel. I have created situations which parallel the events in a novel and asked students to respond in writing. For example, to get my students engaged with one of the major events in *A Face in Every Window* by Han Nolan, I asked them to answer the following:

> If your family suddenly got a much larger house, how would you feel if your parents started taking in young people who needed a home, people you didn't even like and who lived with you like family? What might your parents, who see this as a way to help out others, say to you if you complained? How might your friends react? What would be the hardest thing for you to accept about this new arrangement?

After writing and discussing their responses, students found JP's reaction to his home situation realistic since they had thought about the issue in terms of themselves.

What about Reading Aloud?

As I'm reading a novel with a class, I try to keep in mind my goals for involving students in novels. I want students to interact with the themes and issues in terms of themselves and their own worlds. I want them to be able to step back and objectively look at the way someone else handles a situation and think about how they might handle it differently. I want them to enjoy the book, the unfolding of events and characters, and to feel empathy for the characters, to see how they themselves are alike or different from the characters. If students are unwilling or unable to read a book themselves, I do make allowances because I don't want to punish them for their simple lack of compliance. I still want them to get as much out of the book as possible.

In the last several years, I have had several ninth-grade general English classes in which it was difficult to interest more than half of the students in reading. That is why we read novels aloud. Although even in my own building English teachers would say, "I expect them to be responsible for their own reading!," I ignored their opinion and did whatever it took to get the students reading, helping them to have a positive reading experience. So when my students are really into a book such as *Tears of a Tiger* by Sharon Draper or *Don't You Dare Read This, Mrs. Dunphrey* by Margaret Peterson Haddix, I listen to them when they say they want me to keep reading. They don't want to stop and write; they want to hear the story.

Until I became aware of the work of Kylene Beers of Sam Houston University (I attended a presentation Beers did at the 1990 ALAN Workshop titled "Choosing Not to Read: An Ethnographic Approach to Understanding Aliteracy"), I wasn't aware that many kids don't see pictures in their heads as they read. They plod through words, paying attention to decoding skills, not to meaning. Since this is a significant reason many students don't like to read, I feel that reading aloud to them partially solves the problem. I have heard these students say, "It's almost like seeing a movie of it when she reads it like it means something." So, because students can see those pictures and make those connections when they hear the words aloud, I often read to these classes.

While Reading the Novel

Small-Group Work

If you have students write in literature logs or response journals, ask them for ideas and questions as you read the book with them. You might ask them to bring into class one or two questions or issues from the book that they would like to discuss. Collect the questions the next day and either conduct a whole-class discussion or divide up the questions and give some to each small group. With classes that exhibit the "you're-the-teacher,-you-figure-it-out" attitude, I often develop a few questions to get them started. I often generate these questions while we're reading aloud and write them in the margins of the book. I also try to underline quotations that strike me as I read, so I have possible statements students can react to if they do not bring in many questions.

When you do get to a point where students are willing to pause, having them work in small groups is usually effective. Since many students have never discussed a book without a teacher present, I often give them a structure to help them get started. One day I might ask them to focus on characters. I tell them to talk about who they like, who they don't understand, what they'd like to say to a character, and what they wished characters had said to each other. Other times I might ask students to focus on events or the plot line. Did the events seem realistic? Would they have reacted differently than the characters did to an event? Why do they think characters reacted to the event the way they did? Sometimes we'll focus on issues. We make a list on the board before we break into small groups so that each group will have an abundance of material to work with. When we talk about themes and issues, I ask students to consider what the author wants them to think about the issue. I might pose questions such as, "What do you think Angela Johnson is saying about the process of dying?" and "What might Rodman Philbrick be saying about abusive parents?"

Another day I might ask students in small groups to focus on the book itself. Did the plot structure seem workable? Did any events seem out of place or contrived? Did the story move well, or did some parts lag? What did they notice about the language and words used? Was anything repeated frequently? Why do you think the author used a particular strategy? After a while, students no longer need guided responses; they build the confidence to have a discussion without teacher questions.

Student-Generated Questions

Another way to build student involvement while cutting down on teacher burnout is to have students generate questions every few days and then spend time discussing the questions in small groups or as a whole class. When we read *The Giver*, students raised questions and issues such as:

> Do our memories of the past and present shape our futures?
>
> Why did the Giver live in the world passively for so long?
>
> Let's discuss the symbolism of color and music.
>
> The Rules stress the importance of specific, precise language. Should there be a place for slang? Is there only one best way to express an idea? Is there room for variety in language?
>
> Would our lives change if the weather never changed?
>
> People are taught to apologize, accept apologies, not ask rude questions, and to be honest. Do we lack these values in our society?

Other Activities

I have also developed two other activities to involve students while they are reading the novel, activities which combine dictionary skills and vocabulary with character study. I pass out dictionaries and assign every group specific letters of the alphabet to work with. Their job is to go through their section of the dictionary and list words that describe people. They write down the words and a brief definition if the word isn't well known.

When each group turns in the words, I take them home and type them all. The next day in the same groups students try to identify the fifteen words that describe people in the most positive way and fifteen words that describe people in the most negative way. Then students turn to a character in the book we are reading and try to agree on five words that best describe that person. Students note if any of the words they chose were among the most positive or negative ones and then explain why that word does indeed apply to the character. I usually ask each group to select words for three to four characters. Words might include *able, abrupt, academic, aggressive, audacious, apathetic, bawdy, brotherly, charming, childish, cocky, composed, cooperative, cutthroat, fierce, flashy, headstrong,* and *humble.*

Another character activity involves asking students to write down words that describe characters. One day I might ask each student to write down five things that describe two or three specific characters. Another day I'll ask for adjectives on additional characters. We do this after we've read about half of a novel. Then I type up and duplicate these lists.

In groups students circle the words they think describe the character and underline the words they don't agree with, and then we talk about these. When we've finished reading the book, I pass back students' original lists and ask them to add two or three more describers. They then write about whether their original impression of that character changed. The lists I type up also serve as a wonderful resource if you decide to ask students to write a poem about one of the characters--students often include the words themselves or use the words to help them generate more ideas.

Culminating Activities

Word Test

Once I truly understood, through reader-response theory, that each reader pays attention to different things in a reading, I stopped giving multiple-choice tests. In my quest to find other means of assessment, I stumbled on the word test. After reading *The Giver,* for example, I selected fifteen words from the novel that I felt were important because they illustrated a concept or belief essential to the society depicted in the story. I asked students to select any twelve of these words (which included *love, release, bike, twins, color, war, grandparents*, and *sameness*). For each word, students had to write what they knew about the word in terms of the novel. For instance, if the word was *bike*, they could write, "Bikes are given to every child when he or she turns nine. It is perhaps a sign that the child is now old enough to go out into the community." Students also had the option of adding two words of their own choosing. Like me, you'll be amazed by how much students get out of a book. Since they are freed from having to pay attention to teacher-chosen details, they have the time to think about the major issues. These tests are easy to correct and interesting to read since students' explanations are so varied.

Essay Writing

Another culminating activity I used with that novel was to have students list on butcher paper all the pros and cons of living in *The Giver* society. We hung up the lists in the room and examined them for commonalities. Then, with the lists still prominently posted, I asked students to write an opinion essay on whether they would want to live in *The Giver* society. Because they understood the book, had discussed the pros and cons of the society, and had the posted lists as references, it was not difficult for students to write their rough drafts.

The next day I helped students revise their drafts by giving them the following directions:

In paragraph 1: Take a stand on whether you would want to live in *The Giver* society. Make sure (a) that your first sentence is written so that someone who has not read the book can understand what you're talking about, and (b) in the second and third sentences, give at least three major reasons for your decision.

In paragraphs 2 through 4: Elaborate on each of the three reasons.

In paragraph 5: Explain in three to five sentences what you wish our society has that *The Giver* society has. [I suggested they start the paragraph with wording like "Even though I would/would not like to live in *The Giver* society, there are some things I wish our society did have from them." If they took the position that they would like to live in that society, I asked them to use the paragraph to show in what ways that society was not perfect.]

In the last paragraph: Wrap-up your paper in two or three sentences.

Bingo

When my class finished *The Crazy Horse Electric Game*, I devised a game of bingo as a method of reviewing characters and major events before students scripted a scene. I wanted them to think back over the whole novel, which was a long and complicated one. This method of review was not tedious or boring; indeed, students loved playing bingo. Although it may sound overwhelming to construct such a game, I found shortcuts.

To make the bingo cards, I drew twenty-five squares on a sheet of paper, which I then photocopied. Then on the board I listed all the words that could be used in the bingo game. I tried to come up with about thirty-five names and events so there would be variety in the cards. I passed out a blank sheet to each student, gave each one a number, and told them to begin copying the words from the board, beginning with their number. They were to start with square one, go down to square two, and so on, then come back up the top of the row and work their way down again. By following this method, no two cards were the same. Of course, as students were copying down the words they were chatting about who each person was and what the terms referred to.

I have found that creating these "illegal" opportunities for students to help each other works exceedingly well to get everyone involved. Students often don't realize that I don't care how much help they give each other; I just want them to have the novel in perspective and be aware of the main events before we start writing scripts to flesh out events in the novel. For *The Crazy Horse Electric Game*, I used words such as *Willie, Telephone Man, acid trip, Bisquick, Lacey*, and *cane*.

Playing the game was noisy and fun. Before class I had written each word on a slip of paper. During class I drew the slips out of a bag. I had also written the "definition" of the word on the back of the paper, so I read that to the class. Since a sugary treat and extra credit were at stake, every ninth grader took the game seriously, and even the students who hadn't paid close attention or had not become involved extensively in the story wanted to know who these people and things were. This version of bingo worked marvelously as a way to review the book. Once students felt they had all the pieces in place, it was easier for them to find significant scenes to script.

Options: Writing, Drama, Art

As another culminating activity, I create a list of options that include writing, drama, and art. As I read the novel with students in class, I try to write down ideas in the margins of the book as they come to me. I have found that ideas often fall generally into these six categories:

1. *What a student would like to say to a character.* (Mr. Doom is cruel to the children in his care in *Dave at Night* by Gail Carson Levine. Write out what you would like to say to him to get him to reconsider his actions.)

2. *What a character never got the chance to say to another character.* (Finn in Katherine Jay Bacon's *Finn* still thinks about the members of his family, who were all killed in the plane accident he survived. Write up the conversation he would like to have with his friend Julia about his feelings for his family.)

3. *How things would be different if the point of view was changed.* (How would Coly Jo, one of the "juvies" in *The Buffalo Tree* by Adam Rapp, tell the story of his time in the detention center and what it was like for him?)

4. *Essays or stories or videos on issues brought up in the book.* (Death of a sister; accident; father making fun of you; hearing parents fight; struggling with disability—which of these situations sounds toughest to deal with? Create a story or video or write an essay in which you show someone in one of these situations and how they handle it.)

5. *Art and poetry responses.* (Write several poems about characters or themes or places in the book. If you are artistic, draw a picture of how you visualize something in the book, such as McNab's house or the frogball game or Grayson's funeral.)

6. *Extending the novel through such things as creating brochures, writing radio shows, writing new endings.* (Write the next episode in Willie's life when he returns to Los Angeles.)

Using New Novels with Traditional Materials

If you teach classes in which students are more receptive to reading, there are other satisfying ways to use new books. When we were reading Emerson and Thoreau in an American literature honors class, I knew that the two writers' observations seemed far removed from the lives of my students. I had just read Gary Paulsen's *Woodsong* and was taken with his descriptions of nature and his observations about what he learned from nature. I assigned my students to read the book and was delighted by their responses. First of all, students liked it because it was short and readable. But they also felt plunged into nature along with Paulsen. Instead of asking for projects or more complicated assignments, I asked them to do three things with the novel:

1. Write about what struck you or caused you to think as you

read *Woodsong* by Paulsen. Explain at least three things that made an impact on you.

2. Write about what you think the author learned about himself from his experiences in the woods with his dogs. What does Thoreau say he learned from *his* time in the woods?

3. Look back over Ralph Waldo Emerson's "Nature" and "Self-Reliance," and in as many ways as possible, explain how Emerson's ideas applied to Paulsen's experiences in *Woodsong*. You may also show what parts of Paulsen's experience do not fit with Emerson's views.

I did similar comparison and contrast activities when my students read Walter Dean Myers's *Fallen Angels* as an accompaniment to Stephen Crane's *The Red Badge of Courage*.

Using a new novel does not have to be a great deal of work for the teacher. Once we begin spending our energy to involve the students and stop feeling that we must have a very detailed, traditional plan, we can relax and enjoy the book with students.

FIFTY ALTERNATIVES TO THE BOOK REPORT

Students tire of responding to novels in the same ways. They want new ways to think about a work of literature and new ways to dig into it. This diverse group of suggestions should whet students' interest in exploring new directions and in responding with greater depth to the books they read.

1. Character Astrology Signs. After reading brief descriptions of the astrology or sun signs, figure out which signs you think three of the main characters from your book were born under. Write an explanation of why you think they fit the sign, drawing on their actions, attitudes, and thoughts from the book.

2. Heroes and Superheroes. Select two or three people your character would think of as a hero or superhero. Describe the characteristics of the hero and why those characteristics would be important to your character. Also describe which characteristics your character would most want for himself or herself that the hero or superhero possesses.

3. Create a Childhood for a Character. If your main character is an adult, try to figure out what he or she would have been like as a child. Write the story of that character's childhood in a way that shows why that character is the way he or she is.

4. Critique from the Point of View of a Specific Organization. Select an organization that might have a lot to say about the actions or portrayals of characters in the novel you read, and write a critique of the book from the organization's point of view. For example, the Society for the Prevention of Cruelty to Animals might have a lot to say about Lennie's treatment of animals in *Of Mice and Men,* the National Association for the Advancement of Colored People might comment on the portrayal of Crooks, and the National Organization of Women might have an opinion on the portrayal of Curley's wife and the fact that she was never given a name.

5. Social Worker's Report. If the events in the novel merit it, write up a report as a social worker would on the conditions in the home and whether it's a good environment for a child. For example, if a social worker went to the McNabs' house in *Maniac Magee* by Jerry Spinelli, how would she describe Mr. McNab's home and parenting style? What would her recommendations be? In her report, she would have to respond to issues such as reason for the visit, conditions observed in the home, parenting style of the father, children's adjustment to the current situation, recommendations on removal/retention in the home.

6. College Application. Create the application that a character you have just read about could write and submit to a college. Use all the information you know about the character, and infer and create the rest of it. On the application include these sections: *Name, Academic Rank in Class, High School Courses Taken and Grades, Extracurricular Activities, Personal Activities,* and *Work Experience.* Choose one of the following questions or issues to discuss from the character's point of view in a two-page essay: What experience, event, or person has had a significant impact on your life? Discuss a situation in which you made a difference. Describe your areas of interest, your personality, and how they relate to why you would like to attend this college.

7. School Counselor's Recommendation Letter. Write a summary appraisal from the school counselor's point of view that assesses the character's academic and personal qualities and promise for study in college. The college is particularly interested in evidence about character, relative maturity, integrity, independence, values, special interests, and any noteworthy talents or qualities. Why do you feel this student would be well suited to attend college?

8. Talk Show Invitation. Select a character, think about his or her involvements and experiences, and then figure out which talk show would most want your character on as a guest. What would the producers of the show want the character to talk about? Who else would they invite on the show to address the issues the character is involved in? Write up the correspondence between the talk-show host and the character in which the host explains what the character should focus on while on the show. Have them exchange one more letter after the show mentioning how they felt about what happened.

9. Radio Exchange. Your character calls into a radio show for advice. Choose the show your character would call, and then create the conversation he or she would have with the radio advice giver.

10. Movie Recommendations. From all the movies you've seen in the last couple of years, pick five you would recommend that your character see. Give a brief summary of each movie and explain why you think the character should see it.

11. Create a Homepage. Select several characters and design a homepage for each of them, picking out appropriate backgrounds and pictures and then creating information that would tell a viewer about your character. Also, create links to at least five different sites that you think your character would be interested in. Then write up and post on the page an explanation of how you made the decisions you did and what you believe this tells us about the character.

12. Chat Room Conversations. Imagine that your character has found other people to talk with while in a chat room he or she found while surfing the Internet. Describe the chat room your character was in and why your character would be drawn to the kind of group that operates the chat room. Then construct the conversation your character had with others while in the chat room.

13. E-mail Directory. Create the e-mail directory of all the people you can imagine your character keeping in touch with through e-mail. Explain why you selected the people you did and what it shows about your character. Then construct several exchanges between your character and some of the people in your character's directory.

14. Title Acrostic. Take a sheet of construction paper and write the title of the book down the side of the paper. For each letter in the title, construct a sentence that begins with that letter and that tells something significant about the story.

15. Cartoon Squares. Create a series of six drawings in six squares that shows a significant event in the novel. Under each picture or cartoon, write a few lines of explanation.

16. Word Collage. Write the title of the book in the center of a sheet of paper. Then look through magazines for words, phrases, and sentences that illustrate or tell something about your book. As you look, think in terms of the theme, setting, and plot line, as well as characters. Work to get fifty such words, phrases, or sentences so that the whole sheet of paper is covered. The visual impact of the collage should tell a potential reader a lot about the book.

17. Yearbook Entries. Imagine what three or four characters from your novel were like in high school. Cut out a picture of a person from a magazine to represent each character. Mount one picture per page, and under each picture place the following information, which you will create: nickname of character; activities, clubs, sports they were in and what years; class mock award such as "class clown"; quotation that shows something about the person and what is important to him or her; favorites such as colors and foods; a book that has had a great impact on him or her; voted "most-likely-to" what?, plans after high school.

18. Letter Exchange. Create a letter exchange between a character and the author, or write a series of self-reflective letters from several characters on what the character learned about himself, others, and life.

19. Awards. Create an award for each of the main characters based on their actions in the novel. One might be awarded "most courageous" for fighting peer pressure, another might be awarded "wisest" for the guidance he or she gave other characters. For each award, write a paragraph that explains why this character deserves this award.

20. Talk Show on Issues in Novel. Create and perform a talk show around one of the major issues or themes in the novel. For example, after reading *Tangerine* by Edward Bloor you might want to discuss the issue of the brother's violence and the way the parents dealt with it. Include people to represent several points of view on the issue. You might include characters from the book, a social worker, a police officer, a psychologist, etc.

21. Dream Vacation. Where do you think your character would most like to go on a vacation? Pick a spot, describe it, and explain why he or she would want to go there or download information from the Internet about the place. Then write a day-by-day itinerary of what the character would do each day and why you think the character would enjoy this activity.

22. Scrapbook. Think about all the kinds of mementos you would put in a scrapbook if you had one. Then create a scrapbook for your character, cutting out pictures from magazines or drawing the mementos he or she would include in a scrapbook. Think about Willie in *The Crazy Horse Electric Game* by Chris Crutcher. He would probably have something in his scrapbook to represent his baby sister, his love of baseball, his accident, his experiences in Los Angeles, and so on.

23. Photos or Magazine Pictures. Find two or three photos or magazine pictures that would have special significance to your character. Mount them on a sheet of paper and write an explanation of why they would be important to your character.

24. Music. After reading a novel, figure out how you would divide up the book into sections. Then select a piece of music that you think captures the feel or tone of each section. Record the pieces and, if possible, do voice-overs explaining what is happening in the novel during the piece of music and why you felt this piece of music fit the section of the novel.

25. Poetry. Write three poems in response to the novel. The poems can be about the characters, where the book took place, or the themes in the book.

26. Twenty Questions. Three classmates are each assigned the role of one of the characters in the book. You and your fellow classmates have to figure out which person is which character. You may ask only twenty questions. Create the questions that you and your classmates can use to figure out the identity of each of the three students.

27. File a Complaint. Adopt the persona of one of the characters who you feel was portrayed in a sexist or racist manner. Write up a complaint explaining what you feel was unjust in that portrayal, and explain the actions you would like the author to take to remedy the biased portrayal.

28. Tangible or Intangible Gifts. Select a character and figure out what two or three things you believe your character most needs or wants. Draw or cut out pictures to represent these "gifts," and write to your character an explanation of why you picked these things out for him or her.

29. Talk to the Author. Write a letter to the author of the book explaining to him or her why you think he or she wrote the book and what he or she was trying to show through the book. Be sure to explain what you got out of the book. If the author is still alive, send the letter to the author via the publisher of the book.

30. Point-of-View Column. Write an opinion column like those that appear on the editorial page of the newspaper. Choose a theme or topic from the novel you just read and write the column from the point of view of one of the characters. Your character might write about the importance of education or why we should accept people who are not like us.

31. Character Monologues. Select an event in the story about which characters have different views. (For instance, in *Life in the Fat Lane* by Cherie Bennett, Lara's mom, dad, brother, and boyfriend all had different views on her weight gain.) Write up two or three characters' opinions on the same event in the form of a monologue (one person talking to himself or herself). Present these monologues to the class, with different students reading the various monologues, to show all the points of view on the one topic.

32. Make Up a Word Test for the Novel. Think of fifteen words that are essential to the understanding of the book. Explain why you picked the words you did and how you would define them in terms of the story.

33. Answering Machine Message. Answering machine messages have gotten more and more creative over the years, reflecting the interests and idiosyncrasies of the owner. Select five characters from the novel you have just read and create an answering machine message from each of them. Pay particular attention to diction and tone.

34. Found Poems. Select a chapter from the novel you have just read that you consider powerful or interesting. Then select words, lines, and phrases that you think project strong images, and show the impact the chapter makes by arranging this material into a poem.

The following example comes from Chapter 20 in *Spite Fences* by Trudy Krisher:

> **Violence at the Lunch Counter Sit-in**
>
> Fist slammed into George Hardy's face
> Glasses slid to his chin
> Shattered into a spider's web.
> River of red blood

Running from his nose.
It was the red color of the fence
The red color of the earth
on which I stood
It was red
The color of my life this summer
The color of Kinship.

35. Name Analysis. Select a few of the characters from the novel. Look up each of their names in a name book to see what the name means. Write down all the meanings, and then write a short essay for each character explaining in what ways the name is suitable and in what ways the name does not fit the character.

36. A Character's Fears. One way we get to know characters is to think deeply about them and make inferences based on their actions and on what they and others say about them. Through a person's actions, we can learn what they fear and what they want to avoid the most. Select several characters from your novel and write short essays on what you believe they fear the most and what evidence you used to come to this conclusion.

37. Current Events. Select five current news or feature stories from television or newsmagazines that you think your character would be interested in. Then explain how your character would respond to each of the stories and the opinions your character would have about what was happening in the story.

38. Advertisements. To show your understanding of a character, go through several magazines and newspapers looking for advertisements of goods you think your character would like. Cut out the pictures, mount them on a poster board, and under each picture write a few lines about why this product would appeal to your character.

39. A Pamphlet. Think of an issue that was important to your character. Then create a pamphlet aimed at persuading others of the importance of the issue. Include factual information, testimonials, pictures or graphics, and so forth. For instance, Sura from *The Buffalo Tree* by Adam Rapp might want to create a pamphlet explaining why the juvenile justice system needs to be changed.

40. Draw a Scene. If you are artistic, think of an important scene in the novel you just read and draw it the way you see it. Place the characters in the scene too, and then figure out where you were in relation to the characters when you read the book. Then write or tape your explanations of why you drew the scene the way you did and why you think you were in that particular place in the scene. What does your drawing or explanation reveal about who you related to in the novel?

41. New Acquaintances. Select two characters from the novel you're reading. Then think about three to five people, living or dead, who you would like your characters to meet. Write about how you selected these new acquaintances and what you would like the character to learn from the people you introduced him or her to. For instance, after reading *Monster* by Walter Dean Myers, you might want the main character to meet Malcolm X, who learned who he was while in prison, and Frederick Douglass, who understood the importance of freedom.

42. Book Choices for Character. Select a character and then choose five books for him or her, thinking about what this character might like and also what you think he or she needs to know more about. Scan library shelves, the Internet, or use the library's computer card file. Why did you select the nonfiction books you did? What do you hope your character will like about or get out of the fiction?

43. Community Resources for Characters. After looking in the phone book and on the Internet, create a file of community resources that would help a character in your novel cope with an issue. If the main character has alcoholic parents, you could collect pamphlets, names of self-help groups, and any agencies that address the problem. Then create a display board so others can see what is available.

44. Family History. Create the history of the family of one of the main characters in your novel. For instance, in *Harry Potter and the Sorcerer's Stone,* what would the life of Harry's aunt, Mrs. Dursley, have been like? What major events affected her family? How were such things as holidays and birthdays celebrated? How did her sister (Harry's mother) get along with her? Try to create events that help us understand why she is the uptight, doting mother and magic hater that she is.

45. Detective Work. If a detective or police officer suddenly showed up in your novel, who or what would this new character be investigating? Write about what the detective is looking for, how he or she knew something was awry or needed investigating, and what was recommended. For example, in *Spite Fences,* a detective could show up at Maggie's home to investigate the physical abuse, or an undercover police officer could be in town investigating civil rights violations.

46. The Dating Game. Imagine that some of the characters are writing up resumes so they can appear on *The Dating Game*. What would they say about themselves and what would they say they would like in a significant other?

47. Create a Character's Room. We learn a lot about people by what they keep in their closets, what they have on their walls, what they choose to put in a room. Select a character you know well and create a living room, bedroom, kitchen, or some other room that would mean a lot to the character. Draw it or write about it, making sure to include an explanation of why you designed the room as you did.

48. CD Collection. Design a CD collection for a character you know well, being sure that the collection includes music that expresses as many aspects of the character as you are aware of.

49. Photo Album. Think about the events in your novel. Decide which scenes or pictures from the novel a character would want to remember. Then draw several of these "photos" for an album page or write about which pictures the character would want in his or her album. For instance, in *Dave at Night* by Gail Carson Levine, Dave would want a picture of himself with his father, a group picture of his buddies sharing food on Sunday night, and a picture of Irma Lee at the party in her home.

50. A Character Alphabet. Choose a character you like and then create sentences based on the alphabet scheme that demonstrate your knowledge of the character. If after reading *Spite Fences* you decided to write Zeke's alphabet, it could start like this:

> A is for the ABUSE Zeke took at the hands of a racist mob.
>
> B is for his BENDING OVER BACKWARDS to make sure the visiting civil rights activist could work in obscurity.
>
> C is for the CAMERA he gave Maggie so she could begin to look at the world in new ways.

USING SHORT STORY COLLECTIONS TO ENRICH THE ENGLISH CLASSROOM

Excellent short story collections are now in abundance, and since many of them are in paperback, they are economically available to the classroom teacher. These short story collections can be used in a variety of ways and can inject new life into a tired unit; they can be used as a stand-alone assignment when substitutes will be in your classroom; and they can provide opportunities for students to connect literature to life and to other literature.

Teachers sometimes draw a blank when they see short story collections minus teaching guides. Thus the intent of this section is to show several ways in which short story collections can be integrated into your curriculum and how you can use individual stories.

Students Make the Connections

When we teach something, we learn more than our students do. We have to think deeply about the material, extract important ideas and concepts, and figure out how to involve students. We look for points of connection, figure how it's related to other things in class, and how we can have students respond through writing and talk.

Instead of remaining the chief learner in the classroom, why not let the students engage in this kind of critical thinking and learning? Short story collections offer an excellent opportunity to introduce students to these critical activities.

Short Story Fair

Explain to students that the purpose of a Short Story Fair is to have them read a collection of short stories, pick one, and interest their classmates in reading the story through a display they will create. On the day of the fair, these displays are set up in the classroom or in the library, and students go from one station to another reading, viewing, and even listening to the displays. It works well and adds further excitement if other classes are also invited. To begin, bring in as many copies of short story collections as you can find from the library, the book room, and your own shelves. Have students select, individually or in pairs, one of the collections. Ask students to begin by skimming the collection, looking for one short story they find interesting and that they think their classmates would appreciate. For their display, they will do the following for each story:

1. Bring in one physical artifact to interest people in the story. This object can be symbolic, representing something important to the character, a setting or mood, or a response to the story.

2. Select a piece of music or a song that in some way illustrates something in the story. Audiotape it so it can be played during the fair.

3. Find or write a poem that illuminates some aspect of the short story. Write it out neatly, illustrate it if desired, write an explanation of how it connects to the story, and post it on your display.

4. Create a collage or mobile that illuminates the setting or theme or some other aspect of the story.

5. Complete and post in the display sentences such as "If you like [to feel really connected to a character], this story is for you"; "This story will make you [wonder about death, want to be in love, nudge you to think about your relationship with your parents]."

6. Write and post a letter to the class explaining why this story should be used as a whole-class story and what it would fit with thematically.

7. Create a brief plan stating how you would introduce the story to the class—would you ask classmates to think about themes, ask them to write about a similar incident, create a few surveylike questions to spark interest? What would you ask your classmates to write, draw, or talk about in response to the story?

8. Create an advertisement for your story. It can be a print ad, a radio ad, or a TV ad if video equipment is available. What about the story would you highlight and market?

9. Write a process piece explaining the easiest and most difficult parts of the assignment, as well as explaining the thinking that went into the choice of the artifacts, poems, and so on.

On the day of the Short Story Fair, students carry sheets with them in order to respond to a short series of questions for each exhibit. (What did the piece of music remind you of? Which piece of the exhibit was most interesting to you? What kind of impact did it make on you? Explain why/why not you'd be interested in reading the short story.) Students move from area to area in groups of two or three so that no "exhibit" is ever overcrowded. By the end of the fair, which may last two or more days, students have been exposed to at least twenty stories.

Short Story Hunt

After finishing a novel or unit, ask students to find short stories that in some way relate to the novel or the unit. Does the theme, topic, character(s), setting, plot, mood, or effect of a short story connect to any of those elements present in the novel or the unit? This kind of activity gives students an opportunity to pursue areas and topics they are most interested in. For example, after completing *Spite Fences* by Trudy

Krisher, some students can look for stories on family relationships, racism, civil or human rights, friendship, child beauty pageants, segregation, assault, harassment, neighbors, and so on. Some might find stories they think would provide Virgil Boggs, an unsavory character, with some life lessons he needs. Others might find stories that also have a character who exudes quiet dignity in the face of adversity (like George Hardy), or a character who shows a great deal of practical wisdom (like Zeke), or a character who deals with difficult parents (like Maggie). When students skim short story collections to find connections to novels and units, they are also finding one more way to respond to the novel or unit.

In small groups, students can share summaries of the short stories and their explanations of all the connections they found between the short story and the novel or unit. Each group could then compile lists of the kinds of connections group members found and the names of the short stories that provided these links. If classes become very involved in ferreting out these connections, they could prepare an annotated bibliography arranged by the topic of the connection. That way, future students would have a resource of fiction with which to follow up their interests.

The Teacher Creates the Context

Since we don't always have the time or the place in our curriculum to involve students in taking the lead in the ways just described, the following strategies can be implemented as the teacher creates the context for the story's use.

Using Single Short Stories to Extend a Unit

Oftentimes, short stories slide in nicely to fill the spaces in a unit. While doing a unit on internal versus external conflicts, bring in short stories such as "Fourth of July" by Robin J. Brancato and "She" by Rosa Guy in Donald R. Gallo's *Sixteen*. The first story shows Chuck dealing with multiple dilemmas. The same is true of the main character in "She." Gogi has tremendous external conflicts with her stepmother, but she also struggles within herself. To make these conflicts apparent, students work in groups to prepare one of the following kinds of presentations, which are videotaped:

For "Fourth of July"

> Script and perform the scene in the courtroom when Sager is on trial, making sure to represent Sager's point of view.

Using information from the short story, script and perform a puppet show that reenacts Sager's and Chuck's interactions the day the money was stolen. Try to include Sager's thinking on the issue—perhaps by having him talk to himself.

Chuck arrives at the Fourth of July celebration late. According to the story, he didn't feel all that good about not giving Sager any gas. Script and perform the discussion he has with Katie and Bobby about what has just happened.

Write and perform a monologue (one person talking aloud) from Sager's point of view when he runs out of gas. Will he think he deserves this? Illustrate his point of view and how he really feels about taking the money.

For "She"

Script and act out Dorine's first visit to Gogi's house. Try to show it from point of view of Dorine, the new stepmother. You may have to use some "asides."

Script and act out the next scene. What happens the next morning? How will Dorine and Gogi act around each other?

Create and perform an Oprah Winfrey show on stepparents. Invite Dorine, Linda, Gogi, the father, a social worker, and other stepparents and stepchildren. Focus on trying to understand the various points of views and the conflicts characters experience as they deal with this issue.

Script and perform a puppet show dealing with how kids try to get out of doing housework in a family and why they feel justified in getting out of it. Also try to include the parents' point of view.

Using a Short Story by Itself

Highly interesting short stories make excellent backup lesson plans and plans for substitutes since they can usually be completed in one class hour. If students know they will have to figure out how the story connects to other work in the English language arts class, then they won't find the story unrelated. The following plan works to involve students in the story and to encourage them to write in response to the story.

Create prereading activities to pique student interest.

Read the story together or, if you have highly motivated and involved readers, let them read it themselves.

During the story, occasionally stop reading and ask students to predict, or write a piece of advice to a character, or explain the pictures they are seeing in their heads as they read.

Allow time for students to discuss the story and mull over the issues in it and to generate ways it can connect to other work in the English class.

Offer students a variety of options that will extend their response to the story and demonstrate their involvement with it.

The example that follows is based on "Shadows" by Richard Peck in Donald R. Gallo's *Visions*.

Before Reading

How do you feel about the dark? Are you afraid of it? Think back to a memory you have of the dark and write about it.

People often feel that children should be raised by their parents, yet grandmothers, friends, and relatives often raise children of parents who are still living. In what situations do you believe it is best that children be raised by someone other than their living parent?

During Reading

Close your eyes and imagine what this small child must be seeing after reading page one. Sketch or write down the pictures you have of her and her room when she is being "visited."

Why would the two "aunts" agree to raise this child? Do they seem to be doing a good job?

Before the main character started school (p. 6), she saw her ghost almost every night. Who do you think this is? Why would he come so frequently?

Discussion after the Story

What do you consider to be the hardest thing to understand about this story?

What obligations do you think parents have toward children?

Do you think the main character could be as happy as she says she is?

Why do you think the main character was not given a name?

What other characters we have read about would relate to any of the characters in this story?

If you were to become a character in the story, which one would you become? Would you do anything differently as that character? Explain.

Response Options

1. The main character really believed that *money* was her aunt's middle name because the other aunt said so. Do you remember a time when you believed exactly what an

adult said and later found out it wasn't true? Write the story of this experience.

2. "I thought a mother who had no time for me wasn't worth missing." Write the letter the main character would like to write to her mother explaining her feelings.

3. The main character said, "I'd already explored all the world allotted to me" before she went to kindergarten. Where were you allowed to go by yourself before you went to kindergarten? Draw a map showing your neighborhood and the boundaries you remember being imposed on you. Then write a narrative about a memory sparked by drawing the map.

4. Create a story to explain why some of the ghosts haunted this house. For instance, who were these "gaunt women who wept silently," and why did they weep? What is the story behind the "gray military men who stared sadly at their empty sleeves"?

5. In seventh grade, the main character didn't like boys "because they were too loud and never alone. They moved in a pack and would not be taught, even by teachers." Think back to seventh grade. Write a story about seventh graders of the opposite sex. Include whether anything annoyed you or confused you about the opposite sex.

6. Seth must have had deep feelings for his mother. When he says to the main character, "But for you, there'd have been no one to learn from, or love," he acknowledges his neglect. Construct the conversation he would like to have with his mother.

7. Why was Seth so neglected as he was raised in a little cabin at the edge of the property by an old woman? Create the story of his background, including such things as which aunt was his mother, why the choice had been made to raise him as he was raised, what the aunts would have said about him when they talked to each other.

8. Many interesting terms are used to describe people in this story, such as *rednecks, spinsters,* and *eccentrics.* After figuring out what each of these words means, bring together a group of about four people (including the three types mentioned) at a brunch at a southern house they are touring. Write up the conversation they would have, and make sure they do some "sniping at Yankees."

9. If you are artistic, draw a picture representing this story.

10. Write a collection of three or four poems in response to this story. Some might be written from the point of view of the characters, some might address the themes, others

might include images you see in your head from the story.

11. Richard Peck is a master storyteller. Even though this story is short, he manages to embed many elements that make us want to read on. Look at how he creates the mystery that drives us to keep reading. Where is foreshadowing used? What else does he do to create a sense of mystery? Write a letter to your fellow or sister classmates explaining as much as you can about the techniques Peck uses.

Using a Collection as a Whole

Oftentimes teachers will want to use an entire collection of short stories. After having students respond to and talk about each story, the following ideas help tie the stories together. Ask students to do the following:

Choose a character who interests you from one of the stories. Go through several poetry books and select poems you think that character would like. Share your poems and the reasons for your choices with the class.

In groups, write a script that includes four or five characters from different stories. Decide where they'll meet, what time period they'll be in, and what they'll talk about.

Imagine that the Public Broadcasting System (PBS) has decided to do a series based on five of the stories in this collection. Decide which five stories should be filmed. Then write up a proposal which includes a rationale for placing these stories in the same series, a title for the series, and a short synopsis for each story.

Put together a collage made up of words and pictures depicting a specific character or a theme from a story or an issue the story deals with.

Look at how these stories are grouped. Discuss how each story fits into its group. Then create new ways to group the stories. Think of new group titles and explain why you put each story into the category you did.

Think about the characters, and then pick three characters from different stories who you think could become good friends. Write about why you believe they could like and appreciate each other.

Which story made the biggest impression on you? Write a letter to the author telling him or her why this story so struck you.

Which character would you most want for a brother or a sister? Explain in writing what it is about that person that appeals to you and why you think he or she would fit into your family.

Select five or so characters and think about what they'll be like in high school. Then go through magazines and cut out a picture that could represent each character you chose. Now mount the pictures (yearbook style), and write under each picture the clubs and organizations you imagine the character would belong to, a quotation the character would use, any awards you think he or she got, and what he or she plans to do in the future.

Think back over the characters, focusing on their positive and negative qualities. Now create several award categories (such as the best friend, worst parent, most mixed-up, and so on), and then figure out to whom you would want to give each award.

Examples Based on Donald R. Gallo's *Visions*

Create an annotated book list that would provide helpful information and resources for the characters in the stories about the issues they face: "The Good Girls" (child abuse); "The Fuller Brush Man" and "What Happened in the Cemetery" (dealing with very ill parents); "The All-American Slurp" (adjusting to a new culture); "Playing God" (runaways); "Saint Agnes Sends the Golden Boy" and "The Beginning of Something" (young love); "Great Moves" (divorce); "Shadows" (abandonment by parent); "On the Bridge" (peer pressure); "Cousin Alice" (the supernatural—ghosts); "The Beginning of Something," "Jeremiah's Song," "The Sweet Perfume of Goodbye" (death); "Jason Kovak—The Quick and The Brave" (self-confidence).

In "What Happened in the Cemetery," Fan was in desperate need of a good friend who could listen to her and perhaps give her advice. Think back over all the characters you encountered in *Visions* and choose the one person you think could be helpful to Fan. Write about why you chose that person.

Think about the parents in "Amanda and the Wounded Birds," "The Beginning of Something," "Words of Power," and "What Happened in the Cemetery." What are the strengths and weaknesses of each parent? Which family would you most/least like to live with?

Using Short Stories as Part of the Focus on Writing

If students have worked with a specific short story collection already, this approach seems to work well since students usually want to consider craft and how authors put stories together only after they've first had the opportunity to read and respond to the stories.

Beginnings. Students go through the whole collection of short stories looking for provocative beginnings—those that make the reader want to read on. Students then work to explain what made the beginning effective. Students might want to adapt the structure or idea behind the beginning and use such a beginning in a piece they are revising.

Endings. Students read the last several paragraphs of each short story, focusing on the three or four they consider the best or most effective. Again they work to make some generalizations or to create categories of kinds of endings authors use. Students can then go back through their writing folder looking for a piece that they could improve by crafting a new ending modeled on one they just discovered.

Details of Characterization. Students skim the short stories to refresh their memories about which characters they felt were especially well drawn. They select one or two characters, go back through the short story looking for details of characterization, and then work to categorize all the ways the author brings the character to life. In the next piece they write, students can incorporate the methods of characterization they admired.

Voice. This quality is often elusive and difficult to explain to students. It often helps to first read a short encyclopedia entry to illustrate what *lack* of voice is. Then, to move students toward understanding that voice means we can hear a person behind the words on the page, ask students to select a few paragraphs of a short story and rewrite them in such a way that "voice" no longer seems present. For example, the first paragraph of "Shadows" reads:

> From the very beginning I knew the place was haunted. I wasn't frightened. Far from it. Ghosts were the company I came to count on.

To remove much of the voice from this piece, it could be rewritten as:

> I knew the house was haunted but I wasn't frightened. I considered ghosts as company.

Students can then begin to grapple with how much word choice, sentence structure, and detail affect voice as they work to make the voice in their writing stronger.

Plot Development. Have students write down all the events in a short story to create a story map. Are the events told in chronological order? What effect does this ordering have on the story? Can the events be written in chronological order? Why would the author decide not to use this order? Which event would you consider the high point of the story? Which events build to this point? What can you learn about plot development from analyzing this short story?

Transitions and Sentence Variation. Students go through a short story or two writing down the first two words of every paragraph. What do they notice about the kinds of words each paragraph starts with? Does the author vary the way sentences are started? How often are transition words used?

Language Use. To help students become aware of vivid, descriptive language, have them create "found poems" from a short story. When constructing a found poem, the reader gathers colorful phrases and words from the story and places them into a poem structure. The reader can take them from any place on the page, choosing words or phrases that make an impact. If students have a hard time doing this, it usually indicates that the text doesn't contain much figurative language. This example comes from page 5 of "Shadows":

> One moonlit night
> there was a new shadow in the room
> dark against the moon-white wall
> hardly taller than I
> I saw the suggestion of bare feet
> the moonlight playing on white flesh
> the eyes deep-set and dark.
> I was interested at once.

Short Story Resources

To get a taste of some of the wonderful short story collections available, begin with some of these. This first group includes stories which were written especially for young adults:

> *American Dragons: Twenty-Five Asian American Voices*, by Laurence Yep
>
> *Am I Blue? Coming Out from the Silence*, edited by Marion Dane Bauer
>
> *Athletic Shorts: Six Short Stories*, by Chris Crutcher
>
> *Book of Enchantments*, by Patricia C. Wrede
>
> *Connections: Short Stories by Outstanding Writers for Young Adults*, edited by Donald R. Gallo
>
> *Curses, Inc., and Other Stories*, by Vivian Vande Velde
>
> *A Haunt of Ghosts*, edited by Aidan Chambers
>
> *The Heart Is Big Enough—Five Stories*, by Michael J. Rosen
>
> *Join In: Multiethnic Short Stories by Outstanding Writers for Young Adults*, edited by Donald R. Gallo
>
> *A Knot in the Grain and Other Stories*, by Robin McKinley

Living Up the Street: Narrative Recollections, by Gary Soto

Mothers and Other Strangers, by Budge Wilson

145th Street—Short Stories, by Walter Dean Myers

Places I Never Meant to Be: Original Stories by Censored Writers, edited by Judy Blume

Sixteen: Short Stories by Outstanding Writers for Young Adults, edited by Donald R. Gallo

A Starfarer's Dozen: Stories of Things to Come, edited by Michael Stearns

Tales from the Brothers Grimm and the Sisters Weird, by Vivian Vande Velde

Teller of Tales, by William J. Brooke

Thirteen—13 Tales of Horror, edited by T. Pines

Time Capsule: Short Stories about Teenagers throughout the Twentieth Century, edited by Donald R. Gallo

Tomorrowland: 10 Stories about the Future, edited by Michael Cart

Twelve Shots: Outstanding Short Stories about Guns, edited by Harry Mazer

Ultimate Sports: Short Stories by Outstanding Writers for Young Adults, edited by Donald R. Gallo

Visions: Nineteen Short Stories by Outstanding Writers for Young Adults, edited by Donald R. Gallo

When I Was Your Age: Original Stories about Growing Up, edited by Amy Ehrlich

The following collections mainly have teen protagonists but were not written especially for adolescents: *First Sightings: Contemporary Stories of American Youth*, edited by John Loughery; *Going Where I'm Coming From—Memoirs of American Youth,* edited by Anne Mazer; *Into the Widening World: International Coming-of-Age Stories*, edited by John Loughery; *Leaving Home*, stories selected by Hazel Rochman and Darlene Z. McCampbell; and *Show Me a Hero: Great Contemporary Stories about Sports*, edited by Jeanne Schinto.

CONNECTING SHORT STORIES

English teachers like to use short stories. They keep students involved. They don't take weeks to finish. They can be read in one night. They can be squeezed into the small spaces left by all-school assemblies or impending vacations. They can spark great discussions. Unfortunately, instead of using these short stories to their fullest potential, we often fall into the rut of having students read the story, answer the questions at the end, discuss the literary elements in it, and write a response or essay. Then we start all over again. We usually don't have the time to figure out how to help students make connections between the stories, help them see how stories can speak to each other as well as to issues in students' own lives. In the heat of being prepared for hourly infusions of students, we often don't have the time to step back ourselves and prepare units that help students make these connections.

Whether or not I have time to prepare as thoroughly as I'd like, I usually try to figure out ways to get students interested in the story. My next step, as I gain the time to do it, is to create writing activities based on the story. The last thing I do, and this can take place over several years, is create ways in which students can connect more directly to the stories and can connect the stories to each other. I would like to claim that each group of stories I use in my English classes is always well organized with well-thought-out activities. But alas! It's simply not true. Developing connections takes time. This section should provide ideas on how to go about this and in the process save you the time it took me to work it out!

Grouping Stories

After teaching American literature for several years, I started to look at new ways to group stories so that they would more directly relate to students' lives and concerns. In skimming through my text, I found that many stories related to the theme of parents and parenting and what our culture expects from parents. Since this is an issue very much on the minds of many high school students, I planned to weave this concern into the unit.

By creating connections to their lives and to other stories, I hoped that students would begin to see short stories as slices of life teeming with characters and themes that can speak to us. I started developing writing options and connections between stories after hearing again and again, "What did we read that for?"

I began by framing the unit in terms of parents and what we expect of them. When I create a unit, I work to develop an introductory activity that will involve students and raise many of the issues that the stories present. For this unit, I developed a brief true/false questionnaire after rereading the stories. I worked to create statements that could be provocative and generate discussion.

For this group of four stories, I ask students to answer "true" or "false" to these statements:

1. Parents should give the same amount of time and attention to each of their children.

2. Mothers should be more a part of their children's lives than fathers.

3. Parents should have a big part in selecting or approving of their children's marriage partner.

4. Parents should give up important things in their lives so that their child may be happy.

5. It is hard for teens to deal with a parent who has a low self-concept.

6. It is almost impossible for parents to embarrass a teen through their language, behavior, or dress.

7. Parents usually understand the important issues teens are dealing with even though they might not discuss them with the teen.

8. Adult children usually have an easier time talking about important issues with their parents than teens do.

After students respond individually to these statements, they move to small groups, where they talk about their choices. When students report to the whole group on their discussion, they pick out the areas of most disagreement in their group to explain to the class.

Developing Introductory Questions

Next I develop introductory questions or scenarios to be used for each story. In the first story, "Winter Night" by Kay Boyle, a mother is shown in a poor light for leaving her child in the evening to go out. To encourage students to think about whether there is any gender bias in the expectation that a mother is always available to her child, I created a scenario to elicit students' opinions and attitudes on this topic by reversing the situation. I ask students to respond to this situation: "If a mother was away in the Persian Gulf War and the father worked hard all day and then came home and took care of their child, how would you feel if he hired a baby-sitter several evenings a week to go out with his friends?" I ask students to write down their responses and the reasons behind them. Students then read the story for homework.

When students come to class, I ask them to write down quickly everything they can, describing the baby-sitter, the little girl, and the mother in the story. We then talk about who they looked favorably on. We continue our discussion by comparing their responses on what a mother's duty is versus what a father's duty is from their response to the hypothetical situation.

When I reread a story, I focus on what struck me or what I noticed. Then if student reactions become sparse, I use my reactions as the basis for questions for discussion. For this particular story, I come prepared with questions such as these: As a child, what were your fears? How do they compare to Felicia's fears? The dark seems to be a frightening, lonely time for Felicia; what did the dark mean to you when you were a child? Felicia sits looking out the window before the baby-sitter comes; what memories do you have of looking out the window as a child?

Literary Elements

I then look at the story in terms of what literary elements will help us dig deeper into the story. I do not ask students to plot out the story and pick out such things as the rising action and the climax, because I think that trivializes literature. We try to examine elements that give us new ways to look at the story. For "Winter Night," I draw attention to setting by asking students why they think the author chose an apartment and not a house as the setting. I ask them to look at what creates the suspense and makes us want to read on by posing questions such as, "What moves this story along? What is it we want to find out?"

To encourage students to think about theme, I ask them to write down three words that capture the essence of the story. To look at characters and their place in the story, I bring up the little girl in the concentration camp who, while not an actual character in the story, plays a big role. I ask students about the author's purpose in using her. Then we try to discern the author's attitude by looking at word choice, especially in regard to the mother. For example, I ask students: "By this line in the ending, 'as startling as a slap across her delicately tinted face,' the author seems to be implying much about the mother. What does this seem to say about what the mother realized or became aware of? What are the author's unstated assumptions about a mother and her 'duty'?"

Usually the title of a story gives the reader information about the author's intentions. I ask students what images they have of winter nights from their past. Are these images mostly positive or negative? Then we move on to talking about why they think the author titled the story as she did.

Students usually bring up issues and themes as we discuss the story. If they don't, I try to think about what they might react to, and I bring up questions such as the following: "How much do parents owe their children? To what extent should parents have aspects of their lives that their children are not a part of? What makes a good parent?"

Writing Options

After finishing a story, I think about what I still want to know more
about or what issues the story touched that students would perhaps like
to write about. I always leave the option open for them to create their
own writing assignments, but I've found that having suggestions helps.

When I develop writing options, I try to include some that ask
students to look at the story from another point of view; some that focus
on issues and themes in the story; some that connect issues in the story
to students' lives; some that ask students to extend what they learned
about the characters by putting them in new situations; and some that
ask students to develop or explain something that was only alluded to
in the story. For this story, I offer the following options:

1. Tell the story from the mother's point of view. What is her life
   like? Why does she want to go out so much?
2. Write the scene of what happens the next day. What will the
   mother say to Felicia? What will Felicia say to her mother? Will
   the mother go out as frequently?
3. Write a letter from the baby-sitter to the mother.
4. Write a short story that begins with you as a child looking out
   a window.
5. Write a poem about childhood fears or about loneliness.
6. Construct the baby-sitter's diary beginning with her experience in the concentration camps and ending the day after she
   baby-sits for Felicia.
7. Write the story of your experience with a baby-sitter and compare and contrast it to the experience Felicia had.
8. Write up monologues spoken by the mother, the baby-sitter,
   and Felicia in which each speaks of her loneliness and longings.

Three Stories

Although I originally used six stories in this unit, in the interest of space
I will only include three and give brief overviews of some of the ways
these stories can be approached.

"The First Seven Years"

Bernard Malamud's story revolves around an old immigrant shoe-
maker, Feld, who has dreams for his only daughter and who doesn't see
Sobel, his apprentice, as being part of those dreams. When introducing
the story, I ask students if they think their parents would choose a
spouse for them who would be an acceptable match and what they

think their parents would look for in a spouse. We also discuss what personal qualities are most important to them in friends or potential spouses and what kind of sacrifices they would be willing to make for love.

Issues to discuss as the story is being read include: How would students feel if a parent set up a date for them? What does Miriam seem to want from a relationship? Since Sobel has lived through the experience of a concentration camp, what does he see as being important in life? How does this differ from what Feld considers important? What do your parents want and wish for you in life? What does Feld basically want for his daughter? If Feld were your father, how would you two get along?

After-the-story writing options include:

1. Write the letter to Miriam that Sobel would like to write.

2. If Miriam was able to have a meaningful conversation with her father, what would she choose to tell him or ask him? Construct that conversation.

3. Sobel is obviously a man who gains much from reading and is excited and interested in the ideas he reads about. What ideas do you like to talk about and consider? Where do you encounter these ideas? Books? TV? People? Movies? Music?

4. The concept of duty to parents seems to have changed over the years. Compare and contrast your views of duty to parents with those of Miriam.

5. Construct the conversation you would like to have with Sobel.

6. Write the love poem that Sobel would like to give Miriam.

7. If Sobel could speak honestly to Feld about their differences in values and goals, what would he say?

"The Lucid Eye in Silver Town"

John Updike's story is about a young boy who is going on a trip to New York City with his father to visit an uncle they haven't seen in years. The boy is very critical of his father. I introduce this story by asking students to write about a time they've been embarrassed by their parents *or* to write about the kinds of things parents do that embarrass their children. We also talk about what makes an exemplary parent, what personal qualities such parents have, and how they treat their children. We brainstorm a list of the qualities we admire in parents and then talk about the qualities which are hardest to accept in a parent. During the story, students often discuss whether they would like Uncle Quin for an uncle, what the tension seems to be between the father and mother, and what behavior exhibited by Jay's father would have embarrassed them the most.

After-the-story writing options are:

1. Write the story from the father's point of view, emphasizing how he perceives his son.

2. Jay is obviously embarrassed by a great deal of what his father does. Write the letter he would like to write to his father the day after they got home.

3. Do you have relatives like Uncle Quin? Make up a story about a relative who is not very available to the family and make up a reason for his absence.

4. Assume the mother is upset with the father and how he acts. She wants to talk to him about his lack of confidence but doesn't want to hurt him. Write the letter she would write to Ann Landers seeking advice.

5. If Jay had a best friend he confided in, what would he say to him the next day about his father's behavior?

6. Jay was very embarrassed by the eyelash-in-the-eye incident. Have you ever gotten ill at an inconvenient time or thought you were ill and found out you were just overreacting? Write the story of this experience.

7. Jay doesn't seem to appreciate his father much. Look back through the story at the way his father treats him and the things he says to him. Then write Jay a letter pointing out the positive things he may not have noticed about his father.

"A Visit to Grandmother"

The last story of the unit is by William Melvin Kelley. It's about a grown man who hasn't seen his mother and siblings in over fifteen years. He stays away from them because he believes he is not loved. To introduce the story, any of the following can be discussed: Children build up resentments toward parents for things parents aren't even aware of. What do kids often hold against their parents? What do children expect from their parents? Do you expect to be treated the same as your siblings? What does this mean? Have you ever visited relatives you've never met before? Was the visit uncomfortable? Interesting?

After reading the story, students may want to discuss some of these questions: As you get to know GL, what draws you to him? What don't you like? Do you believe the mother should have been as involved in his life as much as she was? Was she overprotective? What did she feel for this son? What did she feel for Charles? Is it ever possible to love children in the same way and for the same reasons? What does the story of the horse tell us about GL?

After-the-story writing options include:

1. If Chig were to write his reactions to this visit in his journal, what would he say? What do you think he has learned?

2. Charles became the kind of parent he wished he had had. Write a letter to his children from him explaining why he is the kind of father he is and what he felt he didn't get from his parents.

3. Write the letter Charles's mother would like to write to him explaining why she gave him a different kind of attention and why she expected so much more of him.

4. Charles became a doctor and a successful adult. He used his hurt and bitterness to push him into proving his worth. What might he say to kids on the streets today who feel they have a right to be criminal because of their pasts?

5. Almost all of us have memories of visiting relatives we didn't know well. Write the story of such a visit.

Activities and Assignments to Connect Stories

Connecting stories is important so that students can see that the English class is working toward making sense out of literature and using the stories for a purpose. Students get confused when one story is "done" and then they are asked to read another and another. When I construct connecting activities, I start with similarities or differences I see in characters and try to create options which explore those similarities or differences, as demonstrated in the first six assignments below. I use student knowledge of literary elements and characterization to encourage students to evaluate the literature:

1. What would the fathers in "The First Seven Years" and "Lucid Eye in Silver Town" have to say to each other about raising children and what parents owe their children?

2. What would the mothers in these four stories say to each other about their lives and their children?

3. Which characters would like each other? Dislike each other? Pick a pair and write up a conversation between them.

4. If asked, what would each character feel thankful for?

5. Imagine that Sobel and the baby-sitter from "Winter Night" meet and share their experiences. What would they talk about or consider important in life after their concentration camp experiences?

6. Which characters could you see becoming good neighbors? Explain why you chose the characters you did and why you think they might get along well.

7. Write the script and perform a talk show on the topic of what kids would like from their parents. Invite Felicia from "Winter Night," Miriam in "The First Seven Years," Jay in "Lucid Eye in Silver Town," and Charles in "A Visit to Grandmother." You may also invite current experts such as Dr. Benjamin Spock and Dr. Joyce Brothers to participate.

8. Construct the conversation that Rose and Charles's mother might have had about his leaving home when he was fifteen. How would they make sense of this event?

9. Which story deserves the Pulitzer Prize for fiction? Nominate your choice and write up the qualities that make it deserving of this award. After all nominations and reasons have been read, have the class decide the winner.

10. Which story has the most defined or structured plot? Least structured? Explain these differences and the effect on the story.

11. All of these stories deal with parents and/or grandparents. What is each author trying to communicate? How are themes similar and different? Which stories seem most closely related thematically?

12. The teacher will read the name of each story, giving you time to write down what you remember about the setting. The entire class will discuss which settings were most vivid, what this tells us about the importance of setting, which settings were absolutely essential to the story, and which ones could easily be changed without affecting the story a great deal.

13. Which major character did you feel you got to know the best/least? Look back at the stories in terms of what narrative voice was used. Write a paper discussing the advantages and disadvantages of each narrative voice.

14. Without going back to refresh your memory and working only from the story title, explain which characters stand out the most in your mind. Write about what you remember about these characters and why they stand out in your memory.

15. Read the poem "The Fish" by Elizabeth Bishop. Which of the characters in the stories you have read would make the same decision as the person fishing in the poem?

16. Rank the characters from the stories you have just read using the following personality characteristics: caring, nurturing, devoted, confident, compassionate, flexible, unselfish.

17. Bring in poems that you think speak to a character, issue, or theme in any of these stories. The teacher will collect them and

read them one at a time to the class; after each one is read, write down who or what you think this poem relates to and why.

18. Pick at least five characters from these stories to interact with each other. Choose a setting, have the characters meet, and then exchange conversation that reveals something about them and what they believe in or what they are concerned about.

19. Which characters in which stories would probably most enjoy the following poems: Walt Whitman's "When I Heard the Learned Astronomer," Countee Cullen's "Any Human to Another," Langston Hughes's "As I Grow Older," Robert Frost's "Acquainted with the Night," or Emily Dickinson's "Hope Is the Thing with Feathers"?

Students respond positively to these kinds of connecting activities not only because they actually get to use the literature they read, but also because these activities give them more ways to think about and become involved with the literature. They also give students the sense that the literature they read is ongoing; it does not end just because the textbook questions have been answered. They begin to see that they can use the characters and themes in ways that provide information about the world and the people in it. Most important, students see that literature is not simply content to be studied, categorized, analyzed, and forgotten, but instead that literature lives, that it has connections to them and to their worlds.

PUTTING POETRY IN ITS PLACE

Successful teaching ideas and practices do not come easily. It's never as simple as dropping in a good writing idea on Monday or turning to a new language game on Tuesday. To work, a language arts class must integrate writing, literature, language, speaking, and listening. The teacher has to see how all these parts fit together; for example, writing outside of a context won't make sense to students; introducing an occasional poem to be analyzed may seem disjointed.

When poetry is woven into the fabric of the class instead of being approached as an isolated unit, students get more involved. The first seven of the following twelve strategies are designed to provide opportunities for students to use poetry in class and to have a reason to read it. The last five strategies can be used to enhance student involvement when specific poetry is studied. All of these strategies are meant to help the teacher put poetry in its place—in other words, in as many places in the curriculum and classroom as possible.

1. Select poetry in response to characters, themes, mood, or setting in works of literature. After reading a short story or novel, ask students to find a poem that speaks or connects to a character, theme, or setting. Students pour through poetry books, select a poem, and copy it down. On the back of the paper, they explain how they think the poem relates to the story or novel. The next day in class, collect the poems, read some to the entire class, and ask students to write a sentence or two explaining the connection they see.

This strategy works well for both college prep and general English classes. The main difference I have found is that the college prep students are willing to do this as a homework assignment and to find the poetry themselves, while many general students may not want to go to the library to look for poetry. What I have done in classes such as these is to provide thirty or so library books on poetry along with my own extensive classroom poetry library.

The most satisfying part for me is watching students, who up to this point have professed no interest in poetry, find poems that delight them. In my general classes, this activity has worked wonderfully with novels such as *The Watsons Go to Birmingham—1963* by Christopher Paul Curtis. Students find poems on winter, family vacations, death, fear, family, violence, racism, and prejudice. They are often willing to read the poem they find out loud to the class. I set aside one whole class period for these students to find a poem, and I have always been pleasantly surprised. The day I read the poems and ask them to generate a connection is a particularly high-energy day since students are bursting with ideas on how the poem relates to the book.

2. Write poems on themes present in the literature being read. I give students lots of writing options. For instance, after reading Edward Arlington Robinson's "Richard Corey," "Miniver Cheevy," and "Mr. Flood's Party," they may write about Richard Corey's background in story or poetic form. They may write a poem on loneliness since it is a theme present in all three poems. They may write epitaphs in the style of Edgar Lee Masters for one of the three characters, telling people what they would like to say to them after their deaths.

3. Create "found" poems from the literature being read. I try to alert students to the poetic language authors use and so encourage them to look for "found" poems. I instruct them to find powerful images within the text and to arrange this writing in the form of a poem, breaking lines and eliminating words and sentences for emphasis. I generate one example from whatever text we're using so they have a concrete example of what it is I want them to do.

While we were reading the biography *Malcolm X: By Any Means Necessary* by Walter Dean Myers, for instance, I shared a found poem that I created from Chapter 17, "A Son Is Buried":

The Funeral

In Harlem
The first light of day came grudgingly
There was a stillness about the streets.

It was cold
Bone chillingly cold.

Mourners had begun to line up
To take one last look
At this son of Harlem.

Malcolm's body lay wrapped.
He seemed so very distant.

The funeral was simple.
Messages of condolence
The eulogy (for)

Malcolm—the manhood of black America.
Then the casket was closed.

I compressed seven paragraphs by extracting what I thought were the most important words and images to create a powerful effect. I instruct students that if they do need to add a word that is not in the text, to place it in parentheses. Students read these poems aloud to the class, and we are often amazed at how many beautiful and powerful images are present in the novel.

4. Introduce a novel through the use of poetry. Before I start a novel, such as *The Pigman* by Paul Zindel, I bring in a collection of poems on one of the novel's themes, such as alienation. An excellent source for poems that genuinely speak to our students is *Class Dismissed!* by Mel Glenn. Each of these poems is about one high school student and focuses on one aspect of his or her life.

The poems "Dora Antonopolis," "Richie Miller," "Benjamin Heywood," "Jason Talmadge," and "Faith Plotkin" speak of alienation in direct and powerful ways. After I read these poems aloud, we discuss what all these teens have in common. Then we talk about teens we are aware of who had similar problems, such as the one Dora experienced—her conflict being the vast difference between what her father wants for her and what she wants for herself. In groups, students then list all the ways teens feel apart from what is going on at home or in school and all the attitudes and expectations that seem to alienate teenagers. I will often follow up this activity by asking students to create a story, script, or poem that in some way illustrates alienation. Students are then ready for the novel and often feel a real empathy for both John and Lorraine, especially once they meet their families, who seem to be their major source of alienation.

5. Follow up the reading of a novel by reading poems that speak to themes or issues in the novel. Students are often ready to deal with more challenging poetry when they can use a novel as a basis to contrast and/or compare the poems. For instance, after reading both *The Red Badge of Courage* by Stephen Crane and *Fallen Angels* by Walter Dean Myers, I bring poems into class such as "Dulce et Decorum Est" by Wilfred Owen, "Beat, Beat Drums" by Walt Whitman, "Carol with Variations, 1936" by Phyllis McGinley, and "5 Ways to Kill a Man" by Edwin Brock. Students look closely at the poems and discuss such things as which poems most closely agree with the views of the authors of the novels, which present views or ideas not present in the novels, how the descriptions of war differ, and in what ways the word choices in the poems vary according to the war referred to.

6. Create poems about characters as a response to a novel or short story. To draw out a wide range of reactions to various characters, I ask students to create, right in class, very short poems about characters. I usually make up a short formula so students don't have to struggle with the form of the poem but instead can concentrate on what they want to say about the character. I'll often ask them to start out with a noun that represents the character; follow up with two or three adjectives describing the character and a few sentences or phrases telling what the character does or is like; and then end with a summary word. Sharing reactions to characters this way often changes the way a class views a character. Once, many members of one class felt extremely negative about Frankie in *The Member of the Wedding* by Carson McCullers. After students had written these poems about her and shared them with the whole class, they were willing to take another look at Frankie.

7. Use poetry notebooks. Every marking period I ask students to create a poetry notebook; the purpose is to encourage students to read poetry. I may ask a class to select fifteen poems every marking period, copy or photocopy them, cite the source, and write on the back of each sheet why they selected that poem. I vary directions but usually insist that students:

- use a minimum of three books
- choose at least one poem from a deceased poet
- choose one poem written by a person of the opposite gender
- choose one poem written by a poet of an ethnic group other than their own
- find a photo or magazine illustration or draw a picture of at least two of the poems

On the day these notebooks are due, students choose one poem that they particularly liked or one that means a lot to them and read it aloud to the whole class or to a small group. These notebooks encourage students to read poetry, find poetry they like, and share the poetry with peers. It is simply another way in class to validate and use poetry.

8. Illustrate a poem. Students select a poem they can relate to and then either draw a picture to illustrate it or find magazine pictures that illustrate it. These can be shared orally in class or hung up in the room for student browsing. Keeping poetry visible in the classroom speaks volumes about the importance and presence of poetry in our everyday lives.

9. Script and perform poems for the class. An excellent way for students to read closely the poems you select for the whole class reading is to break them into groups to script the poem. Students first must read the poem several times to make sure they have a grasp of it. Then they decide how many voices or parts they want to use. They may use one or two or all voices at one time, depending on the effect they wish to create. They decide who will read what parts and practice several times. I have found that this activity encourages students to get creative, and they often add movements to their performance. For instance, when four girls scripted and read "A Square Dance" by Roger McGough, they not only broke the poem into parts, but they also did a square dance to emphasize the ironic tone of the poem. The poem deals with death and suffering in World War I but is written as a square dance and is meant to be spoken very quickly. The other students, who served as the audience, were stunned by both the arrangement of the parts and the performance.

10. Write instant reaction papers. Instead of having students answer teacher-generated questions about a poem, help students understand their own reactions so they might be willing to dig deeper into the poem. After the whole class has read a poem, ask each student to write down a one- or two-sentence instant reaction.

Put students in groups of four or five and have students pass their jottings to another person in the group. That student comments on what the first student writes and may raise questions on that student's comments. Papers are passed a second and third time, then returned to the original writer. Now the groups are ripe for a discussion since they have read three other reactions to the same poem. Students might then discuss the commonalities and differences in their reactions, help each other with parts that were problematic, or try to work toward a common meaning in their groups. Each group then reports to the whole class their reactions, questions, and interpretations of the poem. Lively discussions usually follow.

11. Select an important word or line. After students have read a poem, have them jot down what they consider the most important word or line in the poem and the reasons for their choice. This activity will usually get them to the heart of the poem quickly. Students are then eager to share their choices in small groups. Follow up this activity with a whole-class discussion so that students can see the range of responses and interpretations of the poem.

12. Focus individual responses. After students have read a poem such as "War Is Kind" by Stephen Crane, have them freewrite about what they think the poem means and how the author feels about war. Then ask them to jot down how rhythm, repetition, word choice, stanza length, and the way the poem is arranged on the page contribute to their interpretation. This is an especially good poem to use to get students caring about poetic devices and about terminology because students usually are split evenly between believing the writer thinks war is great and believing he thinks war is horrible. They are willing to dig into this poem to prove their point and even comment on the use of harsh letter sounds such as *b* and *d*. After their initial writing, usually done as homework, students work in groups to try to come to an agreement about the intent of the poem.

USING CHILDREN'S LITERATURE TO SPARK LEARNING

When picture books appear in a secondary classroom, students behave differently. They paw over the books, oohing and aahing at the illustrations, the colors, and the topics. Enthusiasm creeps into their talk. They become unabashedly interested in the books until it suddenly dawns on someone that these are *kids* books! "What do you think we are, babies?" one might ask. If at this point the teacher explains the rationale and students understand the purpose of what they are being asked to do, they will usually plunge into this genre.

Purposes for Using Children's Books

Why would anyone bring picture books into a secondary classroom? Aside from the ways they can build literacy skills, children's books generate excitement. They are fun to use, and students will read them eagerly. Since this is one genre accessible to all of our students, the payoff in terms of what they learn is usually great.

Teaching Literary Elements

Aside from helping to recapture a zest for reading and language, children's books are an excellent way to introduce or enlarge on literary elements in the context of response. Students can much more easily grasp the idea of theme after they read or listen to a book such as Michael Bedard's *The Divide*. Students can clearly see and explore character from the actions portrayed in a picture book such as *Ma Dear's Apron* by Patricia C. McKissack. Students can finally understand mood after they read a book such as *Follow the Moon* by Sarah Weeks. They can also see that point of view *does* make a difference to the story when they read Jon Scieszka's *The True Story of the Three Little Pigs,* which is told by A. Wolf. Any literary element can best be taught by beginning with children's books. The purpose, of course, in teaching about these elements is so students can use them as tools to get into the literature and talk about it.

Teaching the Conventions of Genres

What makes a fairy tale a fairy tale? A poem, a poem? Or how about short stories, myths, fables, fantasy, or even nonfiction? Students can look at what is expected of specific genres by reading many children's books in one genre. Afterward they list the characteristics they see emerging. This kind of work with picture books is not as tedious as it could be with longer, nonillustrated books. Once students understand and articulate the conventions of a particular genre, they will have an easier time writing in that genre because they'll understand the pieces and parts that go into a specific kind of writing. This type of knowledge can expand students' repertoire of writing forms and give them more choices in their writing. Also, grasping the conventions of a genre enables students to talk about the effect the breaking of conventions has on a piece of literature and on the reader.

A good place to begin looking at the breaking of conventions is Jon Scieszka's *The Stinky Cheese Man and Other Fairly Stupid Tales*. This work can then be extended by discussing the works of William Faulkner (who in *The Sound and the Fury* tells the story from several points of view), the works of John Dos Passos (who uses pieces of many genres in his novels), and those of e. e. cummings (who does not use the conventions of punctuation and capitalization in his poetry).

Examining Good Writing

Children's books can be used in many ways to examine writing. For instance, if students need work in creating more interesting beginnings or endings to their stories, bring in picture books. Have students look through the picture books for excellent beginnings and endings. In their small groups, students then name what makes a particular beginning effective—a question is asked that they want to know the answer to, a sense of mystery or wonder draws them in, and so on. Picture books also help students understand how they get a sense of character. Of course, the illustrations give them information, but students can also clearly see that a character's actions and words, as well as comments from other characters contribute to characterization. Students can experiment with some of these techniques in their own writing.

As Models for Stories

Oftentimes when students claim they are out of writing ideas, bringing in picture books gives them a wealth of formats and topics to draw on. Students might want to imitate the format of the book *Sorry, Miss Folio!* by Jo Furtado and Frederic Joos and create their own story along the same plot line. They could create an alliterative story like *Four Famished Foxes and Fosdyke* by Pamela Duncan Edwards. They could write a story like *Now Everybody Really Hates Me* by Jane Read Martin and Patricia Marx in which they write about why everybody hates or likes them. Or students might love imitating the rhyme schemes and rhythm patterns in any of Dr. Seuss's books.

As a Way to Look at Values Embedded in the Text

Using picture books is a good way to introduce to students the concept of values. For instance, in *Miss Nelson Has a Field Day* by Harry Allard and James Marshall, the whole school is in the dumps because their football team hasn't won a game. It takes the tough Viola Swamp to whip the team into shape after the coach has a breakdown. Some of the values students can dig out of the text are that winning is important and that it takes a tough disciplinarian to succeed as a coach. Examining the values embedded in a story encourages discussion, as students talk about the merits of the values.

Extend Students' Knowledge of How Art and Words Work Together to Create an Effect

Students can analyze the art in picture books and talk about how lines, shapes, colors, textures, sizes, and placement of illustrations have an effect on the story. For example, in *Goodbye Rune* by Marit Kaldhol and Wenche Oyen, the story of a small child grieving for her dead friend, everything in the picture book adds to and elaborates on the theme of death. The pictures are stark and seem far away, colors are somber, edges are blurred and muted. Both the simple, direct words and the artwork create a powerful effect that stirs readers' emotions.

Activities for Children's Literature

What else can we ask students to do with these picture books? We have to show students through the way we use the picture books that we want them to do things that will extend their literacy. Some possibilities include the following:

1. Since the text in picture books is so short, everything stated conveys a great deal of information. Have students take a novel or short story they have read and write it as a children's story; then discuss what happened as they made changes.

2. Have students turn a children's story into a radio play. They can flesh out conversations between characters, remaining true to the characterization in the story. Was this difficult to do? Did they get enough information about their characters? How did they figure out what their characters believed and felt?

3. Have students read a dozen picture books and rank them from best to worst. Then list the criteria they used in judging the books, such as interest, pacing, involvement with the characters, and effective use of language.

4. Help students list the themes brought out in several picture books. How do they recognize themes?

5. Discuss book selection for children. Which characters in the books students have read could have a good or bad influence on children? Should some books be kept from children? This topic can lead to explorations of book censorship.

6. As a way to end class, read a picture book, a fairy tale, a few poems from a children's collection. Pose such questions as: What does it make you think about or wonder about? In what ways can you connect the story to anything else we do in this class?

7. If students are doing reports on themes related to books as part of a project, ask them to find a picture book on the same theme and read it as part of their final presentation.

Integrating Children's Books into the Classroom

But what about context? Simply plopping children's books into the curriculum won't work, because students must see how their use connects to what is going on in class. Following are several ideas to help teachers put children's books into a context that can fit into their existing curriculum.

1. After a novel or short story has been read, bring in heaps of picture books. Ask students to think about how a specific character might respond to a specific book. Have students write and talk about their perceptions. For example, after reading *Freak the Mighty* by Rodman Philbrick, students could read several picture books and pick out the three to five that Kevin would like the best or would most want to read. The same could be done for Max. One book that could be included in the selection brought into the classroom is *Goodbye Rune,* which deals with death. Would Kevin, who has a fatal condition, even want to read the book? After Kevin's death, would Max feel comforted or shaken by the book?

It is not essential that the teacher preselect books carefully for this exercise. The important thing is to let kids find connections and explain why they feel the book relates to the character in some way or why it does not connect to the characters.

2. After reading adult stories on a topic such as death, fear, or loneliness, find children's books on the same theme. Discuss similarities and differences and assess how each genre handles the topic.

3. Before beginning a short story unit, bring in picture books and

ask students to look particularly for the kinds of behavior that are valued. Is perseverance something a character is rewarded for? Also ask students to look for connections between the books. Would a character from one story like a character from another story? Which characters are dealing with similar issues? As they read short stories, students do the same thing. They then work to establish connections between the picture books and the short stories they have read.

4. While working on understanding the ways an author persuades a reader to like or dislike characters, having students read picture books makes these strategies much more apparent. Have students work to find all the ways the author leads the reader to feel a specific way about a character. What effect do the drawings have? What are the characters shown doing? What does the character say that causes the reader to feel a certain way? Look at the describers used. Does the author say that a character "sneered" or "whispered" or "giggled" when describing the way a character said something?

Using all the evidence from the book, have students work in groups to figure out what the author is trying to show through the characterizations. Then encourage students to use some of these strategies in their own writing. If students are learning about such things as irony or Puritanism, or are working to understand when such elements as setting and plot play an important part in a story, to extend a concept have them look through picture books to find examples of these concepts.

A NEW LOOK AT NONFICTION IN THE CLASSROOM

I used to view nonfiction as dry and yucky. When I got to the section in my American Literature anthology called Modern Nonfiction, I skipped the whole thing without blinking an eye. I had peeked at a couple of the essays and had no idea how to deal with them or how to involve students in them. English teachers are often hesitant to use nonfiction, partially because most of our training has been in teaching fiction and writing. Also, because we don't have much exposure to nonfiction in college, we don't see the possibilities or the richness of the genre.

After years of avoiding nonfiction, I realized what I had been missing when I took a graduate course in which we were assigned a series of essays. I was bowled over. The essays, all about moths, involved me, carried me away, got me in touch with deeply buried issues and feelings. At that point, I realized I was wrong—essays were not dead hunks of prose; they were pieces chock-full of the stuff of life. After this experience, I began my plunge into the world of nonfiction and slowly discovered many of the possibilities this genre offered. I found that I could teach nonfiction as I taught other literature, and also that I could use it to teach skills that students weren't usually receptive to learning.

The Essay Takes on New Life

Once I stopped thinking essays had to be treated differently from other literature, I had a much easier time dealing with them. Now when we read essays, I often ask students to read several at once. They get in groups to discuss which essays made an impact on them and which didn't. They then select one of the essays and write a response to it. I tell them they may (a) agree, (b) disagree, (c) pick a point of departure and go with it, (d) pick a line they especially like and expand on it, (e) pick a thought they feel has been neglected in the essay and write about it, (f) any combination of the above. When students are finished writing, they select a section or sentence they really like in their writing and mark it. This writing segment usually takes about thirty minutes.

Next, students get back together as a group and share their essays with one or more people. Each of these people marks something he or she especially likes in the essay and also writes a sentence or two in response to it. Finally, each group begins to organize a presentation, which they will give to the larger group the following day. Groups can read portions of each student's essay, turn one of the original essays into a poem or a fable or other genre, discuss what the group learned from the essays or what point caused the most discussion. They can also create a script in which they question the author of the essay.

Because the essay is a provocative form of writing, I bring it into the class in many guises. Newspaper columnists write fresh, up-to-date essays on topics that can grab my students' attention. If I want students to write a persuasive essay, I use newspaper columnists' essays as examples. The opinions expressed often anger my students, and they find topics for essays in their responses to them.

Responding to Autobiography and Biography

Just as I had avoided reading essays in my English class, so too did I shy away from biographies and autobiographies. When we read in this genre, I seemed to focus only on the facts of a person's life and expected only recall from my students. Needless to say, students were not excited by this approach. And just as I was able to take the genre of nonfiction out of the mental straitjacket in which I had placed it, I discovered that biographies were rich in discussion topics and writing ideas. I also found that organizing my planning around the traditional "elements of literature" was a good way to begin, and that the more I saw biographies as a kind of literature to be responded to, the more involved my students became.

Setting

To get at the idea of setting and how it affects character, I asked students to create a visual representation of the places a character lived or visited and to indicate in some way the importance of each place as well as how the character felt about the place. For instance, in Melba Pattillo Beals's *Warriors Don't Cry,* the biggest place on the "map" would be Central High School in Little Rock. The school could be drawn with flames surrounding it since Beals saw it as a hellish place when she was one of the nine black students integrating the high school in 1957.

Plot

Plot in biographies can be approached in terms of the events and actions that made the biggest difference in or impact on the character's life. Students can make a time line illustrating what they perceive to be the most important actions and events in the character's life and then represent them through pictures or words.

Characterization

Even though the people in these books are real people, when students discuss characterization, they can talk about which characters came to life for them, which characters they would like to meet, and which actions of characters seemed hardest to understand. I usually ask my students to respond to characters in nonfiction just as I have them respond to characters in fiction. They write letters to them, find poems the character would like, and create conversations with them. We talk about their values and about what they would be like if they came to our school.

Theme

When we think about theme, we think about the themes and issues that seem to run through the character's life. We talk about the problems the characters were confronted with. We wonder about what the character learned from dealing with these issues. Sometimes I ask each student to write, using block letters and in marker, the five issues or themes they think are most prevalent in the book. When they turn them in, I have a student cut out all the words and paste them on a large sheet of butcher paper. We have thus created a word collage together, and we have a focus for an in-depth discussion of what students saw going on in the book.

Point of View

We don't leave point of view out of our discussion either. We talk about the view we have of the subject of the biography and how that view might have changed had the book been written by the subject's parents or friends or even an enemy. Sometimes, to illustrate that the author of any book selects the information we are given, I ask students to write a brief character sketch of themselves as if it were written by someone who didn't like them. Then I have them write about themselves from the point of view of a friend or a parent who appreciates them.

Other Assignments

Other assignments that can be done with biographies and autobiographies include the following:

> Collect passages that illustrate the attitudes of the subject of the biography.

> Create a booklet about the subject of the biography titled "This Is Me." Include significant quotations from the book, magazine pictures of your vision of the most important people in the subject's life, advertisements of things he or she would like, names of songs or records he or she would like, TV shows and movies that might be favorites, and a copy of one or two poems the subject would like. The booklet could end with a personal narrative, written from the subject's point of view, of what she or he had learned in life about people, about self, and about the lessons life teaches.

> If the subject of the biography was on a TV talk show, what questions would he or she be asked and how would the subject respond? If there is time in class, this could be performed in front of the class. If it is dramatized, add two or three more "guests," making clear their relationship to the issues in the subject's life. What would they say or ask?

> Create a *Dating Game* show with the subject of the biography asking the questions of possible dates. Make sure the questions she or he asks are consistent with what is important to her or him. Have the three contestants answer in different ways.

Building Units and Projects around Nonfiction

My students in ninth-grade English love it when we start with issues important in their lives and build activities around those themes. They call my class "live" when the discussions and readings revolve around their interests. I have found that nonfiction is the genre most likely to get students involved, especially when students are dealing with current issues and problems.

One nonfiction book my students respond to strongly is *Voices from the Future,* edited by Susan Goodwillie. This book contains a series of interviews of teens by teens and is subtitled *Our Children Tell Us about Violence in America* (Crown edition). This powerful, often shocking book deals with issues such as violence in the home, alcoholic parents, gangs, and kids in jail. When we use this book, I read sections aloud to my class. They write responses, and then we discuss reactions to the material and to the people in the interviews. Later, in groups students brainstorm what they would like to know or what they would like to tell others about the topic at hand.

To draw students further into the material, I also look for short stories and videos on similar issues. We talk about how realistic the stories are in terms of what we've read in *Voices* and in terms of what they know personally. One very hot topic is stepparents. Many students feel they are experts since many of them have had several stepparents.

We also write about the teens in the interviews and treat them like other characters we encounter. Students might create stories about them, write a script on something mentioned in the interview, find social service information that might be helpful to the character, or write up reports of what a social worker might observe in the character's home. We sometimes read novels in small groups or as a whole class dealing with the topics.

One novel my classes especially liked was *Freak the Mighty* by Rodman Philbrick. Although mainly about the relationship between a boy with physical limitations and one with mental limitations, this novel also shows the long-term effects on a child of witnessing extreme violence in the home. Another nonfiction book I have used with my whole class is Nathan McCall's *Makes Me Wanna Holler*. Since the book was out only in hardback, I read chapters to my students. (The book is now available in paperback.) Because McCall was attracted to criminal activity and gangs when he was a teenager and writes with such feeling about his experiences, my students immediately connected with him. They especially loved the chapter on respect because it so accurately talks about how as a teen McCall thought respect from others was the most important thing in his life.

My students wanted me to read the chapters and follow up each chapter with discussion, during which they would talk about why McCall's story was so true. I was not totally comfortable just reading and talking, so I worked at developing writing options in response to the book. Each student chose one option or created one of his or her own. I include a few of these options to illustrate that it is as easy to create writing options for nonfiction as it is for fiction:

> Nathan writes a lot about respect and how important it was to him when he was a teen. Write a story on respect showing what kinds of things kids of today are willing to do to get respect.

> Write about a time you felt put down or "dissed" by others and how you handled it.

> "Each learned what the other could do with his hands, and both developed a mutual respect, especially if they'd nearly taken off each other's heads" (52). Is this still true today? Do people who fight become friends? Write the story of two teens who fight and what happens to their relationship as a result of the fight.

> Think back to the circumstances surrounding the time Nathan shot and almost killed a person. Rewrite this part of the story so it turns out differently. For instance, what might have happened if his girlfriend had talked him out of going after the man or if his friend had intervened when he saw the gun?

> Nathan changed himself from a person who wanted to get respect through his criminal activities to a person who is reflective and caring and a good citizen. Have you ever wanted to make a conscious change in your life? Were you able to do it? Tell the story of what you wanted to change and what happened. Compare and/or contrast a part of your life with a part of Nathan's life.

In addition to using nonfiction books such as *Voices of the Future* and *Makes Me Wanna Holler* as the centerpiece of whole-class units, at least once a year I involve students in small-group projects in which each group uses different materials and focuses on different topics. The goal of these projects is to reach people outside our classroom and make an impact on them in some way

As we deal with topics in nonfiction such as teen pregnancy, peer pressure, runaways, suicide, death of a loved one, dropping out of school, pollution/recycling, racism, guns in school, getting good grades, and coping with stepfamilies, I note which issues seem most vital to my students. When we are ready to begin work on our schoolwide campaigns, students choose from the short list of topics that I have developed from topics they seemed most interested in. The class is then divided into groups according to the topic they picked.

Students are encouraged to make informational posters, bumper stickers, brochures, and buttons. They create slogans and make announcements over the PA system. Each group is also responsible for creating a brief list of articles or novels that provides further information on their topic. Before any of this is put up in the halls or presented to classes, students do a presentation to their own class. For teachers who don't have the time or energy to work toward schoolwide projects, presenting student findings to other English classes is often the perfect solution.

Teaching Skills with Nonfiction

Taking Notes

My first foray into using nonfiction to teach skills which students usually resist learning came about as I was struggling with ways to teach my eighth graders to take notes. When I tried to come up with interesting subject matter we could use, I thought of a nonfiction book on vampires that I had recently skimmed. I knew my students loved gore and the macabre, and I thought they would be eager to read and even reread such material. Since the task of learning to take notes requires multiple readings, I guessed that students wouldn't mind reading and rereading the chapter that described all the ways to dispose of vampires. I knew they would quickly pay attention to what was important in the chapter because they would be fascinated by the material. Another aspect of note taking that students vigorously resist is copying down material just to learn how to do it. They view writing as hard work and don't usually see any use in it if it isn't for something real. In one of those rare creative flashes, I realized that to ask students to eliminate or cross out material would not only meet my objectives but would also make students less resistant to the task.

To prepare for the lesson, I first copied several pages of the vampire chapter for students and then made an overhead transparency of the first page. We started by quickly reading the chapter through once. I explained that their goal was to learn to pick out the significant information in the chapter and that they could simply cross out any information they didn't see as essential. What was left would be the significant information or the information they would take down as notes if they were actually taking notes from a book.

Since the first page was on the overhead, we worked together on that page so that students could see how to do the activity and what was expected of them. Then they worked together in groups, eliminating all unessential information in the remaining pages. After all groups had completed the task, they shared their decisions with the rest of the class. Students didn't resist getting involved because they liked the material on vampires and because they didn't have to copy anything down for "practice."

Locating Information

With one success under my belt, I looked for other ways to use high-interest nonfiction to teach skills. I got the idea of using the *Guinness Book of World Records* when I noticed that students loved looking up records and facts in this book but had trouble when using the *Readers' Guide to Periodical Literature* in the library. Since simply placing this book in students' hands guarantees immediate interest, I decided to use it to work with them on locating information, learning to use alternate headings, and finding the parts of a book such as the table of contents.

Students seemed to have trouble figuring out multiple category labels for the information they wanted when they used the *Readers' Guide*. If they wanted to look up something about crime, they didn't realize that categories such as juvenile delinquency might give them more information. Practice with the *Guinness Book* helped. I have a classroom set of these books that I got through book club points, so every student could have a copy.

I started by asking students to figure out how to locate the record for the most human births by one woman. We brainstormed possible categories as I wrote them on the board. We thought *fertility* might work, or *babies*, or *motherhood*, or *reproduction*. When we looked in *Guinness*, we found that the editors had used the category *reproductivity*. We started our search in the table of contents, scanning the categories. Then we turned to the subject index to see which place was easier to find information. Students realized that the index had more categories and often made the information easier to locate.

Because they were using the *Guinness Book of World Records*, which they view as fun, students were patient in learning to locate the proper headings and in talking about category labels. They got used to the idea that categories can be ambiguous and that there is more than one way to list or categorize something. Thus they weren't as frustrated when we next used the *Readers' Guide* because they didn't expect success the very first time they looked up a category they thought their topic would fit into.

Summarizing and Generating Questions

Encouraging students to summarize and generate questions about what they have read can also be done through nonfiction. I usually keep at least ten high-interest nonfiction books in my class, and every two weeks I hold each student accountable for reading and producing a summary with questions on a section or a chapter. Aside from getting kids to read and think about what they are reading, it's also a wonderful way to keep them busy during those stray moments when they proclaim, "I'm done with everything" and imply, "So it should be okay if I talk loudly and disturb others." One of the books the students always clamored for was about the world's greatest disasters. It was so popular that eventually someone carried it off to his or her own private collection! Other books that work well for this purpose include those on animals and sports books, autobiographical vignettes such as those in *I Dream a World* by Brian Lanker, and oral histories of any kind such as *Bloods: An Oral History of the Vietnam War* by Wallace Terry. Students also gobble up books by Janet Bode (*Voices of Rape, Kids Having Kids, Death Is Hard to Live With*) and Susan Kuklin (*Fighting Back, What Do I Do Now?, and Speaking Out*). Any nonfiction books that have short separate entries work well for this purpose. This assignment is also a subtle way to introduce people, ideas, and events into your classroom.

To keep the motivation high, I try to change the books every three weeks, unless students insist I keep a particular one longer. I also invite them to look in the library for books that other students might be able to get involved in. Then, every two weeks in small groups students share what they have learned so that other students get exposure to some of the ideas or information in these books.

Connecting and Relating Ideas

I also try to teach my students how to connect and relate ideas and stories to each other, and I found an interesting way of doing this by using another kind of nonfiction—the newspaper. Our city newspaper is published every day, and extra copies are available to anyone who wants them. So every other week, I go to the newspaper's office and get thirty newspapers.

Before I hand out the newspapers, we list on the board everything we can think of that we did in class the past two weeks, including what we read, what we viewed, what we talked about, and what we wrote. Students are instructed to look for newspaper articles on any issues or ideas we have touched on in the last two weeks. This use of nonfiction in my class is one of my favorites because (a) students learn about writing by seeing a variety of writing forms up close; (b) they all seem to enjoy reading the newspaper and actually do read; (c) they have the time to think about and review what we've been doing in class, and it starts to make sense to them; and (d) it makes for a quiet, laid-back kind of day, which does wonders for my mental health!

Works Cited

Allard, Harry, and James Marshall. *Miss Nelson Has a Field Day.* New York: Scholastic, 1985.

Avi. *The True Confessions of Charlotte Doyle.* New York: Orchard, 1990.

Bacon, Katharine Jay. *Finn.* New York: McElderry, 1998.

Bauer, Marion Dane, ed. *Am I Blue? Coming Out from the Silence.* New York: HarperCollins, 1994.

Bedard, Michael. *The Divide.* New York: Bantam, 1997.

Beals, Melba Pattillo. *Warriors Don't Cry: A Searing Memoir of the Battle to Integrate Little Rock's Central High.* New York: Pocket, 1994.

Beers, Kylene. "Choosing Not to Read: An Ethnographic Approach to Understanding Aliteracy." ALAN Workshop. NCTE Annual Convention. Hyatt Regency, Atlanta. 19–20 Nov. 1990.

Bennett, Cherie. *Life in the Fat Lane.* New York: Delacorte, 1998.

Bishop, Elizabeth. "The Fish." *Adventures in American Literature.* Ed. Francis Hodgins. San Diego: Harcourt, 1985. 728.

Bloor, Edward. *The Crusader.* San Diego: Harcourt, 1999.

———. *Tangerine.* San Diego: Harcourt, 1997.

Blume, Judy, ed. *Places I Never Meant to Be: Original Stories by Censored Writers.* New York: Simon, 1999.

Bode, Janet. *Death Is Hard to Live With: Teenagers and How They Cope with Loss.* New York: Delacorte, 1993.

———. *Kids Having Kids: The Unwed Teenage Parent.* New York: Watts, 1980.

———. *The Voices of Rape.* New York: Watts, 1990.

Boyle, Kay. "Winter Night." *Adventures in American Literature.* Ed. Francis Hodgins. San Diego: Harcourt, 1985. 560–67.

Brooke, William J. *Teller of Tales.* New York: HarperCollins, 1994.

Cart, Michael, ed. *Tomorrowland: 10 Stories about the Future.* New York: Scholastic, 1999.

Chambers, Aidan, ed. *A Haunt of Ghosts.* New York: Harper, 1987.

Crane, Stephen. *The Red Badge of Courage.* New York: Tor, 1997.

Crutcher, Chris. *Athletic Shorts: Six Short Stories.* New York: Dell, 1991.

———. "A Brief Moment in the Life of Angus Bethune." *Athletic Shorts.* New York: Dell, 1991.

———. *The Crazy Horse Electric Game.* New York: Greenwillow, 1987.

Curtis, Christopher Paul. *Bud, Not Buddy.* New York: Delacorte, 1999.

———. *The Watsons Go to Birmingham—1963.* New York: Delacorte, 1995.

Dickens, Charles. *Great Expectations.* New York: Tor, 1998.

———. *A Tale of Two Cities.* New York: New American Library, 1997.

Draper, Sharon M. *Tears of a Tiger.* New York: Atheneum, 1994.

Edwards, Pamela Duncan. *Four Famished Foxes and Fosdyke.* New York: HarperCollins, 1995.

Ehrlich, Amy, ed. *When I Was Your Age: Original Stories about Growing Up.* Cambridge, MA: Candlewick, 1996.

Faulkner, William. *The Sound and the Fury.* New York: Random, 1956.

Fitzgerald, F. Scott. *The Great Gatsby.* New York: Scribner, 1995.

Furtado, Jo, and Frederic Joos. *Sorry, Miss Folio!* Brooklyn: Kane/Miller, 1988.

Gallo, Donald R., ed. *Connections: Short Stories by Outstanding Writers for Young Adults.* New York: Dell, 1989.

———, ed. *Join In: Multiethnic Short Stories by Outstanding Writers for Young Adults.* New York: Delacorte, 1993.

———, ed. *Sixteen: Short Stories by Outstanding Writers for Young Adults.* New York: Dell, 1984.

———, ed. *Time Capsule: Short Stories about Teenagers throughout the Twentieth Century.* New York: Delacorte, 1999.

———, ed. *Visions: Nineteen Short Stories by Outstanding Writers for Young Adults.* New York: Delacorte, 1987.

———, ed. *Ultimate Sports: Short Stories by Outstanding Writers for Young Adults.* New York: Delacorte, 1995.

Giovanni, Nikki, ed. *Grand Mothers: Poems, Reminiscences, and Short Stories about the Keepers of Our Traditions.* New York: Holt, 1994.

Glenn, Mel. *Class Dismissed! High School Poems.* New York: Clarion, 1982.

Goodwillie, Susan, ed. *Voices from the Future.* New York: Crown, 1993. Washington: Children's Express, 1996.

Haddix, Margaret Peterson. *Don't You Dare Read This, Mrs. Dunphrey.* New York: Simon, 1996.

Hawthorne, Nathaniel. *The Scarlet Letter.* New York: Bantam, 1981.

Hemingway, Ernest. *For Whom the Bell Tolls.* New York: Scribner, 1995.

Holt, Kimberly Willis. *When Zachary Beaver Came to Town.* New York: Holt, 1999.

Johnson, Angela. *Toning the Sweep.* New York: Scholastic, 1994.

Kaldhol, Marit, and Wenche Oyen. *Goodbye Rune.* Brooklyn: Kane/Miller, 1987.

Kelley, William Melvin. "A Visit to Grandmother." *Adventures in American Literature.* Ed. Francis Hodgins. San Diego: Harcourt, 1985. 611–15.

Korman, Gordon. *Don't Care High.* New York: Scholastic, 1985.

Krisher, Trudy. *Spite Fences.* New York: Delacorte, 1994.

Kuklin, Susan. *Fighting Back: What Some People Are Doing about AIDS.* New York: Putnam, 1989.

———. *Speaking Out: Teenagers' Take on Race, Sex, and Identity.* New York: Putnam's, 1993.

———. *What Do I Do Now? Talking about Teenage Pregnancy.* Putnam's, 1991.

Lanker, Brian. *I Dream a World: Portraits of Black Women Who Changed America.* New York: Stewart, 1989.

Lawrence, Jerome, and Robert E. Lee. *The Night Thoreau Spent in Jail.* New York: Bantam, 1972.

Levine, Gail Carson. *Dave at Night.* New York: HarperCollins, 1999.

Loughery, John, ed. *First Sightings: Contemporary Stories of American Youth.* New York: Persea, 1993.

———, ed. *Into the Widening World: International Coming-of-Age Stories.* New York: Persea, 1995.

Lowry, Lois. *The Giver.* Boston: Houghton, 1993.

Malamud, Bernard. "The First Seven Years." *Adventures in American Literature.* Ed. Francis Hodgins. San Diego: Harcourt, 1985. 594–601.

Martin, Jane Read, and Patricia Marx. *Now Everybody Really Hates Me.* New York: HarperCollins, 1993.

Mazer, Anne, ed. *Going Where I'm Coming from—Memoirs of American Youth.* New York: Persea, 1995.

Mazer, Harry, ed. *Twelve Shots: Outstanding Short Stories about Guns.* New York: Delacorte, 1997.

McCall, Nathan. *Makes Me Wanna Holler: A Young Black Man in America.* New York: Random, 1994.

McCullers, Carson. *The Member of the Wedding.* London: Cresset, 1947.

McKinley, Robin. *A Knot in the Grain and Other Stories.* New York: HarperCollins, 1994.

McKissack, Patricia C. *Ma Dear's Apron.* New York: Atheneum, 1997.

Myers, Walter Dean. *Fallen Angels.* New York: Scholastic, 1988.

———. *Malcolm X: By Any Means Necessary.* New York: Scholastic, 1993.

———. *Monster.* New York: HarperCollins, 1999.

———. *145th Street—Short Stories.* New York, Delacorte, 2000.

Nolan, Han. *A Face in Every Window.* San Diego: Harcourt, 1999.

Paulsen, Gary. *Woodsong.* New York: Bradbury, 1990.

Peck, Robert Newton. *A Day No Pigs Would Die.* New York: Dell, 1972.

Philbrick, Rodman. *Freak the Mighty.* New York: Scholastic, 1993.

———. *Max the Mighty.* New York: Scholastic, 1998.

Pines, T., ed. *Thirteen—13 Tales of Horror.* New York: Scholastic, 1991.

Rapp, Adam. *The Buffalo Tree.* New York: HarperCollins, 1997.

Rochman, Hazel, and Darlene Z. McCampbell, eds. *Leaving Home: Stories.* New York: HarperCollins, 1997.

Rosen, Michael J. *The Heart Is Big Enough—Five Stories.* San Diego: Harcourt, 1997.

Rowling, J. K. *Harry Potter and the Sorcerer's Stone.* New York: Scholastic, 1998.

Schinto, Jeanne, ed. *Show Me a Hero: Great Contemporary Stories about Sports.* New York: Persea, 1995.

Scieszka, Jon. *The Stinky Cheese Man and Other Fairly Stupid Tales.* New York: Viking, 1992.

———. *The True Story of the Three Little Pigs.* New York: Viking, 1989.

Shakespeare, William. *Romeo and Juliet.* New York: Washington Square, 1992.

Soto, Gary. *Living up the Street: Narrative Recollections.* New York: Dell, 1985.

Spinelli, Jerry. *Maniac Magee.* Boston: Little, 1990.

Stearns, Michael, ed. *A Starfarer's Dozen: Stories of Things to Come.* San Diego: Harcourt, 1995.

Steinbeck, John. *Of Mice and Men.* New York: Penguin, 1993.

Taylor, Mildred D. *Roll of Thunder, Hear My Cry.* New York: Dial, 1976.

Terry, Wallace. *Bloods: An Oral History of the Vietnam War.* New York: Random, 1984.

Thomas, Rob. *Satellite Down.* New York: Simon, 1998.

Updike, John. "The Lucid Eye in Silver Town." *Adventures in American Literature.* Ed. Francis Hodgins. San Diego: Harcourt, 1985. 603–9.

Vande Velde, Vivian. *Curses, Inc., and Other Stories.* San Diego: Harcourt, 1997.

———. *Tales from the Brothers Grimm and the Sisters Weird.* San Diego: Harcourt, 1995.

Weeks, Sarah. *Follow the Moon.* New York: HarperCollins, 1995.

Welty, Eudora. "The Worn Path." *Adventures in American Literature.* Ed. Francis Hodgins. San Diego: Harcourt, 1985. 575–84.

Wilson, Budge. *Mothers and Other Strangers.* San Diego: Harcourt, 1996.

Wrede, Patricia C. *Book of Enchantments.* San Diego: Harcourt, 1996.

Yep, Laurence. *American Dragons: Twenty-Five Asian American Voices*. New York: HarperCollins, 1993.

Zindel, Paul. *The Pigman*. New York: Harper, 1968.

5 Writing

Diana Mitchell

Students will write in our classes, especially if they see a reason for the writing and if they have a chance to do something inventive. This chapter addresses the many facets of student writing and offers ideas on using scripts, writing-to-learn activities, and student-generated questions and ideas as sources for writing. Newspapers and magazines, often overlooked in the English classroom as a basis for writing, are also explored, as is that all-important project, the research paper (in a section by teacher Endre Szentkiralyi of Nordonia High School in Macedonia, Ohio). Finally, Diana presents twenty-five "surefire" writing assignments designed especially for spring, the time it is most challenging to keep our students focused and working.

SCRIPTING FOR INVOLVEMENT AND UNDERSTANDING

I stumbled across the idea of scripting in the English classroom one very warm day in Michigan when my very warm classroom (right next to the boiler room) was made even hotter by the short tempers of my five groups of eighth graders. I can't say that I thought deeply about the theoretical or pedagogical aspects of this activity; at the time, I simply wanted something that would happily involve these adolescents. Since my students loved to talk and work with each other, I came up with the idea of having students in groups write scripts for either a news show or a puppet show and then perform them.

So we worked on scripts. I remember noisy, intense classes in which the students were working together, talking together, laughing together. On the days of the presentations, students actually listened to and enjoyed each other's productions. I recall this script making and performing as a wonderful way to involve students and absorb that extra energy that middle schoolers seem to come equipped with. But I also felt a bit guilty and wondered if we were doing the expected work of an English class, especially since I hadn't asked the students to script any particular piece of literature or to relate the scripts to anything we were doing in class.

It took me several years before I could see how this activity could be integrated into my language arts classroom rather than used simply as an add-on activity to direct students' energy in positive ways.

As an Alternative to the Book Report

The first time I used scripting in conjunction with literature was the year I wanted my ninth graders to try a new approach to the book report. Because students were reading a novel of their own choosing, I explained that I wanted each of them to write a script from their novel that would make other students want to read that book. I encouraged each student to carefully choose a chapter of their novel, write a script out of it, and read/perform the script to the entire class. My last-hour-of-the-day basic class took a liking to the idea. To get them started, I wrote a script for a novel I had just finished, made enough copies for all the characters I had written into the script, and had students perform it for the class.

Since these very verbal students loved performing, they realized they would get to do more of it if they read their novels and wrote their scripts. I explained how to choose a chapter and how to decide what to put into the script. We talked about action, dialogue, and suspense. We looked at why it was important to include a narrator who could give details of setting, provide necessary background, move the action forward, and even report the thoughts of a character. They began to see that the narrator could be the bridge between the scenes and the events. When we discussed selecting a chapter, we decided it should be one important to the book, that it should have lots of dialogue, and that it should have enough action to keep their classmates interested when it was performed.

We started work on scripts in class so that each student could get an idea of how it was done. When the first person was ready with her script, I made as many copies of the script as there were characters in it. Performances were spaced out so that only two or three novels were presented each day. Because the student who wrote the script got to choose the readers for that script, students saw this as a privilege to be taken seriously. The more they read the scripts aloud, the better their oral reading became. Students who took the job seriously and who read with expression were most often picked by their peers.

The wonderful thing about spacing out presentations was the effect this had on the laggards. They too wanted their moment of glory when they passed out their own scripts to readers of their choosing. So they read and finished their books and wrote their scripts. Everyone in the class ended up completing this project, even those students who often appeared to be unmotivated learners.

Now I had evidence of the power of scripting and performing. I could see that it acted as a stimulus for kids to read because it encouraged them to think about how they could interest others in their book. They also liked it because they were not answering teacher-created questions. They had the power to create a script that they thought was representative of the novel.

Some students selected chapters that would involve the audience in the plot; others worked at showing what the characters were like. The following excerpt of a script from *In the Middle of a Rainbow* by Barbara Girion shows how a narrator can be used and how carefully chosen dialogue reveals character concerns. The student put the necessary background information into her own words when she wrote the narrator's part:

> *Narrator:* We are sitting in on the school newspaper meeting. Jennifer Dayk, the editor, is getting heated up at the jocks in school, forgetting Todd, Corrie's boyfriend and also a soccer player, is there.
>
> *Todd:* *(disgustedly)* Do you all think you're the only ones who listen to music, or read and write? Just because a guy wears padded shoulders to play football doesn't mean his brain is padded, too.
>
> *Jennifer:* *(sarcastically)* Well, I never thought of that, but it sounds good to me—about jocks having padded brains I mean. *(laughing, then angrily)* You Neanderthals don't bother to support the school publications or even stop to read the things we *(sweeping her arms around the table)* work so hard at. Did you ever stop to think that someone can sit up night after night writing a poem? Then most of you sports heroes will take the magazine and make airplanes out of it?
>
> *Todd:* *(just as mad)* Hey, what about the athlete who's working on his body and memorizing game plans all week, for the sake of the school? Why don't any of you come out to watch and support the team? What is it? Is pushing pencils the only sport you're interested in?

Students appreciated scripts such as this one because it gave them a taste of what the characters were like and because they enjoyed the lively language, as well as the issues raised. When every student had presented his or her script, each member of the class selected the five novels from the presentations that they most wanted to read. Thus students got more feedback on how well they had succeeded in interesting others in the novel they had scripted.

As a Way into Themes, Characters, and Issues in Short Stories

Students have also written scripts to show their understanding of characters and themes in short stories. After reading a story such as "The Devil and Tom Walker" by Washington Irving, they develop scripts showing what they think happened in the woods when Mrs. Walker confronted the Devil. Students use what they know about characters to create dialogue that is "in character." For "The Devil and Tom Walker," they used such clues as the tufts of hair scattered about the woods and the apron found to create their view of how this clash played itself out. Working to be consistent with the tone of the story in these scripts, students try to make sure the characters' language and attitudes are portrayed as they were in the story.

I have also had students create talk shows based on issues that unfold in a short story. For instance, in "She" by Rosa Guy in the short story collection *Sixteen*, the major conflict is between stepparent and stepchild. Although the story is written from the point of view of the stepchild, students often explore both sides of the issue in their scripts. One year, when some of my ninth graders read this story, they decided the Oprah Winfrey show would be the perfect format. They invited to "the show" all four characters from the short story, plus a psychologist (played by a student) as well as members of the class who felt they were experts on the issue because they lived with a stepparent. In this case, there was some scripting to keep the show on course and some ad-libbing.

I was amazed by how well the students could adopt the point of view of the character and speak as if they were that character. I was also impressed by how well they all seemed to understand both sides of the conflict even though they tended to empathize with Gogi, the stepchild. This activity not only got students more involved in the issues and characters in the short story, but it also had the benefit of helping students reflect on issues very close to some of their own lives.

As a Way to Increase Comprehension of More Difficult Literature

A one-day workshop, "Out of Their Seats and Up on Their Feet," conducted by Joan Silberschlag at the 1987 NCTE Spring Conference in Louisville, showed me even more possibilities for scripting. Silberschlag had taken poems and arranged them to be read in many voices. She had created in script form an introduction to *The Red Badge of Courage* by Stephen Crane. In addition, she had scripted a chapter from that novel. When it was performed, I was surprised at how powerful the piece became.

As I thought of my own classroom, I realized that my students didn't get as much out of reading *The Red Badge of Courage* as we did watching an enactment of a chapter. A lightbulb went on in my head, and I was suddenly able to see that scripting could be done with almost any literature.

For my first efforts, I had students read Joan Silberschlag's script and carefully look at what she had omitted and what she had included. Since many chapters contain more of Henry's internal thoughts than dialogue, I suggested to students they might want to have more than one narrator to carry the heavy load of narration needed. I chose selected chapters that I thought were important to an understanding of the novel, and students wrote their own scripts. When completed, small groups read and discussed scripts and selected the ones that they thought should be read to the whole class. One student wrote the following as part of his script of Chapter 8:

Narrator 1:	The youth got up carefully, and Wilson led him among the sleeping forms lying in groups and rows. Presently he stooped and picked up his blankets. He spread the rubber one upon the ground and placed the woolen one about the youth's shoulders.
Wilson:	There now, lie down an' git some sleep.
Henry:	Hol' on a minnit! Where you goin' t' sleep?
Wilson:	Right down there by yeh.
Henry:	Well, but hol' on a minnit. What yeh goin' t' sleep in? I've got your_____
Wilson:	Shet up an' go on t' sleep. Don't be making a damn fool 'sa yerself.
Narrator 2:	An exquisite drowsiness spread through the youth. His head fell forward on his crooked arm, and his weighted lids went slowly down over his eyes.

Afterward, students commented on how much more they got out of the novel by scripting it and listening to readings of the scripts. The emotion so often swallowed up by Crane's extensive description burst through in these student-written scripts.

Based on this success, I utilized scripting the next year in my American Literature classes in still another way when we read *The Scarlet Letter*. I had seventy-three students in two classes, so I divided the chapters among small groups of students. Two to three students worked together on a script to try to capture the essence of their particular chapter. Much negotiating went on in the groups as they wrestled with the problems this very descriptive novel presented. A common challenge they all faced was cutting each chapter extensively and simplifying the language.

Between the two classes, students had written two or three scripts for each chapter. On the day the assignment was due, students again got into groups. I gave each group three scripts from the same chapter (but not the one the group had worked on). They had to evaluate the scripts by answering the following questions:

1. Briefly describe what each script emphasized.

2. Which script(s) captured the essence of the chapter? Why?

3. What was particularly effective in any of the scripts?

4. Did any of the scripts include unusual narrative devices? Were they effective?

5. Did you think any of the dialogue was too long?

6. Was the language changed in any of the scripts? What effect did this have?

7. What made some scripts more interesting to read?

8. As a group, pick out the script for each chapter that you would say is most effective in capturing the meaning of the chapter and in keeping the reader interested. Explain.

9. As a group, discuss what makes a script effective. Now list all the advice you would give to someone about how to write a script.

Students' responses to the last two questions included such comments as "Don't leave out main points"; "Detail is good but not when you use too much"; "Don't summarize"; "Make it clear"; and "Don't change the tone of the story."

When students explained why they chose one script over another, they made comments such as "It brought you into the story and made you feel what Hester felt"; "We liked the way she used a conscience as a character, it was more interesting"; "It made you feel and understand what was happening. Others used too much slang and weren't formal enough." This activity managed not only to get students engaged in *The Scarlet Letter*, but it also made them more aware of what makes a script effective.

As a Way to Evaluate Students' Ability to Synthesize What They Know about Authors and Characters

One of my most successful scripting ideas came from an adaptation of a teaching idea I found in *Ideas Plus: Book Three*. Sharon Summers's exercise titled "Guess Who's Coming to Dinner?" (28) gave me the seed of an idea I later expanded on. Summers had her students invite nine authors or characters they had read about to dinner. She asked students to write an essay about how they arrived at the seating arrangements and what topics of conversation would take place around the table. I decided to give this assignment as part of the final exam in American Literature. The first time I gave the assignment, one boy asked me if he could write it in play form. I was delighted with his idea, his script was fabulous, and so over the years I've changed the assignment. Now students bring nine authors or characters together in any way they want, write the encounter in script form, and complete it one week before the final exam. The focus of the script must be on showing how the characters interact in terms of issues that will illustrate what the characters or authors were like.

For instance, in this script by student Luke Waltzer, the characters talk about the death penalty:

Roger Chillingworth:	I think all criminals should be killed.
Dr. Heidegger:	I think we should use criminals in laboratory experiments.
Henry Thoreau:	That's absurd. Whatever happened to human compassion? What about giving each other a second chance? We should do everything we can to rehabilitate our criminals. We must not give up on them.
Roderick Usher:	Death! I dread the day I die! If I were to be murdered, I'd want my killer tortured and then killed!
William Cullen Bryant:	I think death is something to look forward to. It will be exciting and may be even better than life. Until we make sure we are punishing the criminals, we must not use capital punishment.

These scripts, which showcase the thoughts and beliefs of the characters and authors, are shared during our final exam period. I read each script, select about ten of the more interesting and well-written ones, and make ten copies so that each student who reads a part will have a script. During final exam period, we read the scripts aloud and have a wonderful time, while knowledge about authors and characters from the semester is reinforced.

Each year I am stunned by the students' creativity. They have brought characters together in such venues as Ted Koppel's *Nightline,* a wax museum, a golf course, and even Dr. Heidegger's study. The student, Angela Poneta, who set her script in Dr. Heidegger's study wrote the narrative parts using a rhythm and rhyme scheme similar to Edgar Allan Poe's "The Raven." She ends her script with the following words from the narrator:

> And the Raven, never flitting,
> Still is sitting, STILL is sitting.
>
> It lost its life just after flying to
> Heidegger's study door.
>
> And those who longed for truth
> in the legend of the Fountain of Youth
> Are now buried six feet under,
> underneath the earthen floor.
>
> And the magic water left a stain
> upon his study floor.
> It remains forever more.

As with any activity, if scripting is used too often it loses its appeal. It does, however, work wonderfully once or twice each semester. When students script parts of novels for book reports, the activity encourages them to focus on meaning and how best to create an interest in their books. As a response to a short story, scripting allows students to get deeply involved with characters, issues, and themes, and reinforces the idea that literature is meant to make an impact on the reader. When students write scripts on more difficult pieces of literature, they must grapple with the literature to get at the heart of the author's message. As a final exam, scripting encourages students to synthesize what they know about characters and authors by placing them in new situations.

Above all, scripting works because scripts are student created; students have invested themselves in the product. Students share their insights through performance, which expands the audience from just the teacher to the whole class, providing a more realistic and more interactive forum for their writing.

WRITING TO LEARN ACROSS THE CURRICULUM AND THE ENGLISH TEACHER

Other teachers think English teachers know it all. After all, aren't we the ones trained in writing? With the big push for more writing in the content areas, English language arts teachers are often looked to for advice and answers about writing. Engrossed in our own content concerns, however, it's often difficult to offer quick advice to other teachers, especially at the beginning of the year when we want to think about our own classrooms. So after initial questions from content area teachers, we're usually happy to let these writing-across-the-curriculum or writing-to-learn concerns drift slowly out of our awareness. After all, don't we have our students writing stories, poems, and essays? Why should we bother with this writing-to-learn stuff? What's in it for our students?

In a nutshell, writing to learn involves getting students to think about and to find the words to explain what they are learning, how they understand that learning, and what their own processes of learning involve. Oftentimes we forget that although we have a wonderful teaching plan in our head and see all the connections between the poetry, the short stories, the essays, and the surveys we bring into the class, the students might view the work of the class as disjointed and unrelated. So writing to learn, in its most basic sense, is a tool we can use to see how students are thinking about and understanding what they are doing and learning in the classroom.

Thus the intent of the following is twofold: (1) to provide language arts teachers with specific ways to help content-area teachers begin to integrate more writing into their classrooms and (2) to help us all take a new look at how our own classrooms can be enhanced by using some of these formats to encourage students to write about their learning. Sample writing ideas from many curricular areas follow each format suggestion so that you can see how writing to learn can be used in specific content areas.

Writing Formats

1. Learning Logs or Journals. Students are asked to write about their learning in a log or journal, which often takes the form of a spiral notebook to avoid unmanageable stacks of loose paper. Teachers can pose questions and students can make observations, create lists, ask questions, raise concerns, write reflections, and explain their understanding of something. The notebook provides them with a place to think about, learn, and understand the course material. Many of the next nineteen formats can be done in these learning logs.

Teachers can build interest in the day's activities and encourage the beginnings of whole-class discussion by asking questions such as the following:

How are the last two stories that we read connected?

Why do you think George feels responsible for Lennie in *Of Mice and Men*?

Why is five-eighths bigger than one-half? Why do we use the term "half past" and "quarter 'til" when we tell time?

Why it is colder in the winter?

Describe what happens to molecules as they are heated.

Explain why Haiti might have problems becoming democratic.

Write about this painting in terms of color, shape, texture, and value.

Explain what you need to do vocally to create a warm, dark tone or a bright, cooler tone.

2. Content-Area Autobiographies. Students write about their experiences with math or science or reading or gym from as far back as they can remember. They talk about how they felt about what they were learning, positive and negative experiences, whether their families helped them, and so on. These autobiographies help teachers determine where their students are in relation to their subject by giving them information about students' attitudes, achievements, and shortcomings in their subject area.

3. Making Connections to Your Own Life. Students work to find ways that material and concepts in their classes relate to their own lives. The questions that drive this activity help them see how class work is connected to the real world.

What metaphor would describe your life this week?

Do any of the characters in this story seem similar to someone you know?

What three geometric shapes have had a direct influence on your life today?

Where in your life have you seen examples of positive and negative numbers?

Who have you read about in history that you want to be like?

What has a plant done for you today?

What would your life be like if calcium was absent from all foods?

What do you think the lyrics of this song are trying to express?

Which piece of music that we have played can you relate to the most, and why?

What are your assets? Make a list of them and explain how they affect your life.

4. Making Judgments/Evaluating Concepts. Students are asked to use higher-level thinking skills as they draw on content knowledge to come to conclusions.

> Which character seems to have the worst self-concept? Explain why you believe this to be the case.
>
> Which planet, aside from Earth, seems superior to you? Explain how you came to this conclusion.
>
> After hearing two recordings of the same piece, which arrangement was best? Why?
>
> Are high heels a physics nightmare? Explain.
>
> This piece is more difficult for me to play/sing because . . .

5. What if . . . ? This format also taps into higher-level thinking skills. It often asks students to figure out how the absence of something would have an impact on something else.

> What if the setting in this story changed?
>
> What if George had not killed Lennie in *Of Mice and Men*?
>
> What if we had no moon?
>
> What if your heart had only three chambers instead of four?
>
> What if the liquid on the surface of the earth was methyl instead of water?
>
> What if you had to get common denominators when you multiplied fractions?
>
> What if there were no fractional parts in real life?
>
> What if there had been no Abe Lincoln?
>
> What if there were no black or white pigments? How would it affect your painting?
>
> What if people didn't sweat during and after exercise?
>
> What if spark plugs didn't exist?
>
> What if there was no copper?
>
> What would music sound like if there were no major modes?

6. Fiction. Students create stories to demonstrate their understanding of content.

> Write a story about travel from one planet to another, with your hero or heroine telling what he or she observes.
>
> Imagine you are so tiny that you are mistaken for a potato chip and eaten; describe your journey inside the body of the person who ate you.

Imagine that your whole family has been turned into geometric shapes: write a story explaining what shape each person is and how that works to each person's advantage or disadvantage as he or she interacts with other family members.

When you were trying to get the school computer to work, something went horribly wrong, and you find that you have been hurled back in time. Because of the music playing and the clothes worn, you realize you are somewhere in the 1920s. Describe where you are, how you spend your day, what you see, and how others react to your hair and clothes and language.

Create a story in which you pretend you are an atom of hydrogen in a water molecule. Describe in detail how you would feel and what would happen to you if you went through two different types of changes—physical and chemical.

Imagine that you are a scuba diver traveling from New York to London. Write a story that describes the features of the ocean floor you would observe.

7. Scripts or Conversations. Students write a conversation between two people, animals, plants, objects, etc. to show their understanding of content.

Write the conversation between a tarantula and a scorpion. Through their talk, be sure to show what happened in this confrontation.

Construct a food chain conversation between a mouse and a hawk.

Construct a conversation between a negative number and a positive number showing some similarities and differences.

Construct a conversation between an auto mechanic and a customer in which the auto mechanic tries to convince the customer that oil changes are necessary to the running of the car.

Create a conversation between watercolor brushes (round, flat, liner), water color paper (#90 weight and #140 weight), and watercolor paint about how they make a watercolor painting.

Write a conversation between Booker T. Washington and W. E. B. Du Bois.

Write a conversation between a nut, a bolt, and a washer.

Write a conversation between potential and chemical energy.

Write a conversation between the bench press and pectoral muscles.

Write a conversation between a musician and his or her instrument.

Write a conversation between a composer and the notes he or she is writing.

8. Take a Stand. Students defend or debate issues arising in a course.

> Every seventh grader should/should not read Jerry Spinelli's *Maniac Magee.*
>
> Newly emerging nations should simply adopt a democratic form of government.
>
> Gerrymandering other than by geographic locations should be prohibited.
>
> Genetic testing should be required of all potential parents.
>
> Predictions of the earth being overpopulated by 2020 are/are not supported by mathematical projections.
>
> The age for obtaining a driver's license should be raised to eighteen.
>
> Rock music should be studied in school.
>
> Abstract art is confusing/great because . . .
>
> People should use credit cards.

9. Monologues. Students brainstorm several points of view on one issue, concept, or event. Then students select one point of view and write in the first person about their object's or character's position on the issue, concept, or event.

> Louis Pasteur and his discovery that germs cause disease were ridiculed at the time. Fellow scientists, doctors, midwives, people on the street, and so forth could state their views on these smaller-than-the-eye causes of disease.
>
> Vietnam War. Find enough information to do monologues from the following people's point of view: returning vet injured in the war; U.S. soldiers fighting in Vietnam; Vietnamese soldiers (both North and South); South Vietnamese government; Ho Chi Minh (leader of North Vietnam); Vietnamese people in the countryside; Vietnamese people in the cities; American activist against the war; U.S. President Lyndon Johnson; the Pentagon; U.S. citizens for and against the war; parents whose sons are fighting in Vietnam.
>
> Stamp Act. Create monologues from the following points of view: the merchant's, the shopper's, the British government's, the colonial government's, and the people's.
>
> The recall of a popular car. Present the points of view of Ralph Nader, the car manufacturer, the line workers, the dealer, the customer, and the police.
>
> Animals, plants, and land forms and how they interact around the mouth of a delta. Include the points of view of the silt, the river, the ocean, the delta, the fish, and the alligators (both salt and freshwater).

CPR. Should it be given? Write monologues from the viewpoints of the victim, the rescuer, the victim's family, and the EMT personnel.

10. Awards. Students create awards based on any criteria the class or teacher develop.

> In English, awards could be based on character behavior in a novel such as most supportive person, greediest person, etc.
>
> In science, students could nominate lab experiments that were most exciting or the most demanding; they could give an award to the most important ingredient in protoplasm.
>
> In math, students could give awards to the most important formula.
>
> In physical education, students could nominate most accessible sport, or the sport that works large muscle groups.
>
> In social studies, students could nominate and give awards to people, eras, actions, and events.
>
> In foreign languages, students could give awards to the least desirable grammatical concept or favorite verb.
>
> In music, awards could be given for such things as composition with the best phrasing, most romantic sounding, hardest to play/sing.

11. Three Words. Students are asked to choose three words that best describe this novel, era, chapter, etc. They then explain why they chose those words and how those words capture the essence of what was just read or studied.

> What three words describe the problems in the American diet?
>
> What three words best describe the Bill of Rights?
>
> What three words best describe the mossy stage of a climax community?

12. Personification. Students become an object and discuss it in the first person (using "I").

> I am a comet heading toward the sun. I'll describe what I see and feel.
>
> I am Joe's stomach. Here's what I experience.
>
> I am a muscle, and I'll tell you what I like and don't like about my life.
>
> I am an equilateral triangle.
>
> I am a decimal point. Here's what my life is like.
>
> I am an electron. Come with me as I describe my journey through the GM cranking circuit all the way back to the battery.

I am a Kandinsky painting.

I am a Beethoven composition.

I am an *-ar, -er, -ir*, or irregular verb. I will explain the advantage to being this kind of verb.

I am the words to [specific song].

13. Scenarios. Create a situation. Have students write about it.

Your grandmother just moved from the coast of Florida to the west side of Michigan on the shores of Lake Michigan. She is deathly afraid of hurricanes, and when she looks out on the huge expanse of Lake Michigan, she feels sure that someday a hurricane will strike there. What would you tell her to convince her that she will never have to worry about hurricanes?

You are on the jury of the Sacco and Vanzetti case in the 1920s trial. Of the twelve jurors, you are the only one who thinks they are innocent. Write a letter convincing the other eleven of the defendants' innocence.

You are sitting at your desk at work. You have a balance sheet and income statement that have to be done by 5 P.M. All the information is computerized, and the power goes out. What do you do?

14. Press Release. At the end of the week, students write press releases (which possibly could be read over the PA system) explaining what the class accomplished or was involved in during the week. Make the language lively and interesting. These also could be shared with other classes in your content area.

Create a press release on owl pellets. What are they? What's in them? What do we learn from them?

Write a campaign press release on various historical presidential campaigns.

Write a press release for a new product discovery.

In science, write false press releases. Then explain why they are wrong.

15. Letters. This is a favorite form for students to work in. They can address the letters to themselves, younger students, a grandmother, or a parent. This kind of assignment lends itself to being displayed in class.

Write a letter home about your first week as a Civilian Conservation Corps (CCC) recruit.

Write a letter to yourself explaining what you feel you need to work on so you can better use the periodical chart.

Type a letter to a friend about the proper format of letters.

Write a letter from Mozart to you at the time he is writing his final mass.

Write a letter explaining to next year's students what they can expect from this class.

Write a letter to Salvador Dali trying to convince him to donate a painting to your school.

16. You-Are-There Scenes. Students are transported to a different time or place and act in the capacity of a reporter, describing for viewers or radio listeners what they are seeing. If people are involved, they can ask them questions. This project makes a great alternative to the basic report.

It is the time of the dinosaurs. Explain where they are, what time period you are in, what the land and plants look like, and what kind of dinosaurs inhabit the place.

You are at the scene of the Boston Massacre. Describe what kind of people are present. How are the British soldiers being treated? How are they reacting? How does the dispute start? Be sure to interview members of the crowd.

You are there when the existence of black holes is confirmed. Describe who was there, how they determined what a black hole was, how others reacted.

You are there in Picasso's studio when he is in his "blue period." Describe what is happening.

17. Memos. This is a good way to rotate the job of writing down what was done in class so that absent students can get the information without bothering the teacher:

To: Absent Students

From: Your Name

Re: What We Did in Class on September 16

This form can also be used after tests so that students can remember what worked when they studied and what didn't.

Write a memo on the proper use of current laboratory equipment.

Write a memo of a list of art supplies needed for a project.

18. Interviews. Students can interview imaginary people, each other, or adults on what they know about something specific. If these interviews are written up and posted in the room, they will usually generate interest and stimulate even more learning.

In biology, after students dissect pigs, the questions constructed might look something like this: "What did you think when you first heard you were going to dissect a pig? What were the best and worst parts for you? How do pigs' systems compare to humans'?"

In English, students could interview each other about novels they are reading with questions such as, "How do you feel about the book so far? What parts seem most real to you?"

Interview your parents about the labor and delivery your mother experienced having you.

Pick a sports figure and write questions you would like to ask. Answer them as you think the person might respond to them.

Make up a list of questions you would like to ask composers about their music. Each student picks a composer and constructs the answers that that composer would be likely to give.

19. A Member of an Organization. Ask students to imagine they are members of some national organization. Have them write up a critique of an issue/person/era/concept/event in terms of the point of view of that organization.

What would People for the Ethical Treatment of Animals say about pig dissections?

What would the National Organization of Women say about the works of Ernest Hemingway?

What would the Handgun Control organization supported by Sarah and Jim Brady say to members of the Michigan Militia?

What would a member of the National Endowment for the Arts say to school board members who think that music and art are "frills"?

20. Write Your Way into Our Next Unit. Ask students to write an "Everything I Know About [whatever you are going to involve students in next]." This activity helps teachers determine what students already know about a topic. These pieces can be read aloud as the teacher jots down responses on the overhead and groups them by themes. Students will have an opportunity to let others know what they know, and questions will arise as a natural lead-in to the unit.

Benefits of Writing to Learn

After trying some of these writing-to-learn activities, you will probably become aware of some of the following benefits:

Students become more involved in the workings of the class because the writing motivates them.

Students discover what they know and what they have questions about.

Students become more aware of their own learning as they write about it.

Students demonstrate higher-level thinking skills elicited by the writing.

Teachers can assess what the class understands and doesn't understand through student writing.

How Can Writing Become a Successful Part of the Classroom?

These writing activities and formats will not work if they are only occasionally dropped into the class work. Students must feel that writing is an important part *of* the class before they will put effort into it. Writing can become a successful part of your class if you:

- show students you value it as part of the class.
- provide audiences for the writing (other students, other classes).
- keep content at the center of the writing process and look at what the writing says.
- realize writing is an act of trust on the part of students and that they must feel safe about sharing their writing.
- design writing activities that stretch students' knowledge and ask students to structure and synthesize what they know, not merely regurgitate what they are told.
- give students choices about the form of the writing assignment whenever possible.

USING STUDENT WORK AS THE BASIS FOR CLASSROOM ACTIVITIES

Students write in our classes almost daily. They write journals, they write responses to literature, they write answers to questions we ask them. They also brainstorm lists, write about characters, and write about their own experiences. Too often this "paper trail" is a quick round-trip between student and teacher: students write, we read, we return. Their work ends up as merely a grade in our grade books. Thus we usually don't see any connection between the work students produce and our constant search for fresh ways to involve our students. Instead we read to find new teaching ideas; we rack our brains to think of clever new lesson plans. I found that part of the solution to student involvement was to use the work students generate as the basis of activities in class.

Student-Generated Questions and a Short Story

This finally occurred to me one day when my American Literature students had just finished reading Stephen Crane's "The Open Boat." They came into class with all kinds of questions, ranging from "Why was this story so long?" to "Why didn't the one who worked the hardest live?" In response to so many student inquiries, I asked each of them to write down all their questions so we could discuss them the next day.

After class, when I read the students' concerns and saw the scope of their questions, I was astonished. They asked things I would never have thought about. But they also focused on many of the areas I wanted them to consider in this story. I quickly realized that I had to make use of all this valuable student input. Instead of picking out only a few questions that interested me for discussion the next day, I typed up all of the student questions. Although this sounds like it takes time that most teachers don't have, I simply put both of my classes' questions together and started typing. I left out questions that had been asked in some form already and ended up with a list from two classes of fifty-seven questions that took me less than an hour to complete. I later realized that this time investment paid off because students loved the activity that grew out of these questions and because the "products" were oral reports.

The day after students handed me their questions, I passed out the list, divided students into groups, and asked them to sort out questions that couldn't be answered and to consolidate those that were similar. When that was done, I assigned each group about five questions. They got started that day discussing and figuring out answers that satisfied them. When they finished the next class period, each group reported their answers to the whole class. They also answered questions that their responses raised.

Although I would like to include all fifty-seven questions the students generated, I selected just a sampling:

1. Why does the author keep repeating, "If I am going to be drowned"?
2. Why didn't the sailors in the dinghy swamp the boat at St. Augustine instead of waiting a whole night?
3. Do the waves and sea gulls and sharks have any symbolism?
4. Why was this story tedious, long, boring, depressing, dull, and stupid?

5. What was the significance of the oiler dying? Why was he the only one with a name?

6. What are the themes in this story?

7. Why does the story start in the middle?

8. Why is there so little dialogue? It seems if you were stranded you'd have a lot to talk about.

9. Why did the author have us enter the thoughts of the characters—it seemed confusing.

10. The sea jargon—what does it all mean?

11. The man who saved them—was he a saint or a normal person?

12. Why is the story called "The Open Boat"?

13. Why did Crane concentrate so much on detail?

The students had questions on terminology, on why things happened, on style, on plot, on symbolism, on people's behavior, and on what it all meant. Since the students were the creators of the questions, they seemed more interested in discussing and answering them as they furthered their understanding of the story. Using this technique seemed to encourage students to go further into the story than they had done when I was the one asking all the questions. Additionally, they felt that what they had been asked to do (write questions) had been used, and that pleased them.

Students' Questions and Poetry

Once I saw the benefit of beginning a study of a short story with student questions, I decided to try the same technique with poetry. I was hoping this would work because getting students into the nitty-gritty of a poem and its construction is usually not easy to do. Students are often not interested enough to want to dig deeply.

Because Stephen Crane's poem "War Is Kind" generates diametrically opposed interpretations, I thought it would be a good poem to use to encourage students to look at the craft of poetry and how craft contributes to meaning. I gave students the following directions:

> Explain the meaning of the poem "War Is Kind," discussing all of its poetic and literary devices. Also discuss how the use of these devices adds to the meaning of the poem. Remember, it is not enough to identify a literary device such as alliteration; you must also explain what it does in the poem or how it adds to it.
>
> Include in your discussion the arrangement of and difference between stanzas, and the literary and poetic devices used such as repetition, alliteration, diction, etc. Also, discuss sentence length,

sounds of letters and words, and their effect on the poem. Discuss anything else that will contribute to your intelligent discussion of this poem.

Since students did this literary analysis during class time, I took their responses home that evening and read through them as I typed them up. I tried to eliminate only duplication but still ended up with five full pages of student responses. Several students thought Crane was extolling the virtues of war, while others felt he was antiwar. They gave many reasons for their interpretations. A brief sampling follows:

> The poem is very ironic because war is not at all kind. War is very indifferent, war does not care for those who it hurts. It is ironic that he tells the maiden, the lover, and the child not to weep because it seems that it would almost be unkind for one not to weep.

> It tells that the soldiers are born to fight and die when their time comes. People, family, and friends should not mourn the deaths of soldiers because that is why they are here.

> Stanzas 2 and 4 are tighter, line length more even, perhaps to show the order and regimentation of the military. The syllable count of these two stanzas does not vary much from line to line going only from 6 to 10 syllables, perhaps to show how in the military and in war there is little room for difference, men must all fall in and obey orders.

> The alliteration in the second stanza is hard: *glory, god, great,* and *drill* and *die.* These are hard sounds which contradict the title.

Before students came to class, I had decided which groups they would work in since I wanted groups to consist of students with varied interpretations. Their job was first to read over all the responses and try to come to a group consensus about what Crane intended through his poem. They were to do this by using as much information as possible from the responses to support their position. Two days of lively discussion and presentations followed as students explained how line length, word choice, repetition, and letter sounds contributed to their interpretation.

Students' Generalizations and a Novel

I used this strategy next when we read a novel. After we finished the novel, I asked students to brainstorm and then list all the recurring themes and motifs they could find in the work. I've varied how I do this; sometimes I ask classes to do it individually and sometimes I ask them to do it in groups. Then I typed up student responses and gave them to the class for further work.

Following is a list of some of the recurring themes and motifs students identified from *The Adventures of Huckleberry Finn:*

1. honesty vs. lies
2. religion—preaching—prayer
3. making moral decisions (right vs. wrong)
4. how people dress—appearance—stereotyping people
5. the river—woods—islands
6. quest for freedom
7. lack of backbone—going along with the crowd—cowardice
8. deafness—not hearing what others say
9. attempts at new lives—escape—running away
10. death—murder—violence—feuding
11. facades vs. reality
12. poetry—drama—putting on a show
13. treatment of slaves—prejudice—bigotry
14. use of darkness and light
15. education vs. ignorance

In groups the next day, students looked at all the themes and motifs they had identified and worked to come up with generalizations about them that were supported by the novel. They were to answer the question: What was Mark Twain trying to show us through this novel? Following are samples of student generalizations:

1. Real education does not always come from books.
2. Some people are literally deaf and some are deaf to what other people say, especially if it's the truth.
3. When people are insecure, they are more likely to follow the crowd instead of listening to their own instincts.
4. People stereotype others to try to figure out what they are like without really having to get to know them.
5. The people's willingness to believe in con artists shows how insecure they are with themselves. They do not know what to believe themselves, so they think that someone else knows what's good for them.
6. The river is life, which has twists and turns and turbulence but keeps flowing until it empties into the ocean, where it goes to eternal life.
7. People are hypocrites because they are trying to correct things in other people that they don't like about themselves.
8. The treatment of slaves shows the moral injustices of that day

and that the institutions of society such as the churches and government supported these moral injustices.

9. Throughout the story, some of the characters use religion to cover up who they really are. They feel that if they go to church loyally, people will excuse them for all the bad things they do.

10. We are always trying to be free from something. You are a slave to whatever it is that you let control you. No matter how many men see you as a free man, you are not truly free until you can say it yourself.

I have cited only strong generalizations to illustrate the ideas students could come up with, but many generalizations were weak or not very focused. Since I had typed up all the generalizations that were not duplicates and the weak ones were included, the next day students were asked to rank a few. I asked them to identify the fifteen they thought were the strongest and to give reasons for their choices. Then they were to select the five they thought were the weakest and explain why.

Students were actively engaged in reading their peers' generalizations and in working to make connections between the generalizations and the novel. This activity took a whole day; the following day, members of each group reported their decisions to the whole class, supporting their explanations with evidence from the novel. They answered questions on their work as we looked at which generalizations got the most support.

This type of activity—using what students believe about the novel as a starting point—is effective in getting students in deep discussion and dialogue about the book. They are not responding to a teacher's interpretation of the novel but instead starting with their own reactions. It makes sense to begin this way because then students feel ownership in what they are doing and are much more eager to get involved in the activity. Additionally, they are not burdened with the teacher's views, which may be the result of reading the novel as many as ten times before. Students start with their own understandings and build from there.

Making Inferences

The year I used *The Giver* by Lois Lowry in my ninth-grade English class, I wanted students to notice the values on which the "perfect society" in the novel was built. I wanted students to understand that the activities and behavior allowed in a society are based on that society's beliefs. It was my hope that after looking at the values in the novel's society, students would more clearly see what our society values.

To move toward this goal, I asked students to make inferences from facts I selected from the novel. I explained that *inference* meant "to derive or draw a conclusion from facts given." Then I gave them a list of ten facts and asked them to draw inferences from those facts. As an example, I gave them the fact that "Mirrors are rare in this society." I showed them that one possible inference from this fact would be that "Appearance is not highly valued, and people spend time doing other things."

Two (of the ten) facts from *The Giver* that I asked students to respond to were:

1. Citizens were released (killed) the third time they were brought before the court.
2. All children are given bikes at age nine.

Students responded to the first fact with such statements as:

They are very strict. It's either straighten up or leave.

They don't want violence.

Everybody gets treated the same.

They don't have jails and they want a good society.

They value a peaceful society.

So people don't keep doing bad things.

Forgiveness was not a part of their society.

Students responded to the second fact with statements such as:

Because they know how to ride them.

All children have the same life.

Everyone is treated equally in this society.

To show they are responsible to take care of something.

So no one would get jealous if someone got their bike before they did.

Because it shows that they are mature enough to go out into the community alone.

To show maturity.

It is obvious that not all of the students' statements were inferences, and part of my goal was to help students understand how to make inferences. So once again I typed up samples from student work, and as a whole class we went through them to try to figure out if they were indeed inferences. We talked about which were the strongest inferences and what we could learn about the society by looking closely at some of the facts in the novel. We then turned our attention to our own society, looking especially at the numbers of people in jail and at the amount of violence in our society. Students came to the conclusion that our society seems to value personal freedom over almost everything else. They did realize that the people in *The Giver* valued a peaceful society more than anything else and did whatever was needed to achieve that end.

Figuring out how to make inferences was difficult for many students, but it seemed to help to use the material they had generated. They could all see good examples of inferences as well as figure out why some statements were not inferences simply because they didn't draw conclusions. We were starting with *their* understanding of what an inference was and moving from there.

Student Brainstorming and Writing

In addition to using student responses as a basis for class activities when we're reading novels, I also use students' brainstorming ideas as the basis of writing assignments.

Childhood Games

One year in my ninth-grade classes, when we were looking at the folklore of childhood, I asked student groups to list all the games they remembered playing as a child. The groups were lively and boisterous as students began not only listing games but also sharing their memories of those games. At the end of the hour, each group had quite a long list of games to turn in. The next day, I brought in typed lists of all the games they had mentioned. This list included:

> curve ball, freeze tag, Mother May I?, monkey in the middle, hopscotch, dodge ball, bloody murder, hide and go get it, king of the mountain, knock-knock, zoom zoom, manhunt, I spy, shoot the moon, red light- green light-stop, red rover, follow the leader, cops and robbers, double dare triple dare promise or repeat, duck duck goose, Simon says, hand clap games, hot potato, I'm going on a trip, bombardment, statues, kick the can, skunk in the barnyard, school, cooties, eraser tag, cowboys and Indians, prison, house, prank calling, sevenup, TV tag, ring around the Rosie, marbles.

The following day students shared memories aloud about these games, and then each student wrote a personal narrative about playing one of them. Students loved this assignment and were eager to share their work with the class. I then asked students to get back into groups and try to categorize or find commonalities among the games. What made some games like other games? Which games had leaders? I also asked students to try to figure out what the rules for these games were and what children learned from each category of game they identified. After the groups looked at these issues, they wrote a joint essay on what children learn from playing games.

The activity started with brainstorming and ideas students came up with. Because most of them had fond memories of childhood games, they were more than willing to think about, talk about, write about, and analyze them.

Being a Teenager in the 1990s

Another way I have begun units is by tapping into what students already know or are already interested in. In my ninth-grade class, I loosely structure a unit around the theme of "Being a Teenager." I start by asking students to complete ten sentences that begin with the phrase "Being a teen in the 1990s means . . ." The results are startling, and samples follow:

Being a teenager means . . .

always being on the alert for the gun that you may die by.

accepting responsibility a lot faster and a lot sooner.

constantly adjusting to keep up with friends.

having a harder time growing up than any generation before us.

loud music and dangerous thrills.

having sex at an early age.

excessive violence.

expect the unexpected.

doing as your parents ask you.

having fun while I can.

going to parties, dancing.

worrying about who are your real friends.

you're going to get shot or killed for dressing a certain way or because of mistaken identity.

not paying bills or taking care of kids.

dealing with racism.

worrying about AIDS.

shopping with friends, going to college, getting an education.

trying to pay attention in class.

suicide.

teen pregnancy.

there is no respect.

We used these lists in many ways. First we tried to look at the big picture to figure out which things seem most burdensome to teens today and how much time they spend thinking about these things. We did this by passing out the list and working in groups to rate the ten issues that students felt most affected them. Then we shared views and listed on the board the top issues. Students made copies of the lists from the board. Afterward, they were to watch at least three TV shows that week that focused on teens and then list the issues that surfaced in these shows. They compared our list to the issues repeated in TV shows.

Then we read many short stories in collections, such as the ones Don Gallo has edited in *Visions* and *Connections*, and talked about the stories in terms of teen life. Are they realistic? Do they show concerns that students in our class share? Are they good examples of specific issues? Is this what teen life is really like? At the same time, students were reading individually chosen young adult novels and looking at their books in the same light.

Later on, I also asked students to look again at the list we generated and write a brief persuasive essay explaining to adults what it is like to be a teenager today. Students looked back over the lists, jotted down notes, and wrote essays that presented their point of view. Excerpts follow:

> Growing up in the 1990s means being strong against peer pressure or becoming another nobody or dope head.

> You must have at least one role model or someone who looks after you and knows what is ahead for your future. If not, you will turn to other means for support. We are the kids of the so-called Baby Boomers and they were just kids themselves so they knew nothing about raising kids. (Well, the majority didn't anyway.) So you have to set high goals for yourself and try your hardest to reach them and don't fall prey to "the easy way out."

> A kid of the 1990s sees guns, dope, dope heads, and dope dealers every day. It is not a surprise or something new. It's just a shame.

> Growing up in the 1990s isn't as easy as it was in the past. Times have changed. Adults always say things like "these are the best years of your life" or "don't wish your life away."

> Well if these are the best years of our lives I'd hate to see the worst. We have to worry about drugs, getting shot, sex, having kids too early, and even AIDS.

> Adults don't think we have a lot to worry about. What they don't realize is every teen has seen, used, or sold drugs. That is, if they finish high school. I don't like school and I don't plan on going to college, unless I get an opportunity to get a high paying job for taking certain classes. That is my opinion about teens in the 1990s.

These students could articulate what they considered was important partly because they had other students' responses to stimulate and further their thinking. The whole idea of using what students know and their responses as the basis for class activities has endless possibilities. Students are filled with ideas. They burst into our classrooms chattering about movies, problems, relationships. Harnessing this energy and their ideas is our great challenge, but since students seem more interested in getting involved in what their peers say and in what they know, it is to our benefit to find as many ways as we can to use student input in our classrooms.

USING NEWSPAPERS AND MAGAZINES— THE MULTIPURPOSE TEACHING TOOLS

Many English language arts teachers shy away from using newspapers and magazines in their classes, feeling that they only apply to journalistic courses. As this section demonstrates, however, newspapers and magazines can be the perfect vehicles to teach a variety of skills, as well as a way to heighten student interest. There is something almost magical about flipping through the pages of magazines and newspapers. Students feel in charge of the experience. They usually get a chance to create, to make something of their own when newspapers and magazines are used, thus capturing their attention.

Newspapers and Novels

The newspaper can provide variety for class activities centered on the reading of a novel. Bring in newspapers and ask students to go through an issue to locate at least ten connections to the novel. Put in the position of thinking about themes, setting, and characters, students learn from this assignment that what they are reading *does* connect to their world and that they are capable of critical thinking as they make the connections. For instance, as they read *Of Mice and Men,* they might find newspaper stories about migrant labor, the mentally impaired, caregivers, bullies, women who feel trapped by circumstances, unintentional murder, racial crimes, or discrimination. They can write about which character would respond most strongly to the article and explain why. They can also explain what the character would say about the article.

A sampling of connections from one daily paper to *Of Mice and Men* follows:

Frightening manhunt

> Lenny and George, after reading this article, might want to urge the hunters not to assume that the hunted are always guilty.

Deer is state's official mammal

> Lenny would probably argue with the choice, explaining why he thinks it should be the rabbit.

Female chimps sneak off to have trysts with males outside their social group

> Men in the bunkhouse might take this as more evidence of the dangerous nature of women.

Barbie puts doll in wheelchair to portray diversity

> Candy would especially like it that people of different abilities are finally being shown.

Graduate triumphed over life's terrible times

> All the men in the bunkhouse would like this story because it could offer them hope.

An article on unions

> The men in the bunkhouse might have a good discussion about this concept and how it could possibly change their lives.

Students can also identify which comics, personals, and ads would appeal to characters. They can locate objects that different characters might relate to, or want, or admire. Students can locate pictures in magazines or newspapers that remind them of the characters and explain why they chose the picture.

Cut-up Words and Phrases

Have students peruse magazines to find fifteen to twenty interesting or intriguing phrases, mainly from advertisements (since very small print is too hard to work with). Collect all these offerings and staple or glue them to a sheet of paper and photocopy them for the class. Working in small groups, students then compete to create the most connections between the phrases and anything they have studied or read in your class during the last marking period. This activity pushes students to think and bring into play all they have learned or been exposed to in your class.

Have students cut out single words from magazine or newspaper headlines that in some way connect to what you have been doing. Students then create a dictionary out of the words. After pasting words alphabetically in a booklet, students find the definition and such things as what part of speech the word is. Then they write a sentence explaining how the word relates to a novel or unit. Encourage them to find at least twenty words that begin with different letters of the alphabet.

Ask students to write a letter from one character to another or to create a dialogue between two characters using words and phrases in each sentence that have been cut from magazines. Students glue down or staple the words or phrases and then complete the sentence. This forces students to be creative because it taps into their knowledge of a novel.

Teaching with Tabloids

Bring tabloids to class or select several articles from tabloids and make copies for your students. Also have a supply of regular newspapers available. After students have read a few newspaper and tabloid articles, have them compare and contrast the characteristics of newspaper and tabloid writing. (Students love doing this since they seem to enjoy the sensational writing in the tabloids.)

Next, ask students to form groups and select a newspaper article which the group will turn into a tabloid article. Noise levels can get high as students work to create a story as outrageous as the ones they have read. Ask groups to share their new stories orally. Because of the nature of these rewritten stories, students will listen attentively and enjoy the writing immensely.

Finally, students discuss what it takes to change the writing, what kinds of words were used, and what principles guided them as they changed one kind of writing to another. Implications of the assignment are discussed, and students usually begin to realize that not everything written has to be "true." They also realize that different kinds of writing have different conventions or rules that may be unique to the genre. (Thanks to Deb LaFleur of Williamston [Michigan] Middle School, who first acquainted me with this idea.)

Looking at Point of View through Newspaper Articles

Bring to class a newspaper story based on a socially relevant issue. Students take turns reading parts of the article aloud. In the example that follows, the article was about a drunk driving accident that killed four young people, leaving the teen driver severely injured. The article was discussed in terms of whose perspective it seemed to be written from and whether it seemed objective. Students then brainstormed other perspectives the article could be written from. They suggested the drunk driver, the passenger who lived, the Emergency Medical Team (EMT), a nurse, a parent or relative of one of the accident victims, a police officer, a bystander, the boy who the driver of the car had had an argument with minutes before the accident, a coach of one of the boys, the store owner who had sold them the beer, the mother of the driver.

In small groups, students each chose a different perspective and a different genre (if they wanted to) to use to write the story of the accident. Stories were shared, and the writers explained what information they chose to include or exclude and why. Group discussion followed in which group members talked about what was the most difficult part of the assignment and what each person needed to know to write from another's point of view.

The police report was written on a quickly made-up accident report form, so the student who wrote from this point of view had to be familiar with the form. The Emergency Medical Team had to describe the conditions of the bodies and generate that information since it wasn't mentioned in the newspaper. Others who chose to write from the EMT's point of view wrote a stream-of-consciousness narrative of what they thought about as they headed to the accident and when they got there. In the piece from the point of view of the coach, he discussed the good things about the dead boys and what he had tried to teach them. The mother of one of the dead boys composed a poem that told the story of her son's life.

Students quickly saw that each point of view considered the same event through a slightly different lens. They also learned that the same material can be written about in several genres. The original newspaper article was posted in the middle of a bulletin board, and all the pieces created from it were stapled around it. Thus this assignment continued to have an impact on the students long after they had finished it.

This assignment can be followed up by having students pick out five newspaper articles and listing five different points of view each article could be written from. Then, when it is time to do other kinds of writing assignments, students can be urged to consider using a different point of view to make a different kind of impact. (Thanks to Diane Delaney, Hayes Middle School, Grand Ledge, Michigan, who first demonstrated this idea in The Michigan Red Cedar Writing Project summer institute.) These ideas, which can inject a sense of newness and excitement into the class, can be a beginning to periodic use of newspapers throughout the year.

TAKING THE PAIN OUT OF RESEARCH PAPERS

Most teachers put off thinking about teaching research skills and research writing during the first semester of the school year because we're usually riding a wave of student goodwill and enjoying this "honeymoon" time of year. After the Christmas break, reality often sets in. Students know they'll be with us for at least five more months, activities don't seem as much fun, and so there seems to be less enthusiasm. For some reason, this is the time of year we decide to "get down to business" and tackle the research project—since students are grumpy anyway!

The following should give all of us new ways to think about and approach the research paper. In this section, Nordonia High School (Macedonia, Ohio) teacher Endre Szentkiralyi points out the basic flaws in most approaches used to teach the research paper and explains a wonderfully practical way to involve students in critical thinking as they get further into their research question.

Research Papers and Their Pitfalls

> "He can't even footnote properly."
>
> "I can't believe she really wrote this; it's probably just copied out of an encyclopedia."
>
> "My students won't write complete sentences, so how will they write a research paper?"

Do these and similar protests sound familiar? We teachers frequently complain of our students' inability to write, especially when it comes to research papers. Yet research papers will not go away; they are part of the curriculum of almost every school district in the country. In my district, for example, we start introducing the concept to eighth graders. But if we continue to teach research papers the same way we were taught, such complaints are likely to persist. Only with a careful look at the assumptions underlying research papers can we hope to improve the situation.

Myths of Research Papers

One of the persistent myths about research papers is the importance of correct form. The title page needs to follow X or Y format exactly, the margins need to be precisely one inch, the paper should be double-spaced, endnotes should have superscripted numbers, the bibliography needs to be reverse indented; the list goes on and on. We spend weeks talking about the placement of colons and commas and whether to underline a title or to place it in quotation marks, but are surprised when the actual writing received is not quality prose.

Another prevalent myth is that students cannot think for themselves, that they cannot draw conclusions. I have seen students rehashing other people's arguments, quoting from various sources, their papers becoming mainly summaries of other people's ideas. When confronted with such papers, I sometimes found myself concluding that this student did not have an original idea and, furthermore, was unable to comprehend the necessary concepts at all. I have even heard colleagues declare that since the student at his or her present stage of cognitive development is unable to think analytically, he or she will only plagiarize.

What is interesting is that one finds these myths spoken by eighth-grade teachers as well as by first-year college instructors. What follows is a dangerous thing to say because people do not take kindly to being told they may be wrong, but perhaps the fault lies not so much in the student, but in the way the research paper is taught, the process by which we approach the concept of research papers. Our underlying assumptions, then, are what we may be able to change.

Observations about Learning

A number of writers in the composition field have made observations which, when looked at from the perspective of teaching research papers, shed light on the mythical way research papers are being taught today. Janet Emig, for example, examines composition, and teaching in general, stating that "to believe that children learn because teachers teach and only what teachers explicitly teach is to engage in magical thinking" (21). By this she means that it is not so much what teachers try to accomplish that students learn, but rather that what students personally experience is what they will eventually learn.

Margaret Donaldson's work in child psychology also sheds light on the way in which students learn. In *Children's Minds,* she challenged the prevailing view that children are incapable of abstract thought, as supposedly proven by Piaget and other psychologists. She found that in fact even quite young children are capable of reasoning deductively, provided the situation makes sense to them (57–74).

Emig's and Donaldson's ideas have enormous ramifications for teachers of research papers, for they dispel two prevailing myths. First, if students are given instruction mainly in forms—if we as teachers provide them with circumstances in which bibliographic forms and conventions are foregrounded—then they will concentrate on these forms at the expense of the thinking and analysis that should go into the writing of a research paper. Second, if our students concentrate on incorporating other people's ideas into their papers without first having drawn their own conclusions, the writing will reflect that and will not be well thought out. To be able to judiciously quote from other sources, the student writer first needs to formulate his or her own thoughts and questions.

Starting the Research Paper

To avoid these pitfalls during the course of my own teaching of eighth graders, I refined a unit on research papers that seems to work better than the process I was taught in high school. I decided that the first key to writing effective research papers is personal relevance. Thus my first step in teaching the research paper was to have the students freewrite a page on their personal experience with the topic they had chosen. This freewriting was not graded; its purpose was merely to bring out inherent feelings, thoughts, and experiences with the topic. This incorporated the learners' models of reality; it engaged their worlds, forcing them to muster the resources at their disposal.

The Answerable Question

The next step was to devise a thesis statement. To keep from using abstract terminology, I referred to this as an answerable question. This question was what students wanted to answer or explore; in other words, it dictated in what direction their research would lead them. It needed to be concrete and specific. The question sometimes changed as a result of their diggings, but it served as a good starting point or focus for their research. This step is important since so many research papers crash and burn because of initial lack of focus.

I then showed students a sampling of personal experience extracts and their resulting answerable questions so that the students got a general idea of what was expected (answerable questions are in **boldface**):

> My dad always buys American, but my uncle says that American cars just aren't built as well as Japanese cars. My dad says that the Japanese are ruining our economy, but my uncle says that we're digging our own grave. . . . I wonder what kids my age think. . . . **How many people would buy a car just because it's American, or just because it's cheap, or just because it's good?**

What reasons do people have for buying U.S. or foreign cars?

I listen to heavy metal music all the time, and I don't consider myself violent. How would I measure the impact of music on me or on other people? Maybe I could describe my (or other people's) feelings before and after listening. . . .

Does listening to heavy metal music cause violence?
Does listening to rap music cause violence?

I bought this on sale, but I know someone who works in a store who told me that it's not really a sale—it's just a business tactic . . . .

Are sale prices really low prices?

Encouraging the Thinking Process

At this point, students were fairly clear about the direction in which their research would go. They knew the question they wanted to answer and were ready to begin looking. But here awaited another pitfall of common research papers: looking in books, they may be led from one tangent to another, they may adopt one perspective and then discard it in favor of another, and when their thoughts are completely mixed up and scattered, they finally throw up their hands and turn in a hodgepodge of writing. No wonder the teacher surmises that the student can't draw conclusions. The reason for the confusion, the reason the student is often unable to effectively generalize, is that when writers write books, whether science or history or literary theory, they do so convincingly. And when the student has not yet formulated an answer to his or her question, when the student is on shaky terms with his or her own conclusions and is confronted by such convincing prose, then it is easy to be swayed from one opinion to another and back again.

So, before focusing on form, students need to think through their topic before they write. Nancy Sommers compared the revision strategies of students writers and experienced adult writers and found that the primary objective of experienced writers when revising was "finding the form or shape of their argument" (50). This is important, for it means that the student must first come to terms with what he or she wants to say and only then develop a concern for the readership. Mina Shaughnessy supports this argument:

> The conditions under which the student is writing have not allowed for the slow generation of an orienting conviction, that underlying sense of the direction he wants his thinking to take. Yet without this conviction, he cannot judge the relevance of what comes to his mind, as one sentence branches out into another or

one idea engenders another, gradually crowding from his memory the direction he initially set for himself. ("Diving In" 238)

Shaughnessy meant her comments for general basic writing, but it applies to research papers too; without this conviction, students cannot judge the relevance of what they encounter in their research, especially if it is convincingly written.

In fact, the reason for writing a research paper is to interpret and analyze data and to deduce logical conclusions. These are the skills we as teachers want to develop in our students. As long as the circumstances—the research paper assignments—are structured correctly, the act of writing can indeed be a helpful way for the student to learn. But if students have too many possibilities to choose from, their reasoning will be overwhelmed with choices. This is simply a matter of information overload, and looking in the library without directions or without a conviction can skew thinking. Shaughnessy addressed this issue, stating that as teachers, we must lead basic writers slowly up the ladder of abstraction, perhaps beginning with inferences from small pools of data, or with nonprint media (*Errors*).

Two Options: Interview or Survey

Although at the time I was not acquainted with Shaughnessy's views in this matter, this is exactly what I had my students do. Instead of going to the library, our next step after writing the personal experience and identifying the answerable question was one of two options, depending on which option best lent itself to the student's choice of topic. The first option was to interview several knowledgeable people about the topic. The second option was to conduct a survey to find answers to the answerable question. Each option in its own way forced students to come up with the raw data and do the thinking about the topic before doing any writing. The actual assignment was as follows:

> *Option 1:* Prepare an anonymous questionnaire which you will distribute to fellow students. Include at least five open-ended questions which you feel are pertinent (to get the information you are looking for). "Why?" should be one of them.
>
> *Survey Audience* (write half a page on the following): Who will complete the survey? Will it be one class, two classes, social studies classes, math classes, a homeroom? Will it be only boys, only girls, the whole lunchroom, a random sampling? Who are you targeting to make your evidence acceptable?
>
> *Option 2:* Interview a knowledgeable person on your topic. The more people you interview, the more points you will get. You

must write at least five questions which you will ask the person during your interview.

Person Interviewed (write half a page on the following): Who is the person being interviewed? What are his or her qualifications? Where did he or she get knowledge about the subject? How long has he or she worked with this topic?

The Survey Audience and the Person Interviewed sections served to prod students into thinking consciously about the research choices they made. These parts of the assignment forced students to reason and to open their procedure to critical inquiry; they must be able to justify their choices. In addition, note that this whole approach will work with any age group, whether ninth graders, seniors in high school, or adult basic writers. The key is to get thought processes active, and the depth of research will incrementally reflect students' ages and life experiences.

An advantage to having students interview or survey is that it limits the pool of initial information. Students develop their skills in drawing valid conclusions and in correctly analyzing information. They are not faced with a library of information, but are presented with only the most important facts or data. Limiting the scope of research gives students a sense of control and accomplishment; they face a manageable amount of information to process.

Using Secondary Resources

Now—when the students had thought about the topic and had come up with raw data to evaluate, whether facts and opinions from interviews or numbers from surveys—they could begin to formulate a thesis. At this point, they actually wrote a significant portion of the paper. After this stage and *only after this stage* were they allowed to go to secondary sources such as encyclopedias, books, magazines, or journals. What this procedure did was allow students to look specifically for information that shed light on their conclusions. They were not using the references to formulate their conclusions but rather to prove and strengthen their arguments.

Their written prose became more focused and relevant, for their purpose in writing the paper was to communicate their results, not merely to fulfill form requirements as would have been the case in the traditional research paper. The problems they were struggling to solve as they were writing were not problems of form and style but rather cognitive problems, such as whether they were drawing valid conclusions. This is what leads to quality writing. The students' finished products dispel teacher myths about the relative importance of forms and conventions and about the lack of student reasoning. Understanding their subject is what empowers students to be authoritative and convincing in their writing. And, whether working with eighth graders or with high school seniors, empowering students is what teaching writing is all about.

Endre Szentkiralyi

SPRINGTIME SANITY SAVERS

April tumbles into May. Then the real challenge begins—how to keep our students happily involved and still learning! While there are no surefire formulas or ironclad lesson plans guaranteed to involve every student, the following ideas have seen me through many a hot spring when student attention was beginning to wane.

Since many of the ideas focus on writing, I have often ended the year with a writing unit in which I require students to complete a set number of writings. They can choose which options they complete. Over the years, I have used these ideas in different ways and in different contexts. The important thing is to make sure the context—the reason students are doing this work—is clear to the students.

While many of these ideas have been presented in other sections of this book, they are presented here as well because they particularly appeal to students and, simply by the nature of the assignment, involve them. Certainly many of these ideas will not be new to English teachers, but I include them here because I know it is helpful to have related ideas in one place. Of course, most of the writing ideas work best if implemented the way you normally handle writing in your class—peer editing, sharing in groups, hanging up finished writings and illustrations in class, making a booklet of class writings.

1. Fractured Fairy Tales. On the chalkboard, have students suggest names of all the fairy tales they can remember. Then ask them to "fracture" or change something about the story. The stories could be told from the point of view of the bad guy, or they could be modernized, or students could introduce characters from other fairy tales. The possibilities are endless, and students enjoy changing an already known story. Participation and willingness to do this assignment are usually high because most students know fairy tales; they can see possibilities for change and don't feel overwhelmed by this task.

2. ABC Stories. Students may write a story on any topic, but each sentence must begin with a different letter of the alphabet, starting with A. The teacher may require only twenty-two or twenty-four sentences and let students leave out a few troublesome letters such as X or Z.

> *Example:*
>
> **A**nxiously I twisted my hands as I waited by the window.
>
> **B**efore I knew it the moment I had dreaded all day had arrived.
>
> **C**ertainly this wouldn't mean the end of my career.
>
> **D**id she really think that confronting me on my own home ground would cause me to waver in my decision?

3. Cut-Word Story. Have students find and cut out of magazines the following categories of words: five nouns, five verbs, five adjectives, five small words, five words over six letters, and five unusual words. Give each student an envelope in which to put his or her words. After all words are in their envelopes, give each student someone else's envelope. They are to write a story that includes all the words in their envelopes. Have them write the story on large paper (11" x 17") and paste down the words they use from the envelope as they fit into the story. The end product is partially written and partially made up of cut-out words from magazines.

4. Letters to Next Year's Students. Ask each student to think back over the year and then write a letter for the students who will take your class next year. Their letters can contain advice and their philosophies on how next year's students can do well in this course or in school in general. Have students copy these letters in ink or marker so that you can hang them up as your first bulletin board in the fall. These students will probably rush back to your room in the fall to make sure you put their letters on the board.

5. Bummer Behavior. At this time of year, everyone is getting on everyone else's nerves. So that others are aware of annoying behavior, discuss and list on the board all the aspects of students' behavior that are annoying to members of your class. They may mention things such as paper-wad throwing, rubber-band snapping, comb stealing, punching, name calling, pencil snatching, hat grabbing, lunch room craziness, running and bumping into others in the hall. Try to get everyone to focus on one behavior that drives them crazy, and then ask them to write a letter to someone (Ann Landers, friend, principal, person who exhibits that behavior) explaining why that "bummer behavior" is irritating and how it makes them feel when they see this behavior. Put letters (if appropriate) on the bulletin board so others can see the type of behavior that some find irritating.

6. Use of Children's Books as a Writing Stimulus. Students can create stories about the unusual pictures in Chris Van Allsburg's *The Mysteries of Harris Burdick* or create their own writing assignments after hearing a book rich with writing ideas such as *The Whale's Song* by Dyan Sheldon. Give each small group a different children's book to read. When they have read a book they like, they then generate writing ideas from it. One student from each group reads the book to the whole class and shares the group's writing ideas. When one book from each small group has been read, students pick the one writing idea they like the best and write about it. These drafts are shared the next day, and students compare how they chose to respond to a particular book.

7. Pamphlets. Students can create pamphlets letting others know about themselves or about issues they are interested in. If students can still be motivated to do any research at this point in the year, have them select a topic they are concerned about or interested in, research the topic, and present the information in a pamphlet. Possible topics include vacation spots; a state or place I would most like to spend the summer; saving the rain forests; reasons not to smoke; why be a vegetarian? Have students fold plain paper in thirds to create the pamphlet. Post the finished products on a bulletin board so others may read them.

8. Name Stories. Ask students to make up a title of a short story or a newspaper headline out of the letters of their first or last names. Example: DIANA—Doctors Isolate Atrocious Neuron Antibodies or Dinosaurs Intimidate Absolutely Nice Animals or Dingbats Invade Antique National Auction. Then have students write a short story or newspaper article about the title they created that they like the best. Stress that vivid nouns in the title make the story easier to write.

9. The Childhood or Adulthood of Comic Characters. Save a few weeks' worth of the Sunday comics to pass out to students or have students bring in a favorite comic strip. Their assignment is to write the background or life story of the comic character they choose, explaining how that character came to be the way he or she is. Or in the case of Marvin, Peanuts, and Calvin and Hobbes, students can write the story of what these characters will be like when they grow up. What kind of jobs will they have, who will their friends be, will they ever be happy? Encourage students to cut out a picture of their comic character and glue it to their final drafts. Students enjoy sharing these stories with the class.

10. Lists. Have students create lists on topics of their own choosing. My students have written lists on such topics as:

> how to be a beach bum
>
> reasons not to get up until noon
>
> what to do when you get bored in the summer
>
> ways to get your parents to let you stay home from school
>
> how to get out of cleaning your bedroom
>
> how to be a teacher's pet
>
> how to tell if a teacher is mean
>
> how to talk a teacher into having a party
>
> how to bother your parents
>
> subtle ways to get back at your parents
>
> things they like/dislike about siblings
>
> things they tell their siblings to do
>
> dumb words or sayings
>
> famous but annoying people
>
> how to tell if someone of the opposite sex likes you
>
> where to put stuff in your room
>
> where to stick gum in the classroom
>
> things to do in class if you are bored
>
> out of the ordinary things you'd like to do in school
>
> why people don't like cats

Once these lists are compiled, put them in a classroom book called "The Big Book of Lists." Students love to read them!

11. Letter Exchange. For middle school students who have fears and doubts about going to high school, set up a letter exchange with a ninth-grade class in the high school. The middle schoolers write to the ninth graders asking them questions, and the ninth graders write back, answering their questions.

12. Yearbook Snapshots. Ask your students to imagine they are now seniors in high school and that they each get a full page in the yearbook. Ask them to capture the important aspects of themselves on this page.

Challenge them to think about the things they would like to accomplish in high school and what they would like to be remembered for.

Have them include as much of the following information as possible:

a. nickname

b. activities, clubs, sports, and what year they will be involved in each

c. class mock award such as "class clown" that they would most like to get

d. quotation that shows something about them or what is important to them

e. a poem that is meaningful to them

f. favorites—colors, foods, music

g. a book that had a significant impact on them

h. if they could be voted "most likely to_____," what word or phrase would they place in the blank and why would they like to be known for this?

i. plans after high school

Encourage students to mount pictures of themselves or cut out magazine pictures which they would like to represent them on their page and then arrange the information on the page in an eye-appealing manner. If all students produce their yearbook page on paper with holes in it, all the finished pages can be put in a binder, and each class can have its own "yearbook."

13. Awards. Have students in groups brainstorm possible awards that could be presented to classmates for the work they have done this year. Possible awards include "author of scariest story," "best editor," "author of funniest story," "most improved writer," "author of best play," "author of best tall tale," "creator of best fable," "best illustrator," "most helpful group member," "creator of most original idea for a story," "author of funniest poem," "author of most beautiful poem," "author of saddest poem." Students make up a list of categories, put them on the board, copy down the categories, and nominate one person for each category. When a winner is decided on, each student must write up one paragraph explaining why this person got this award.

14. Silhouette Collages. Using an overhead projector as the light source, sit students one at a time near the light so the outline casts a shadow on the wall. Tape a piece of 11" x 17" paper where the shadow is cast. Quickly trace around the shadow, and then have the student cut out his or her own silhouette. Have students cut out of magazines pictures and words that represent them and then paste them over the silhouette. The whole silhouette should be covered. After they artfully arrange and glue on their words and pictures, have students write a paper explaining why they selected each word and picture and what it says about them. Tape the silhouettes around the room. If possible, leave them up so that next year's class can see them.

15. Tall Tales. Students tell these all the time without realizing it, especially when they fabricate reasons they didn't bring their homework in! To get them thinking about what a tall tale is, we talk about exaggeration and then about Paul Bunyan. I try to get them to make up an original story, but if they have trouble coming up with a story idea, I encourage them to write about the exaggerations they are familiar with—such as reasons they were late to class. When they finish their rough drafts, have them write their final drafts on two sheets of white paper taped together the long way, thus creating the visual effect of a "tall" story.

16. Stamp Out Dull Stamps. Talk about how stamps that commemorate great people or important events are issued. Have students develop a series of "teen" stamps in honor of people, places, issues, or events that are important to people their age. They might design a stamp for a specific recording artist, sports figure, author, or scientist. They might want to design a stamp to raise teen awareness of the destruction of the rain forests, the importance of recycling, the increase in child abuse, or the fear of the violence they live with. On a stamp form, which the teacher can create for the students, have students design the stamp and then write about why they believe there should be such a stamp.

17. End-of-Year Memory Book. With the cost of yearbooks so high today, many students simply cannot afford to buy one. This activity provides students a place for their classmates to write the kind of thing they would write in a yearbook, and it gives students a chance to record and reflect on the past school year. As I decide what this year's book will contain, I also gather ideas from the clip art on my computer that I can use to decorate each page of the memory book. My goal is to make the pages look so attractive that the students will want to do their best writing because they will want to keep these memory books. When I've got all the pages run off, I pass out the pages only a few at a time, mixing the fun pages with those that require more writing. Page topics include favorite music, memorable movies, activities the student was involved in, here's what I remember about [first hour, second hour, and so on], advice to next year's incoming class, friends [here are some of the things we did together this year], clothes [clothes I like to wear; clothes everybody wears; when I get dressed up I wear _____], how not to get caught doing [_____] at this school, excuses used to get out of class, excuses used when tardy, and the cafeteria [best and worst food, here's how I would describe a typical lunch hour in the cafeteria]. When all pages are complete, students make them into books, decorate them, and have their classmates write notes to them on the pages left for that purpose.

18. Obituary of an Object. Choose an inanimate object, and after thinking about how it met its demise, write an obituary that includes the following information: (a) name of deceased, (b) place of death, (c) cause of death, (d) time of death, (e) general chronology—place of birth, survivors, achievements, (f) funeral arrangements—place, time, officiating minister's name.

Here's an example from one of my high school students:

Poor Percy

Percy Pencil, age four, died yesterday at J. W. Sexton High School. An autopsy showed that Percy Pencil was busted in half by a student.

Percy was born at Wallace Conquest Pencil Co. on September 5. He was the son of Mr. and Mrs. Michael Marker and had just graduated from Ohio University. He had a major in cursive and was going for a Ph.D. in calligraphy. He lived in Columbus, Ohio, on 4073 N. Ink Street. Percy is survived by his brother Pat Pen.

Percy's burial will be in Mrs. Mitchell's room at J. W. Sexton on March 24 and will be presided over by Minister Charlie Chalk.

(Idea adapted from Carter and Rashkis 234)

19. Skeleton in the Closet, or the NOT WANTED Poster. Have students cut out pictures of people who look interesting or unusual from magazines or newspapers. Then have them imagine that this is a relative in their family who everyone tries to pretend doesn't exist. In other words, the family has disowned this person. Students are to create the story of what this relative did that so enraged or embarrassed the family. Staple a piece of paper labeled NOT WANTED with the picture pasted on it on top of the story. If you put these on the board, students will want to lift the picture and begin reading the story. (Thanks to Nancy J. Johnson for the seed of this idea.)

20. Wanted Posters. These can be used in a number of ways. If a story has just been completed, students can illustrate what one character would most want and then write about it. At this time of year, however, students may want to create a Wanted poster of what *they* would most want. It can be concrete, such as a vacation in Mexico, a car, or CDs, or it can be abstract, such as racial harmony, love, or peace on earth. Students draw or find a picture in a magazine to represent what is wanted and then write several paragraphs explaining why it is wanted.

21. Mouth Stories. Students love to write on forms. One form I use is a wide-open mouth which is filled with lines for students' stories. To get them thinking about the experiences and sensations a mouth has, we share our stories of going to the dentist, eating, chewing gum, smoking, having braces, and talking. Then I ask students to write in the first person about a famous person's mouth or about the experiences an ordinary mouth has. Many students give blow-by-blow descriptions of what it's like to get braces. Final drafts are put on the mouths, decorated with markers (some students even draw in their braces), and put on a board titled OPEN WIDE.

22. Sole Stories. Kids like this one too. Discuss with students and list on the board all the unpleasant things a foot can experience (disease, tight shoes, stepping on things, jumping). Then discuss the pleasant experiences a foot can have (walking in the sand, being in water, wearing comfortable shoes).

Next, ask your students to write in the first person as if they were the sole of a foot. They can imagine they are the sole of a famous person, describe their own foot experiences, or just focus on one experience a foot has—such as having planter's warts removed. After their rough drafts have been proofread, have them trace the outline of their foot or shoe on construction paper and write their final draft on that foot. Make sure you have half the class do a right foot and half the left so that you can hang up the finished soles in a footstep pattern around the room.

23. Dialogue Writing. A great way to teach kids the proper way to write dialogue (for instance, begin a new paragraph every time the speaker changes) is to pair them off and have them write dialogue back and forth. I let students choose their partner, and they have to engage in written discussion for twenty minutes, with no talking allowed. Kids absolutely love the chance to write these "legal" notes, and they quickly learn to write dialogue.

24. ABC Scheme. ABC schemes are a great way for students to show off what they know about a topic. In small groups, have students brainstorm lists of what they know a lot about or what they are interested in. Once they have selected a topic, they're ready to begin. They then write twenty-six sentences about their topic by using the order of the alphabet. In the first sentence, they explain something about their topic that begins with A. The second sentence tells something about the topic that begins with B, and so on. Using this scheme makes students think about what they know and often sends them to the dictionary in search of an adjective to describe some aspect of their topic. I also instruct students to make each sentence at least eight words long to avoid the "A is for apple, B is for berries" kind of approach. I have had students do the *Alphabet of Violence,* which included such sentences as: T is for the "Torrents of Tears the survivors shed"; A is for the "Appalling statistics that indicate the number of teen deaths due to violence each year"; G is for both the "Guns and the Gangs which have made our cities into killing Grounds." Students have chosen more lighthearted topics such as baby-sitting, dealing with siblings, and going to school, but they have also worked on such weighty topics as racism and sadness.

25. Last Day Letters. Here's a solution to that last day in English class when almost nothing appeals to or seems meaningful to students. Instruct students to write a letter to themselves. Tell them you will find out their next year's homeroom and make sure they get the letter. The letter should be a personal assessment of the entire past school year. Suggest that students include how they felt about the grades they achieved and why they got the grades they did. Have them deal with successes as well as failures in the areas of friendships, extracurricular activities, and scholastics. Are there things they regret about the past year? What changes would they like to make? The last part of the letter can deal with promises or resolutions they make to themselves for the coming school year. Have them address the envelope themselves. In the fall, you'll hear lots of positive feedback about this assignment.

Works Cited

Carter, Candy, and Zora Rashkis, eds. *Ideas for Teaching English in the Junior High and Middle School.* Urbana, IL: NCTE, 1980.

Crane, Stephen. "The Open Boat." *Adventures in American Literature.* Ed. Francis Hodgins. San Diego: Harcourt, 1985. 386–402.

———. *The Red Badge of Courage.* New York: Tor, 1997.

———. "War Is Kind." *Adventures in American Literature.* Ed. Francis Hodgins. San Diego: Harcourt, 1985. 403.

Donaldson, Margaret. *Children's Minds.* New York: Norton, 1979.

Emig, Janet. "Non-Magical Thinking: Presenting Writing Developmentally in Schools." *Writing: The Nature, Development, and Teaching of Written Communication.* Eds. Carl Frederiksen and Joseph Dominic. Hillsdale, NJ: Erlbaum, 1981.

Gallo, Donald R., ed. *Connections: Short Stories by Outstanding Writers for Young Adults.* New York: Dell, 1989.

———, ed. *Visions: Nineteen Short Stories by Outstanding Writers for Young Adults.* New York: Delacorte, 1987.

Girion, Barbara. *In the Middle of a Rainbow.* New York: Scribner, 1983.

Guy, Rosa. "She." *Sixteen: Short Stories by Outstanding Writers for Young Adults.* Ed. Donald R. Gallo. New York: Dell, 1984.

Hawthorne, Nathaniel. *The Scarlet Letter.* New York: Bantam, 1981.

Ideas Plus: A Collection of Practical Teaching Ideas. Book Three. Urbana, IL: NCTE, 1985.

Irving, Washington. "The Devil and Tom Walker." *Adventures in American Literature.* Ed. Francis Hodgins. San Diego: Harcourt, 1985. 106–14.

Lowry, Lois. *The Giver.* Boston: Houghton, 1993.

Shaughnessy, Mina. "Diving in: An Introduction to Basic Writing." *College Composition and Communication* 27 (1976): 234–39.

———. *Errors and Expectations: A Guide for the Teacher of Basic Writing.* New York: Oxford UP, 1977.

Sheldon, Dyan. *The Whale's Song.* New York: Dial, 1991.

Sommers, Nancy. "Revision Strategies of Student Writers and Experienced Adult Writers." *College Composition and Communication* 31 (1980): 378–88. Rpt. in *Cross-Talk in Comp Theory: A Reader.* Ed. Victor Villanueva, Jr. Urbana, IL: NCTE, 1997. 43–54.

Spinelli, Jerry. *Maniac Magee.* Boston: Little, 1990.

Steinbeck, John. *Of Mice and Men.* New York: Penguin, 1993.

Twain, Mark. *The Adventures of Huckleberry Finn.* New York: Penguin, 1986.

Van Allsburg, Chris. *The Mysteries of Harris Burdick.* London: Andersen, 1985.

6 Thematic Units

Diana Mitchell

The appeal of the unit is undeniable, as it can help students see real connections between disparate works of literature and can invite students to pursue research on unusual topics. In this chapter, Diana demonstrates how a teacher can take an idea or concept and create an inventive, wide-ranging unit of study and reading. American literature, ghostly themes, heroes, and even family stories are all presented as legitimate topics for thematic study. Diana gives suggestions for student projects oriented around a theme, and also explores the thematic focus of race and gender.

CREATING THEMATIC UNITS

Over the years, I have learned that units do not have to be big and cumbersome; they can be short and compact and created with relative ease.

Recognizing the Need for Thematic Units

The first time I taught ninth-grade English the anthology used was organized around elements of literature such as plot, theme, and characterization. At first I was rather dumbfounded. What was I supposed to do with stories organized this way? Was I supposed to point out that "yes, indeed, this story has a plot" and "oh, this one does have a theme"? What was the point?

After surviving a few years reading one story after another with no sense of connection among any of them, I knew I had to go in a different direction. So to do something more with the stories and to find ways they could relate to my students, I slowly moved into the organization I call thematic units. Because I see a thematic unit as an umbrella under which concepts and materials are gathered, I liked the idea of using this loose organization to discuss important issues, to bring together different kinds of materials, and to have my students work toward making connections among the works as they made connections to their own lives.

Getting Started

I started out slowly by building a short thematic unit called "The Way We Were" around the short story "Charles" by Shirley Jackson. I wanted my brand-new ninth graders to have an opportunity to dig back into their memories of childhood as they looked at the way childhood was portrayed in literature. First, we read the story, wrote about our own kindergarten memories, and talked about what little kids are afraid of, how they got away with things as "Charles" did in the story, and how a story changes when told from a different point of view. My students looked at themselves as children and also looked at how childhood was portrayed. The writing connections popped up everywhere. My students wanted to write letters to the main character's parents to tell them to be firmer and not believe everything that Laurie told them, they wanted to write to the parents from the teacher's point of view, and they wanted to do interior monologues from Laurie's point of view as he was making up the "stories" he told his parents.

We brought in children's stories such as "Little Red Riding Hood," "Goldilocks," and "Hansel and Gretel" to see what behavior and actions were attributed to children. We talked about why kids act out at school and even looked for stories in the newspaper about kids. Students wanted to talk about their favorite TV programs when they were small, toys they cherished, the way they dressed, and the games they played. We compared the rather pampered way the kindergartner was treated by his parents in "Charles" to the way we saw children characterized in other texts. We talked about lessons young children learned from the stories they read, the movies they saw, and the way their parents treated them. We ended the unit with projects that included scripts of scenes that students would add to the story, pamphlets advising parents how best to deal with kindergartners, presentations on what fairy tales were teaching children, and videos of children playing games with voiceovers about what lessons and values each game was teaching children.

Organizing a Unit

After feeling successful at "exploding" the story in our text to a unit that captured my students' attention, I decided to proceed in a more organized fashion by asking myself what steps I had gone through to put together this unit. The following steps surfaced:

1. Start with a "big question" or idea. What do you want students to find out, or answer, or explore?
2. Articulate why this unit is important and what it has to do with your students. If you don't know why a unit can be important and how it can be connected to student lives and interests, then students certainly won't see the point of what you're asking them to do.

3. Brainstorm. Write down any ideas that come to you, any writing connections, questions, material, and issues that can be built on. If you find through brainstorming that your overriding question has lots of pieces and parts, then it will probably be rich enough to engage the class. If you run into blocks and dead ends, then rethink your idea for a unit.

4. Select a centerpiece. What will you build the unit around? A video, a short story, an audiotape, a piece of nonfiction, a novel, a play, a specific TV show? Use the centerpiece as a focus and as a way to kick off the unit and get the students involved.

5. Make a list of possible activities that will involve students. If you see ways to incorporate interviews, small-group work, projects, and writing assignments, then you'll know this unit is full of possibilities and will likely involve students.

6. Make a mental inventory of what other materials can be used. Will children's picture books work? How about fables or fairy tales? Can you think of a movie or video that would work with the theme and contribute to the unit? How can poetry be worked in? What about nonfiction? Music? Art?

7. Write down the language arts skills that will be emphasized through work on this unit. Will you focus on having students understand memoirs and learn to write descriptively in that genre? Will you ask students to understand the elements in a fable and be able to write one? Will you work with students on improving their ability to use dialogue in their stories?

8. Figure out what kind of modeling or instruction you need to include so that all the students have the skills necessary to do what you would like them to do. Do you need to draft a script on the overhead together so that students know the necessary conventions? Do you need to construct an activity that includes acting out a scene to help students enter the world of the story?

9. Consider the classroom organization and the structure. How much of this unit is teacher directed, and how much is student centered? Can you see lots of opportunities for students to work in small groups on issues that will concern them? How will you organize class time? What will you expect your students to do each day?

10. Construct introductory activities and possible end-projects and assignments. Have a long-range plan which can be adapted or changed after you see the direction students want to take with the "big question."

11. Reflect on whether the unit is in line with best practice in the field and whether it is consistent with your philosophy on the teaching of language arts. For instance, does the plan for

a unit integrate reading, viewing, writing, speaking, and listening? Are students expected to make meaning and relate this material to themselves, or does the teacher control all the outcomes? Are students being given a chance to raise real issues and answer questions for which the teacher does not have the predetermined answers?

12. Decide how you will access or evaluate student work for this unit. Will you develop a rubric for both oral and written projects? Will you have students write and reflect on what they have learned? Will you construct essaylike questions on skills you want to emphasize? Will you ask students to evaluate group work using such sentence starters as "My major contribution to the group was" and "In our group, here's what we accomplished on our task"? How much will you access through observation?

Developing a Unit around Classroom Concerns

I develop short units and long units, units based on materials in our anthologies, and units based on videos and interviews. I develop units around an author, a kind of writing, a novel, a research project, a single short story, a poem, an audiotape, a genre (such as fairy tales), or even around a concern in my class. For example, when I saw too many of my urban ninth graders get in fights or verbal shouting matches over perceived signs of "disrespect," I decided to confront the problem head-on by developing a short unit on respect. Our question was, "What does respect really mean, and how do people handle it when they don't get the respect they think they should?" I hoped that through this short unit students would at least begin to think about their actions and what they meant. I also hoped students would develop other ways to handle people who they felt disrespected them.

After brainstorming, I could see that this topic was chock-full of issues. Why do some kids consider respect so much more important than other kids do? How do we get true respect? Does our drive for respect cause us to do things we don't want to do? Is this true respect? Who do we respect? What did that person do to gain our respect? What's going on beneath these incidents of "calling someone out of their name"? Are there other ways to handle incidents of perceived disrespect? What can we learn from others about settling disagreements?

Planning the Unit

I could also see that I had plenty of material, so I selected a chapter from Nathan McCall's *Makes Me Want to Holler* called "Respect" as the centerpiece. As a kid growing up, the author felt the way so many of my students felt, that all they had was their name and that they became less if others disrespected them. McCall's chapter is tough and tells it like it is. Since the chapter stops without much reflection on the author's part, I skipped ahead in the book to find passages I could read that would show how he had reconsidered his position on respect as he got older. I also brought in Aretha Franklin's recording "R-E-S-P-E-C-T" to look at how she viewed respect, and two short stories, "On the Bridge" by Todd Strasser in *Visions* and "Fourth of July" by Robin G. Brancato in *Sixteen*, both collections edited by Donald Gallo.

Activities that occurred to me were interviewing older people and peers, writing skits or talk show dramas, writing a narrative on the topic, finding poems on the issue, writing an expository piece on getting respect, writing an editorial on why this issue is so important to teens and how adults can help, alternatives to verbal and physical battles, small-group discussions on getting respect, having the assistant principal for discipline share her insights on kids who fight for respect, having a member of Peer Assisted Listening (PAL) talk about and demonstrate this program's approaches to mediation, and writing up class activities into a newspaper on the topic.

In addition to the materials already mentioned, I also thought I could work into the unit discussions of TV shows to see what models TV offered for getting respect. I would also invite students to go on a children's picture book hunt for books that give younger children advice on the topic of settling disputes. I knew I could count on my students to give me titles of movie or video possibilities and to suggest songs that dealt with disrespect.

When I considered the language arts skills that students would use in this unit, many jumped to mind. Our explorations of literature would allow us to do such things as compare the structures of the genres used looking for similarities and differences; compare our views of respect with the authors'; and evaluate the short stories in terms of how realistic the characterization was and how believable the actions were.

Students would be writing in many formats and genres and focusing on such things as the use of dialogue, the selection of details to make an impact on the reader, the use of persuasion, and how each piece was organized. Thinking, writing, speaking, and listening skills would be combined through creating interview questions and interviewing an older person, sharing responses, and drawing conclusions about what the younger generation can glean from the older generation about respect. Speaking and problem solving would be emphasized when we role-played after hearing the PAL demonstrations on conflict mediation.

Skills Students Would Need

When I looked at what I was expecting of my students, I decided that work would have to be done on using dialogue and on exploring what vivid details look like in writing, why word pictures are important to readers, how to construct interview questions, how to conduct an interview, how to effectively write an expository piece, and what goes into writing an editorial. This modeling or instructional part of the unit could be accomplished using the overhead projector and having students contribute their ideas. For instance, we could construct dialogues on the overhead, paying attention not only to the format but also to what makes a dialogue interesting. When we looked for vivid details, I could put up several sentences from past student writing and have students identify which sentences create pictures in their minds. We would learn to construct interview questions by first generating questions that would give the interviewer little information and then learning to construct more open-ended questions.

I decided that we would read aloud the short stories and the chapter from Nathan McCall's book. Small groups could focus on specific tasks from topics in the stories, using them to create a survey to give to fellow students and to generate questions for interviews on the topic of respect. I wanted to leave lots of room for whole-class discussions.

Activities for the Unit

To begin the unit, I thought I would start in a very simple way by having students write on a large note card their definition of *respect*, how to get respect, how you know you aren't being respected, and possible ways to handle a show of disrespect. Students would not put their names on the cards so that I could collect them, shuffle them, hand out the cards to small groups, and have them read the cards they received and then write up a list of what they learned from the cards. This introductory activity would give us lots of information and raise interest in the topic. When I considered end projects, I looked at some of the activities I'd brainstormed and decided to create end products around them. I wanted to give students the opportunity to construct a pamphlet on what the older generation has to say about respect and another pamphlet on what their peers have to say about it. Others could put together a newspaper by writing articles focused on what we discovered about the topic, as well as stories on guest speakers. I also envisioned a talk show presentation in which students role-played specific points of view on the topic. I knew other projects would emerge as we became involved in the unit.

Best Practice and the Unit

In reflecting on what elements of best practice were embedded in the unit, I could immediately see that the language arts were integrated, that students would be actively constructing meaning through their work, that the skills were being taught in the larger context of the unit, and that students were engaged in authentic, real-life learning.

As I thought about assessment, I knew I would do much of it as we worked our way through the unit. I would ask students to explain and compare Nathan McCall's definition of *respect* to the definitions the main characters in the short stories had and to their own. I would grade these on how well each definition was explained and whether examples were used. I would also look for evidence that students understood how to compare the different definitions. For group work, I would hand out a sheet of paper with a circle on it and tell students to divide up the circle or pie into pieces according to who contributed the most to the group that day. Students would have to explain their reasons for dividing the pie the way they did.

Creating Rubrics for Projects

Since all of the end products were to be presented in public ways (the pamphlet, the newspaper, the talk show), I decided to create a rubric that would include the presentation as well as the content. When I construct a rubric, I always make positive statements which can then be responded to according to the following assessment system:

1. not at all
2. a little
3. a lot
4. a great deal.

Thus a rubric for this kind of end project could include statements such as the following:

1. It was obvious from the way the [newspaper, pamphlet, talk show] was put together that a great deal of time was spent on this project.
2. The project was composed in such a way that readers or viewers gained new insights or information.
3. The project reflected the use of multiple resources to gather information (interviews, stories, poems, informational writing, Internet).
4. Careful attention was given to detail (correctness issues could

be included here for written projects, while thoroughness of coverage could be included for oral projects).

5. Creative or visual elements enhanced the effect on the viewer or reader.

6. Sufficient ideas and information were presented.

7. An excellent understanding of the issues embedded in the concept of respect was displayed.

For written projects, additional items like these could be included in the rubric:

1. A strong writing voice is evident.

2. Sentence structure is varied.

3. Holds the reader's interest and attention.

4. Paragraphing and transitional words make it easy for the reader to follow the piece.

5. Attention is paid to word selection, with powerful verbs and adjectives often used.

For talk shows and other oral projects, additional items such as the following could be included in the rubric:

1. Voice quality was excellent (volume, rate, variation, inflection).

2. Participated enthusiastically in the part played.

3. Stayed in character and never exhibited distracting behavior.

4. Spoke convincingly.

5. Used gestures and movements appropriately.

Creating a Thematic Unit in American Literature

Most of us have some kind of anthology we can or should use, and although many anthologies have a built-in organization, this should not prevent us from creating units with other organizational patterns using only some of the material from our anthology. Plodding through a textbook, moving from story to story, doesn't usually convince students that the work in the language arts class is in any way related to them. Once I knew what was in our American literature anthology, I felt free to develop units that would involve my students instead of focusing so much on the history and characteristics of different literary movements.

Thoreau and Modern Humankind

I am wild about Henry David Thoreau because I constantly learn from his writings. I wanted my kids in Thoreau's face. I wanted them to see why he valued individualism. I wanted them to look deeper into the world and recognize the part nature can play in our learning and in our nourishment. I recognize high school as a stressful time for students and want them to develop some perspective on what might be important in life. Thus I framed the unit around the question: "Does Thoreau have anything to teach modern humankind?"

As we got close to beginning the unit, I asked my students to pick a night when the stars were out and spend five to ten minutes under the stars by themselves, trying to clear their minds. When they came indoors, they were to write about what they had experienced by focusing on the stars. It was fairly easy to tell who had really contemplated the stars and who hadn't. The students who did the solitary viewing seemed to be much more philosophical. This assignment led us to a discussion of what, if anything, we can learn from nature. Then students were ready to meet Henry David himself. I started with Jerome Laurence and Robert Lee's play *The Night Thoreau Spent in Jail,* which we read aloud together in class. Through this play, students saw Thoreau in action, saw what a rebel he was and how he questioned everything in his search for the "essentials" of life.

We also read selections from Thoreau's journals. I felt free to shorten any of the pieces of text I used and to bring in material that was not in the text. I asked my students to find ten sentences or concepts in the selections from *Walden* that they either strongly agreed with or vehemently disagreed with and to explain why in their response journals. I typed up a list of lines from parts of Thoreau's work that weren't assigned and asked students to explain what the quotations meant and whether they agreed with them. Then I asked students to rank the fifteen quotations from most important to them personally to least important personally. In small-group discussions, students shared their views, trying to persuade others to agree with their rankings.

Using Other Texts

An article in the newspaper told of a superintendent who fired a teacher because he refused to conform to the faculty dress code. My students believed the action was ludicrous and so wrote letters to the superintendent from Thoreau's point of view. We posted the letters on the bulletin board, and it was obvious that my students were beginning to understand Thoreau's values and beliefs. Another text I brought into class was Gary Paulsen's *Woodsong,* the story of Paulsen's relationships with his sled dogs and his eventual running of the Iditarod in Alaska. My students gobbled up this book. They loved it and enjoyed thinking about what Paulsen learned from his dogs and from nature. I asked them to respond to the book by writing about what they thought Paulsen learned from nature, what Thoreau and Paulsen had in common, and what parts of the book had the biggest impact on them. Later I asked the students to write a reflective paper about whether they could be a Thoreau in their own time, and in what ways they could connect Thoreau's values or beliefs to their own.

Thoreau Today

The last project we did in our Thoreau unit evolved from an idea I got from Tom Romano's *Clearing the Way: Working with Teenage Writers*. I had my students write short stories or plays about Thoreau appearing in our time with his values intact. They were to include what Thoreau would bring with him from his time period and how he would react to the world today. Some students set their plays in the school and had Thoreau enroll as a student. They shared his comments as he went from class to class and how he reacted to the school culture. One creative student even had Thoreau fall into Walden Pond and enter this time period through a locker at our school!

This assignment captured the imagination of my students, and because they poured so much energy into the project, we ended up with many memorable scripts and stories. On the day the writing was due, students met in small groups in class to share their work with each other. Then each group begged to have at least one or two pieces read to the whole class. We spent the entire next day enacting scripts and reading short stories. To make students aware of how much they had learned about Thoreau and about writing, I had each small group write up a short report on two or three stories or scripts, detailing all the ways the writers showed their understanding of Thoreau. I also asked them to comment on the aspects of the writing that were especially strong. This unit ended on a high note because students had so much ownership in their plays and scripts and enjoyed the chance to use in creative ways the knowledge they had gained.

GHOSTLY THEMES IN THE ENGLISH CLASSROOM

Ghosts in our culture represent fear, terror, mystery, and unresolved questions about the supernatural. When students hear ghost stories or tales of unexplainable happenings, they sit up straighter in their seats, strain to hear every word, and glue their eyes on the teller of the tales.

Thinking about ghosts and fear taps into students' imagination and gives them much to wonder about. Since scary themes seem to entrance students, what better way to involve them in literature, writing, and language studies than through the use of the scary, the mysterious, and the unexplainable?

I began thinking of all the ways we could capitalize on students' interest in the scary and eventually developed a short unit in which all the class work focuses on scary phenomena. Then I looked at other ways to integrate these intriguing ideas into our regular course work so students would look deeper at the literature they read, be motivated to write fascinating pieces, and want to think about how language creates scary effects.

The Unit

I decided to organize the unit around the big questions of "What is scary, and why does what frightens us fascinate us?" and "How do writers and storytellers scare us?" One way to kick off the unit and arouse student interest is to ask them to share stories they have heard about unexplained incidents or the appearance of ghosts. Usually students will share stories of close relatives who had a recently deceased family member appear to them a few days after the death, or they know of instances of objects moving in a room, or doors opening and closing mysteriously, or sites at which strange things happen. When the story sharing is finished, have students jot down in their journal or notebook a few words about the stories they found the most intriguing or the scariest. This may provide them with topics or ideas for their own stories later.

Beginning the Unit

After capturing the students' interest, one way to proceed is to bring in a collection of scary short stories such as *Short Circuits: Thirteen Shocking Stories by Outstanding Writers for Young Adults,* edited by Don Gallo, or a *Haunt of Ghosts,* edited by Aidan Chambers. You'll find many other collections in bookstores or on the shelves of school libraries.

Choose several stories to read aloud to your class. Ask students to rank the stories by how scary they are: a four-star rating would mean extremely scary, while a one-star rating would indicate that it didn't scare the reader much. As the students rank the stories, have them list the things they considered scary about the story. After the readings and ranking are complete, students work in groups to generate a list of all the elements they found scary in the stories. As groups share their findings with the whole class, the teacher can write the list down on butcher paper so it can be posted in the room.

Looking at a Novel

Next, explain to students that they will each examine one scary novel, reading to find the scary scenes. Students can choose from such authors as R.L. Stine, Christopher Pike, Caroline Cooney, Jay Bennett, Stephen King, and Diane Hoh. Students will probably be aware of other writers as well. Once they select a book, they can either skim it or read the book until they locate a scary scene. After selecting a scary scene, students are asked to analyze it in terms of structure and language so they can get an inside look at the craft of writing scary stories. What are the sentence constructions like? Are clauses used? What about sentence length? What verb tenses are used? Are they active or passive? Is repetition used? What effect does all this have? What about the scene makes it scary? Are the characters in control? What does the author do to make them appear helpless? Does he or she talk about what is done *to* the character?

Students are usually more willing to look at highly interesting writing in terms of the craft of writing than they are to look at such things out of context. This activity will be difficult for students if they are doing it for the first time. Be patient and give them all the help you can. Keep emphasizing that they are trying to break the code of scary or horror writing so that they can learn to do it effectively themselves. If you find that students struggle too much, try duplicating one scary scene or chapter and have the whole class work on it together, recording their responses on the overhead so that each student can see what "tricks" or structures an author uses to create the effect he or she wants. This list can be recorded on butcher paper and titled "The Craft of Scary Writing—Tips and Techniques."

Sharing and Writing about Fears

Now that students have talked about scary incidents, heard scary stories, and analyzed how writers make stories scary, they should be ready to think about their own history of being scared. Asking student to share all the things they remember being afraid of when they were younger will elicit a gush of responses. They love to share memories like this, partly because they see it as evidence that they have grown beyond these fears. As students share their fears, create another list on butcher paper of all their suggestions. These will usually include such things as being afraid of the dark, monsters, large animals, big people, getting in trouble, and so on.

Then ask students to create a time line that illustrates all the things they were afraid of, including what they fear today (disapproval, low grades, roller coasters, etc.). Students first draw a line indicating the span of their lives and then break up the line according to the years of their lives. For year one, they will probably have to ask their parents or siblings what they remember the student being afraid of. Time lines for that first year might include fear of strangers, fear of getting shots at the doctor's office, and fear of stuffed animals. The next few years will also probably require input from the family to complete. Students might find out they were afraid to sit on the grass, to leave their mother, to go on kiddie swings. Once they get to the fourth or fifth year of the time line, they will probably remember what terrified them. If they can do so, they can create a picture to represent each fear so that others can see at a glance what form fear took for them.

After sharing time lines and fears, students are then asked to select one of the items on the time line and write a personal narrative about it, working to include as many techniques (using the list the class created) as they can to produce scary writing. When these pieces have been workshopped, revised, and edited, they can be collected in a class book of scary stories or in a notebook to be placed in the library for other students to see.

A writing activity that students can work on collaboratively is to create the scariest story they possibly can. Have them begin by brainstorming a list of scary places (cemetery, inside a store closed for the night, an unlit basement, etc.), scary characters, scary actions, unusual weapons (golf club, knitting needle, meat cleaver), and an unexplained detail (bloodstain, deep scratches on the wall). After lists have been generated, students create scary stories using at least one entry for each category in their story. When groups have completed their stories, create a scary atmosphere in which they can read the stories to the class.

Following these activities, students will probably be in the mood to explore the ideas surrounding fears and scary things. Give students a chance to brainstorm topics they would like to know more about, or provide them with a list of possible projects like the one that follows. Explain to them that they will participate in a Fright Fair, in which projects will be shared with other English classes that meet the same hour. Encourage them to focus on projects that will interest others.

Fright Fair Projects

1. Create a how-to booklet or poster. Topics could include how to build a haunted house, scare your brother or sister, create scary special effects, find information on real haunted houses, or plan a trip around strange or unusual places.

2. Investigate the place of ghosts and spirits in other cultures. How do Native American cultures view spirits and the spirit world? What about Asian cultures, Central American cultures, Irish culture with its leprechauns? Different students could research different cultures and present their findings in a booklet or poster display.

3. Create a scary newspaper which could be distributed to students. A group of students could split up the work, with some writing scary news stories, some interviewing ghosts or people who have witnessed an unexplainable happening, some writing editorials, some creating ads or cartoons, etc. If they have access to a computer, students could produce it through desktop publishing and have copies made so others can be frightened or amazed by their work.

4. Create a booklet titled "Everything You Wanted to Know about Ghosts [or ESP or Telepathy] but Were Afraid to Ask."

5. Research why people like to be scared. Students could do such things as create surveys about what movies other teens watch, whether or not they watch horror movies, and if they do, why they like them. They could look for figures on how well scary movies do at the box office and then perhaps find people who go to scary movies or read scary books frequently and interview them. The star of *The X-Files*, David Duchovny, believes that his TV show (about alien presence on our planet) is popular because when people are scared they forget their troubles. This group's findings could be presented in the form of a TV news broadcast, with visuals such as charts showing movie attendance, figures of how many books Stephen King has sold, and so forth, as well as interviews with people who enjoy being scared.

6. Write and present several scary poems.

7. If you are artistic, create a drawing or a collage that represents people's fears or what they are scared of and present it to the class. If you can draw cartoons, create a frightening cartoon strip.

8. If you are a dancer, create a dance that exemplifies fright or fear.

9. Make a scary video.

10. Search for frightening books in the library. You might want to write annotations on books that deal with tragedies or disasters or scientific issues that are frightening (such as levels of pollution or contaminants in food).

Assessing Fright Fair

Of course, when students complete projects and perform them or share them in some way, we have to assess them. But don't let this daunt you.

As students begin working on their projects, have them help you create a rubric by which the performance or presentation will be evaluated. They might want the information or presentation to be judged based on whether or not the information or presentation had startling or frightening aspects, since everyone is attempting to create or present that effect. Other aspects of the rubric could include whether or not sufficient information and ideas were presented. Following is a list of items that could be included in such a rubric:

1. The presentation had startling or frightening aspects.
2. Sufficient ideas and information were presented.
3. It was obvious from the way the project was put together that a great deal of time was spent on it.
4. Careful attention was paid to detail.
5. Creative elements enhanced the effect on the viewer.
6. The presentation kept viewers' interest.

In addition to implementing a presentation rubric, you can ask students to write papers titled "My Journey to the Fright Fair," in which they discuss the topics they considered, how they went about getting information or creating projects, dead ends they ran into, what worked and what didn't, information or ideas they didn't use and why, and what they learned. Other assessment pieces can be based on teacher observation, group-work responses, and/or spectator evaluation of presentations.

All of these projects could be presented to other classes during a two-day Fright Fair. Written and artistic projects could be summarized and displayed, whereas the rest of the projects could be performed or presented. Students who greatly fear getting up in front of others could be given the option of being videotaped in private, with the tape being played during the Fright Fair.

Integration into Other Activities

Before plunging into activities centered on the scary, you may want to raise the issue of fears with your students and ask them to create a list of fears and then categorize them. They may put "fear of aliens" into a category called Fears of the Unknown, "fear of walking down a dark street alone and being attacked" into the category Physical Fears, "fear of embarrassment" into Social Fears, and "fear of disapproval" into Emotional Fears. After getting students talking about the idea of what people fear, begin to look at the stories you use in terms of fears.

1. Have students address questions such as the following: What does each main character fear the most? What can we learn about people and human nature by identifying characters' fears? For example, if students decide that the biggest fear of Snow White's stepmother was a loss of beauty, they can discuss the pressure on women to always look good and where and why they think this expectation developed.

2. If a ghost could be introduced into a story, what kind of ghost would it be, what would be the ghost's purpose, which character would the ghost appear to, what would the ghost want to tell that character?

3. Have students write tombstone inscriptions in response to literature. They can include name of character, date of birth, date of death, three adjectives that describe the person, three roles the character had in life (mother, teacher, daughter, etc.), cause of death, what the character would like to be remembered for, what the character would like to say from his or her grave. Students can fold an unlined sheet of paper in half, cut a little off the top edges to create the shape of a tombstone, open it, and write on it the inscription. These can be posted in the room under a heading such as "The Graveyard Gang."

4. Ask students to skim poetry books for poems that a character would find frightening or fearful. Share these with the class, explaining the reasons the character might react in a fearful way to them.

5. Share some of the work of Edgar Lee Masters's *Spoon River Anthology* with your students so they can observe how he writes epitaphs in which one character from the grave speaks to the living or to a specific person. Have students create epitaphs about characters they just read about.

6. Ask students to write about how a character would deal with death and/or talk about their own death. What would that character fear the most? What would he or she like to be remembered for?

Further Ideas

Other ways to capitalize on students' interest in this topic include:

1. Each student creates an entry for a classroom encyclopedia about ghosts and the supernatural. First students brainstorm all the concepts they can think of that would be part of such an encyclopedia; then each student selects a topic. Students research their topics and write them up in the format of an encyclopedia entry. This assignment gives the class an opportunity to examine the language and style of encyclopedia entries.

2. Students can write about experiences they've had that are unexplainable.

3. If students could be invisible—like a ghost—to what kinds of places would they want to go? What kinds of information would they want to get? Who would they want to know more about? Have students write on this topic. They might want to consider visiting a famous person for a day as a ghost to see how ordinary that person's life is.

4. How would you react if a ghost appeared? Write that story.

5. Create a ghost dictionary. Brainstorm words that would be in a ghost's dictionary and then follow the format for a dictionary entry but write the definitions from the point of view of a ghost. Example: **cemetery**—a place I go when I want to see my friends.

6. Using the time lines the class created, make a list of all the things people are commonly afraid of. Then have students create categories of kinds of fears, such as fears of the unknown, physical fears, social fears, etc. On the list, indicate which category each fear belongs to.

Students can then decide which fears are most likely to be experienced by people of different age groups. What do little children mostly fear? What are the main teen fears? What about adult fears and the fears of the elderly? Students could conduct surveys to be passed out to different age groups that will identify fears and possible reasons for them. Students could then be asked to write one of the following: short stories illustrating what it's like to have a particular fear at a particular age; skits illustrating child, teen, or adult fears; pamphlets on a specific fear for a specific age that include what that age group says about the issue, as well as the advice other groups would give about that fear; a talk show, in which fears from one age group are discussed from several points of view (this last activity could also be acted out).

7. Students' interest can be stirred by examining the craft of writing a scary poem if they are given copies of some of Jack Prelutsky's poems, especially from the collections *The Headless Horseman Rides Tonight* and *Nightmares*. Ask students to consider how the verbs; the nouns; the descriptive words; the long, drawn out consonants and vowels *(the baleful banshee);* or the word choice contributes to making the poem scary. What about the rhyming pattern? the alliteration? the repetition? Because these poems are so much fun

to read and so scary, students can usually be persuaded to consider how Prelutsky does it. As a follow-up activity, have students create scary poems of their own using Prelutsky's techniques.

Student interest in ghostly themes can be used to your advantage as a teacher and to their advantage as learners.

TAPPING INTO FAMILY STORIES AND THEMES TO HEIGHTEN END-OF-YEAR ENGAGEMENT

Strong material keeps our students involved. We need some kind of focus to pull them in, some compelling reason for them to read, write, speak, and reflect. Focusing on projects and activities that relate to the family seems to meet this need because all students come to our classrooms with family histories and stories. Thus we can capitalize on students' interest and on the accessibility of family stories and themes.

This section sketches out several projects and assignments that focus on the family and then suggests some contexts which can give them structure. It ends with suggestions for using the family as a lens to look back on the year's class work, especially for those advanced placement students who, after taking the test in May, feel the class is over.

Introductory Activities

To help students recognize the richness of exploring the idea of family and family stories, start with an activity that will encourage them to begin to think about the broad expectations we have for families and the many different concepts of family. One way to introduce the topic is to have students complete the following sentence starter ten times to get at how they view families: A family is_____ . These responses are shared in small groups, and then a sampling is read to the whole class. If time permits, one group can take on the task of selecting the most representative statements to post in the classroom.

Another way to encourage students to think about family is to have them examine the ways in which families are portrayed in literature and in the media. Students can peruse stacks of picture books and compile descriptions of how families are portrayed. Do the stories take place in single-parent homes? two-parent homes? How many siblings are shown? Are other relatives considered part of the family? Are friends depicted as part of the family? What seems to be expected of the families?

Since so many students are also TV viewers, ask them to collect descriptions of the composition of TV families and what is expected of different family members. What do the families seem to teach or reinforce? What is shown as being important to the family? Once students have begun thinking and talking about families, they can be asked to participate in several of the following activities.

Name Stories

Parents name their children for a wide variety of reasons. I remember my mother telling me that the final two contenders for my name were Diana and Victoria, names of characters she had enjoyed reading about in novels. After sharing my own name story and explaining where my parents found my name, I asked my students to interview their parents about why they were named as they were, what other names were under consideration, and who ended up picking out their name.

Since students worried that they wouldn't have enough information to write a whole story, I encouraged them to include in the story how they felt about their name and the way others responded to it. When they brought their one- to two-page stories to class, they shared them in small groups, and then each group picked one story they thought the whole class would enjoy. It was fascinating to hear about the different naming traditions of different racial and ethnic groups.

Many of the Latino students had been named after someone special, usually a relative who had a close relationship with the family. Many of the African American students found that their parents had created a name especially for them. The white students were often named simply because their parents liked the name. In some families, a close friend had been allowed to choose the student's name as a sign of the friend's importance to the family.

After sharing these stories, students realized that naming was part of their family history. They also discovered that the reasons other names had been passed over by their parents made an interesting part of their name story.

Celebrations and History

Another rich lode of stories can be mined from family celebrations. Students can tell stories based on a memorable birthday celebration, a family wedding, a baptism, how the Fourth of July is celebrated, or what Thanksgiving traditions their families observe. Also, since many students have never heard the story of how their parents or grandparents met, how the courtship proceeded, and how the wedding was planned, these are stories they may be interested in gathering and writing. Other students might want to find out the story of their mother's labor and their birth or do research on what different relatives remember about them as a baby. I stress that each of us may have a different definition of family. Some of us include friends and unrelated individuals. Others think of family in terms of biological family, stepfamily, adoptive family, or foster family.

Photograph Poems

Memories of family flood back when students see old photographs in family albums. These photographs are another wonderful source that can stimulate writing about the family. For this activity, ask students to bring in a photo that is important to them, such as a picture of themselves at play as a small child, a portrait of a relative, or a picture of a favorite vacation spot. In small groups, students explain their photograph, why it is important, and what kind of memories it elicits. Next, they brainstorm images, phrases, and lists based on the memories associated with the photograph. Then they begin to write.

Because these photos tap into such rich memories, student poems are usually amazingly powerful. Students often write about deceased grandparents, happy summer memories, dear friends, and elementary school events such as being in a play. When students write their final draft, they leave room on the paper to staple the photograph. If these are hung up in the classroom, students from other classes often drop in to look at the display because they are drawn to the photographs.

Points of View

One valuable but difficult thing for young people to understand is that any number of people can witness or participate in an event and yet have very different views on it. To get students to think carefully about point of view, have them compare the way they remember an incident in their family with the way other family members remember it. Students begin by brainstorming events or incidents that more than one family member was a witness to or participated in. Incidents range from learning to ride a bike, to having the best birthday party ever, to participating in a holiday event, to attending a family reunion, to buying a car, to witnessing some kind of accident. Students should make sure this event or incident is one they clearly remember. After taking the story through the normal steps for first drafts, have students revise and write a developed final draft. This draft will be shared with other family members.

Before the students read the story to family members, they ask family members to share their memories of the incident. If family members can be persuaded to do so, they write up the same incident from their own point of view. After the students summarize how the family remembers the incident and how these memories differ from their own, they attach this sheet to the final draft. This assignment not only results in vivid writing but also encourages the family to talk about their common history and often begins student-parent conversations about how other such incidents are remembered.

Conducting Intergenerational Interviews

For this project, students interview a relative of a different generation. Most students choose grandparents, although some interview parents or old family friends. The topics about which they interview these family members can be discussed and decided by each class. What are they most interested in knowing from a different generation? Do they want to know what the subjects were like as kids or what kinds of diseases and remedies they remember? Do they want to know how they celebrated holidays and birthdays or what school was like back then? Although classes can decide to do these interviews on almost any topic, one that always produces lots of material is the older generation's memories of school—how they felt about approaching summer vacations, what they wished they had done better, and what they remember about school in general.

After students in small groups brainstorm the kinds of questions they would like answered, all the questions are reported to the class, and the whole group then makes the selection. It is important to help students see that open-ended questions usually elicit the best information. To test out the effectiveness of the questions, bring another adult into the class (a teacher, librarian, security guard, assistant principal, custodian, etc.) and have the class ask this person the questions students decided on as they jot down the adult's answers. If a question gets little response, students might want to drop it from their list.

Sample Questions

1. Can you tell me what you remember about being in ninth grade (or whatever grade your students are in)?
2. What did students wear to school? What were the hairstyles like?
3. How would you describe attitudes toward teachers? Was there much misbehavior in classes? If so, how was it handled?

4. Do you remember any groups or cliques in your school? Describe the people in the different cliques and their attitudes.

5. Tell me about the extracurricular activities at your school. Which were the most popular? Did many students participate?

6. Was it important to your parents that you get good grades? If it was, what did they do to make sure you kept up your grades?

7. Did you think it was important to graduate from high school? What motivated you to stay in school or what caused you not to finish?

8. What kinds of jobs were available to students who graduated from high school? Did finishing high school seem important?

9. Tell me about the kinds of friends you had in ninth grade. Did any of them ever encourage you to get in trouble?

10. In your day, when kids got "in trouble" at school, what did that mean?

11. What do you remember about the kind of work you did in classes? What did you spend time doing? Do you remember anything about your English classes, such as what you read or what you did?

12. What kind of rules did your parents have for you on curfews, dating, and helping at home?

13. In what ways do you think kids today are different from the kids of your generation?

14. What advice would you give to teens today about getting through high school?

15. Do you remember any special events or activities at the end of the school year? How did kids celebrate the end of the school year?

16. How did you spend your summer vacations?

I also make sure that we discuss and role-play the techniques for conducting a good interview. I explain that showing interest and responding to what the person is saying is very important. I also remind students not to ask interviewees to write down answers to questions, because the information won't be nearly as rich and descriptive. Students are encouraged to tape-record the interview. Once the interviews are complete, students are eager to share them with their classmates. To accomplish this, I have students read their interview or play the tape to a small group of four or five. As each interview is played, students jot down what they learned, what surprised them, how teens' lives seemed the same and different in that generation, and so forth. As a group, students then list several categories or elements that the interviews have in common. Then they draw generalizations about how ninth grade seemed different in these earlier generations. Last, they work to summarize the advice these adults gave. Since students are excited about these tapes and interviews, I try to make time for at least one person from each group to read or play the tape of his or her interview to the whole class.

The following day, each group reports on the questions it answered and on what group members learned from the interviews. I then ask students to write reflective pieces on what they personally got from conducting their own interviews and what they learned from hearing the interviews of others. Next, I ask students to compose a letter to the older generation telling them about how today's generation is different and why some of the advice might be hard to follow or why they thought the advice was good. These letters are sent or given to those interviewed.

Family Member Collage

A collage, which is a collection of pictures, photographs, and words, is a concrete way to illustrate a wide variety of information about a person or a topic. The collage on a family member is meant to show at a glance what this family member is like and what he or she enjoys or responds to. Students first have to choose who the subject of the collage will be. They can choose either a family member they know well or one they would like to know better since this format offers the opportunity for dialogue with the subject. Brothers and sisters are most often selected, although students have collected information on parents, grandparents, and even great aunts and uncles. Students collect photos, magazine pictures, and poetry that the person would find meaningful. After interviewing the person, they write a list of the person's likes and dislikes, best and worst memories, favorite celebrations or holidays, goals and dreams, regrets, favorite books, movies, and TV shows. Excerpts from this material are written on the collage. When the collage is complete, the 11" x 17" sheet of paper should be covered with written and graphic information about the relative.

The collage can also be used to help the student think about the semester's activities in another way. The student writes a reflective paper explaining which novels or short stories the relative would like and which characters he or she would have liked or disliked. Students can also discuss which of their pieces of writing would appeal to the relative the most and why.

Sibling Surveys

Teaching students how to construct a survey and how to use the information gleaned from the survey in various writing formats helps students understand that all information does not come from a book, and shows them how information can be used. In small groups, students generate questions they have about being a brother or a sister. The questions from all the groups are compiled, and the whole class decides which ones will be used on the survey.

Sample Questions

1. How many brothers and sisters do you have?
2. Where are you in the birth order?
3. How many siblings currently live with you?
4. What are the benefits of having siblings?
5. What are the disadvantages of having siblings?
6. What chores are you expected to do?
7. What chores are your siblings expected to do?
8. If you are expected to take care of siblings, do you get paid for it?
9. In your experience, who gets along easiest—brother with brother, sister with sister, brother with sister? Why do you think this is so?
10. What do you believe is the ideal number of years between siblings? Why?
11. Do you believe your parents treat all of their children equally or fairly? Explain.
12. What is the biggest life lesson you have learned from having siblings?
13. If you decide to marry and have children, how many children would you want to have? How far apart would they be?
14. What do you believe are the advantages of being an only child?
15. What do you believe are the disadvantages of being an only child?
16. Which TV show or movie depicts the kind of brother or sister you'd like to have?

Once the surveys are constructed, passed out to different classes, and collected, students work to compile the results and make some generalizations about what they found. News, feature, and opinion stories are written using the information gleaned from the surveys.

Family Dictionary

Students gather words that have special meaning to their family, words their family uses differently than others do, and words that the family has invented or created. Students work to gather twenty-five to thirty words, arrange these entries alphabetically, break the words into syllables, list which part of speech the word is, and write the definition of the word as the family uses it. Encourage students to draw or find illustrations for at least five words. Sample entries include:

> *bub bee* (verb). Word invented by my sister to describe rubbing the ribbon end of the blanket back and forth over her lips. A soothing bedtime activity.
>
> *corn fritters* (noun). The favorite food choice of my family. Made with fresh corn off the cob.
>
> *luke* (verb). Family term used in place of "let" in speaking of letting water out of a basin. We say, "Luke the water out."
>
> *Na na* (proper noun). The term our family uses for grandmother, chosen by our mother because she thought "grandmother" sounded too formal.

This kind of project encourages students to dig into the language usage of their family and to listen carefully to how family members use words. Students also see that words are used differently by different people and how much their family influences their language.

Young Adult Novels about Families

Students choose a young adult novel that revolves around a family. When they complete the novel, they evaluate it in terms of the realism of the family relationships and how the family was portrayed. They can also create dialogues between characters in the novel and their own family members about an issue raised in the novel.

Some excellent novels that could be used include *Children of the River* by Linda Crew, *Drummers of Jericho* by Carolyn Meyer, *A Face in Every Window* by Han Nolan, *Face to Face* by Marion Dane Bauer, *The Falcon* by Jackie French Koller, *Finding My Voice* by Marie G. Lee, *The Glass House People* by Kathryn Reiss, *The Heart of a Chief* by Joseph Bruchac, *If You Come Softly* by Jacqueline Woodson, *Just Like Martin* by Ossie Davis, *Maniac Magee* by Jerry Spinelli, *Memoirs of a Bookbat* by Kathryn Lasky, *Spite Fences* by Trudy Krisher, *Tangerine* by Edward Bloor, *There's a Girl in My Hammerlock* by Jerry Spinelli, *The Watsons Go to Birmingham—1963* by Christopher Paul Curtis, *Wish You Were Here* by Barbara Shoup, *Yolonda's Genius* by Carol Fenner, *Youn Hee and Me* by C. S. Adler.

Contexts for These Activities

Since students need to see how subjects, ideas, and activities connect in their classes and understand the purpose of any activity or assignment, it is important that all assignments be embedded in some kind of context so students can see where their work is leading. If writing activities are included in a writing workshop format, students can collect in a portfolio the work they have done. If the whole class has done several of the activities as part of a unit, they can create a newspaper as an end project or put together individual anthologies of the family stories. If a few of the activities have been done by the whole class, they can be collected in class booklets for each assignment and then placed on display in the library for other students to read. A brief explanation of these end products follows.

"Family Gazette" Newspaper

Students construct a newspaper using the materials generated by the class. Each student writes a certain number of news, feature, and opinion articles and at least one other kind of story (book review, death notice, advice column, etc.). For news stories, students can draw on the results of their work with the sentence starters to report on what students believe a family is; write about the information garnered from the sibling surveys; or construct a story describing the differences in point of view that family members have on the same incident. Feature stories can be written about the name stories, the photograph poems and the stories behind them, the intergenerational interviews, and the family dictionaries. Opinion pieces can be developed about the importance of certain childhood memories and what these suggest teens need from families, or about the advice the older generation gave to the younger generation in the intergenerational interviews. All of these stories are arranged in newspaper format, and the finished product is shared with the class and with families.

An Individual Anthology of Family Stories

Students collect a specified number of finished pieces of writing from the family assignments to create anthologies that their own families would enjoy reading. They would probably want to include their list of what a family is, their name story, several other family stories, the photograph poem, the point-of-view paper, the intergenerational story, and the family dictionary. The collage can be used as the back and front cover. Students end the anthology with a reflective piece on what they learned or realized about their family and its strengths.

Writing Portfolios Focusing on the Family

For this portfolio, students collect their best pieces of writing that represent a variety of formats and genres. Students can include the photograph poem or one they create out of other material on the family; a news, feature, or opinion story on topics suggested earlier; narrative family stories selected to illustrate devices used such as flashbacks, writing in the first person, writing in the third person, or use of dialogue; the intergenerational interview; a book review on a young adult novel. To demonstrate their ability to write informational text, students could include a piece on what they discovered through the sibling interviews. The final piece in the portfolio is a reflection discussing the writing processes students used with each piece, what they found most difficult to write, and which pieces they like the best, as well as a brief analysis of such things as kinds of beginnings and endings, how they varied sentence structure, and where they used colorful language.

After the Advanced Placement Exam: Bringing in the Family

Many advanced placement students begin to "check out" mentally the last month of school after taking the AP test in early May. The test seems to mark the end of the class for such students who, in spite of showing up for class, are usually not willing to engage in much work. One way to get around this reluctance is to have students look at the year in retrospect through the eyes of their family.

Literature Retrospect

To keep students thinking about and analyzing and discussing the wonderful literature used in the class throughout the year, begin a retrospective by having students list as many of the characters they have read about in the past year as they can remember. From this list, students choose five characters they think their family would most approve or disapprove of. Students also address questions such as the following: Which character could most easily become part of the family, or which character would have the most trouble fitting into the family? What would their grandmother or father say if Tom Buchanan showed up? How would they respond to Daisy or Jordan Baker? Which themes they've read about would family members react to most strongly?

Writing Retrospect

As students reflect on their own writing over the course of this year, ask them which pieces their family members would most want to read. Which pieces would surprise them? Which pieces would they be hesitant to read? Students then develop explanations for these choices.

Family Portrayals

Ask students to look back over all the literature read and decide what statements or generalizations have been made about the family through these works. Do the stories, novels, and poems exalt the family? Do they show weaknesses in families? Do stories emphasize a particular role for the mother or father? Write or discuss the findings.

Letters

Encourage students to write a letter to their parents explaining how they've grown in the course of their high school career and what they think they have learned. How do they feel about graduating, what will they miss, what will they be glad to leave? If students feel comfortable doing so, ask them also to write about what they realize their parents have done for them. Additionally, they can write about their worries about going to college, looking for a job, or going to a technical school. Have students bring in a stamped envelope addressed to their parents in which they place their letter. Once the school year starts in the fall and many of them are away at college, mail the letters to the parents.

Poetry for the Family

If students are still willing to participate in a short project, have them bring in poetry books (or the teacher can bring in many from the library) and select poems for family members. They can make a copy of the poem, explain on the back the reasons they selected it for a family member, and then put this collection of poems in a folder and actually give it to a family member. If students view this as involving more energy than they have, simply have them share the poems in small groups and explain their reasons for choosing the poems.

Collecting Short Stories

Short stories are often overlooked in the language arts classroom, yet they can be fascinating and satisfying to read. Bring in several collections from the library and borrow more from other teachers in your building if you need to. Have students look for short stories they think would appeal to a family member, or have them look for stories about families like theirs or a family they'd want to be part of.

HEROES BRING LITERATURE TO LIFE

As teachers we strive to involve students in the work of an English class and to make this work meaningful and interesting to them. The thought of heads down on desks, signaling the tuned-out student, makes us bristle. We think, we brainstorm, and then we come up with ideas that we hope will fascinate our students.

When I read articles about the concept of heroes and superheroes, I wondered if I could get students thinking about connecting these ideas to the novels and short stories they read. Couldn't students use the hero as a measure of a character's actions in a group of short stories or in a novel? After rummaging around in books about heroes and thinking of the kinds of strategies my students respond to positively, I devised the following activities to try with my students.

Prereading Activities

Before we read a group of short stories (or a biography, as we did in one of my classes), we listed on the blackboard all the heroes and superheroes students had heard of. Then they moved to groups and worked at brainstorming characteristics of heroes and what actions and behaviors made someone heroic. After listing student ideas on the blackboard, we pared the list down to those ideas most students could agree with. The next day I brought in a list of characteristics I had culled from Chapter 5 of Joseph Campbell's *The Power of Myth*. They include:

1. A hero gives his or her life to something bigger than himself or herself, to some higher end.

2. A hero performs a courageous act, either physical or spiritual.

3. A hero is usually someone from whom something has been taken or who feels there's something lacking in the normal experience available or permitted to members of his or her society.

4. A hero embarks on a series of adventures to recover what is lost or to discover some life-affirming information.

5. The hero usually moves out of the known, conventional safety of his or her own life to undertake the journey.

6. The hero undergoes trials and tests to see if he or she has the courage, the knowledge, and the capacity to survive.

7. A hero has to achieve something.

8. A hero's journey usually consists of a departure, a fulfillment, and a return.

I asked students to compare Campbell's elements with the list they had developed the day before. They decided which of Campbell's elements they wanted to add to their list. After the class came up with a list everyone generally agreed on, we were ready to apply our knowledge of heroic behavior to the behavior of the characters we had just read about.

Using Comic Books

Another way to encourage students to generate a list of heroic behaviors is to use superhero comic books. Kids love to read them. I asked my ninth graders, who were going to read Walter Dean Myers's *Malcolm X: By Any Means Neces*sary, to bring in their own superhero comics so their classmates could read about superheroic behavior. After each student read one comic book, groups were formed so students could work together. The groups extracted from the comic they read the characteristics of a superhero, which they inferred from the superhero's actions. Students also tried to construct a rough plot outline so they could figure out the typical journey of a superhero. One group of students also compared the class list of heroic qualities with Campbell's elements.

Writing a Hero's Résumé

A third way to get kids involved in thinking about heroes and superheroes is to have each student do a bit of research on a hero or superhero and then write that hero's résumé. They can choose a Greek or Roman god/hero, a hero from history such as Harriet Tubman, a modern-day hero, or a superhero. The résumé can include such items as personal data, strengths, types of jobs the hero is good at, relevant experience, education, achievements, community activities, and references. An example follows:

Superman: A Résumé

Personal data: age 25; single; no living parents or siblings; excellent physique; great eyes.

Strengths: X-ray vision; incredible strength; able to fly; honesty; willingness to fight for right; can blow out fires with superpowerful breath.

Type of job desired: one that involves helping people out of tight situations and saving the good from the evil.

Relevant experience: extensive. I have videos and books that document my deeds.

Education: finished high school.

Achievements: ability to blend in and be considered a regular person in spite of my superhuman abilities.

Community activities: saved the city from disaster several times.

References: Lois Lane, reporter, and Harry White, editor of *The Daily Planet.*

When students have completed these résumés, they could then be asked which characters or stories could use the talents of their hero. For instance, many of the parishioners in "The Minister's Black Veil" by Nathaniel Hawthorne would probably like to ask Superman to peer through the veil and describe the expressions on the minister's face and in his eyes. Or perhaps he would be a welcome addition to "The Outcasts of Poker Flat" by Bret Harte. With his powerful breath, he could blow a path through the snow to the next town. It would be interesting to talk about how the story would have changed through such intervention and how it would have affected the characters.

Other Activities

No matter which of these strategies you use, the important thing is to get students involved in thinking about heroic behavior. Then, armed with the lists or the résumés, students can deal with the literature they have read in any of the following ways:

1. Which hero would a character most admire? Explain. Or, which heroic characteristics would a specific character such as Jay Gatsby from *The Great Gatsby* most want?

2. Which superhero or hero could have helped a character? For instance, could any of the heroes have helped Kenny through his trauma in *The Watsons Go to Birmingham—1963* by Christopher Paul Curtis?

3. If you could add a hero or superhero to the story just read, which one would you add? What would you like that hero to accomplish or change in the story?

4. List the most admirable traits of heroes such as unselfishness,

dedication, or courage. Rank characters in short stories or novels on these characteristics, using one as the highest achiever and five as no achievement in this area.

5. What are a specific character's "dragons" or "monsters"? What is the character struggling against? Does he or she have the heroic qualities necessary to satisfactorily meet and conquer the monsters?

6. Which of the characters just read about seem most heroic/least heroic? What did they achieve/fail to achieve? What made them heroic/not heroic?

7. A hero's journey usually involves a going away, going through a series of tests and trials, and returning changed or having accomplished something. Look carefully at the characters just read about. Could any of them be thought of as going on a heroic journey?

8. In the days of old, courage involved performing dangerous physical deeds. Today courage is usually seen in everyday actions such as standing up for someone getting picked on when the person risks rejection for defending the other person. Look back to the stories or novel just finished and think about which deed or action you consider the most courageous. Describe the action and explain why you found it courageous.

9. After reading several short stories or a novel, create a HELP WANTED poster advertisement for the kind of person most needed in the story. Cut a picture from a magazine showing a person who represents the heroic qualities you are seeking. In several paragraphs, describe what attributes this hero has and why he or she is so badly needed in the story.

10. Who would specific characters have as their heroes/heroines? Describe the characteristics they would pick and why these are important to them.

Once the idea of heroic behavior has been introduced into the English language arts classroom, heroes provide another effective avenue for drawing students deeper into literature and do indeed help bring literature to life.

PROJECTS THAT PROMOTE AUTHENTIC LEARNING

If they are authentic, projects are usually surefire ways to involve students. Students easily become engaged because authentic projects have a genuine payoff—the end products will be used.

Project 1: Creating Videos or Handbooks on "Life as a Ninth Grader"

By the middle of the school year, every student is an expert on what it is like to be in that specific grade. Students know what the traps and temptations are; they know about changing friendships; they know what's expected of them to make it through the year academically. They've tried to balance the social and extracurricular aspects with schoolwork. This project taps into and celebrates that expertise.

Depending on the grade of the students involved, the focus will differ. Ninth graders might call their project "Ninth Grade—What's It All About?" while twelfth graders may want to call theirs "Twelfth Grade: Making It Through." For the sake of brevity, I will discuss here only how this project can be implemented in the ninth grade.

Students can decide whether they will produce a video to show incoming ninth graders next year or a handbook that will be given to these ninth graders. If students know that the project will culminate in a talk show that will be videotaped or a booklet that will be given to incoming students, the motivation to participate fully will be high.

Explaining Goals

Begin by explaining your goals: that you want them to reflect on what they've learned as ninth graders that could help others survive ninth grade, and that you want them to interview adults who may have opinions and information that could be helpful to new students. You might begin in small groups by having the students brainstorm all the areas in which they want to give advice. After they list everything they think incoming ninth graders should know, have them work to categorize the information. Typical categories might include finding your way around the building, getting along with older students, activities that are fun to get involved in, friendships and how not to get burned, keeping your social life under control, and so forth.

Interviewing Adults

Once students know the areas they would like to focus their advice and opinions on, they can then figure out the kinds of information they want from adults. Again, group brainstorming often leads to possibilities the teacher wouldn't think of. Students might want to talk to counselors to find out what kinds of issues ninth graders come to see them about. These same counselors could also be interviewed for any helpful advice they could give ninth graders. Assistant principals and security personnel could also be interviewed and asked about their most frequent interactions with ninth graders. They also could be asked for their opinions on why ninth graders seem to be involved in particular issues (such as smoking and truancy).

Students might also want to talk to cafeteria workers about ninth-grade behavior, asking them how they know a student is new to the school and what are the most common behaviors that distinguish ninth graders in the cafeteria. Older students could be interviewed about how they can spot ninth graders and what advice they'd give them. Bus drivers could be interviewed. All of these people would be providing a picture of how ninth graders appear to others.

Surveying Other Ninth Graders

Next, students can construct a survey to give to other ninth graders so they can represent the views of a larger cross section of ninth-grade opinions. After students decide on the survey questions, they should take the survey themselves to see which questions get the best responses. Survey questions might include such things as what advice current ninth graders would give to incoming ninth graders on friends, succeeding in class, things not to do, ways not to act, the biggest problems they had this year, and what they would change or do differently if they had the chance.

Once students get the surveys back, the topics can be divided up. One group might want to focus on the social aspects of ninth grade while others focus on the academic, the extracurricular, or the personal issues ninth graders seem most concerned about. Each group compiles its information and decides how the information should be used in the handbook or video.

Possible Parts or Sections of a Talk Show or Handbook

According to student input, sections of the handbook or topics on the talk show could include learning the building layout, coping with the first few days, adjusting to classes, selecting friends and social groups, coping with peer pressure, focusing on school work, and so on. According to adult input, topics or sections could include what attitudes a coach likes to see in players; tips from counselors; tips from security guards; tips from the assistant principal for discipline; observations from lunchroom workers, the assistant principal for student affairs, teachers, parents, and the principal. If students choose to make a video, they can play the part of one of these adults and use the information from the interviews to help adopt these adult viewpoints on the talk show.

Putting It Together

Whatever format students decide on, it usually works best if the class is divided into teams. Some teams can process and compile information they have gathered from talking to adults who deal with ninth graders. Other teams can focus on compiling and digesting information they got from the surveys. From the information on the surveys, students should decide what type of student "guests" will appear on the show or what points of view will be represented in the handbook. Someone may want to portray or write about an excellent student who can't understand why everyone doesn't just do the schoolwork given to them; another may portray or write about a student reeling from the effects of family divorce. All of these points of view can be portrayed to show what ninth grade can be like. Of course, other students can appear as themselves or write about their own views.

Once the groups have digested the information they are working with, their major job is to write questions that the host or hostess can ask of the guests or to select and organize the writing. Group efforts must be coordinated to make sure that all important facets of ninth-grade life are covered. Then students have to be sure to include a wide variety of views on the topics to keep the show or the handbook interesting.

Once the video camera is rolling or the handbook is in production, the hardest part is over. After the taping or the selecting of material, students work to edit the tape or booklet so that next year's ninth graders have an accurate picture of the joys and pitfalls of ninth grade.

Project 2: Compiling a Poetry Book for a Special Person

Another project that can quickly engage students is the poetry project, in which they find poems and compile a booklet of poetry for a family member or a friend. One of the goals of the project is to get students to read a wide array of poetry so they can enjoy and appreciate it. Before students look for poems that speak to their chosen person, they should brainstorm a list of their memories of that person.

If the poetry book is for an older brother or sister, students might list memories of such things as "letting me walk to school with you, the time you helped me learn to ride a bike, the time you were mean to me and your friends wouldn't let me play with you." Other memories might include the best Christmas, a birthday to remember, and hobbies or sports the sibling enjoys. Students might also list what they think is important to that person. By gathering these concrete memories and ideas, students have a starting point of topics they can look for in the poetry.

Oftentimes, of course reading a poem will cause students to see how the poem could be connected to the special person. Each student begins his or her search for poetry that this specific person would like.

Guidelines

Usually, guidelines require a set number of poems, and that poems be selected from a set number of poetry books. Other guidelines can include number of illustrations, photos, or magazine pictures required for each booklet. Since one of the purposes of the assignment is to expose students to a wide variety of poetry, have them scan several books. Depending on your teaching situation, you can either bring books from several libraries into the classroom or assign students to find the poetry on their own. I always include children's poetry, not only because it delights students but also because almost everyone, adult and child alike, will have a poem they can relate to from children's poetry collections.

After students select ten to fifteen poems, they handwrite or use a copier to reproduce the poems. Each poem usually stands alone on a page, followed by another page explaining why the student selected the poem for the chosen person. Since students are compiling the booklet for someone they care about, they will usually want to spend time creating an appealing cover. Some students may want to create one on a computer, some will chose to draw their own, some will want to use photos or magazine illustrations, and some may even want to paint a cover.

Presenting the Booklet

When the booklets are complete, they are presented to the special person, who is asked to write a letter back to the student, telling the student such things as which poems they especially liked and what they felt about the student's effort. If the booklets are presented to much younger brothers or sisters, parents will have to help in this effort. Students have the satisfaction of presenting a finished product containing poems they have personally selected, and they get feedback on how the product was received.

Project 3: Creating Research Packets for Next Year's Students

Research skills are tough to teach any time of the year unless the motivation to find out about a specific topic is very high. In this project, students prepare exhaustive lists of resources on a topic of their choice that will be used by your students the following year or placed in the library as samples of available resources. Since students are not going to end up with a research paper as a product, they are often more excited about the opportunities to explore in depth a topic that interests them. These research packets make excellent tools to teach incoming ninth graders about what kinds of resources there are in the community, as well as show them in concrete ways that encyclopedias and books are not the only resources they can use to gain information.

Selecting a Topic

To get your students committed to expending effort in locating resources, take time in selecting a topic. Students can start by brainstorming a list of what they are interested in knowing more about or by writing down questions they would like answered. After each student has generated a list, students share them in small groups, explaining to group members why they might be interested in each topic or question. Sometimes their own explanation is enough to help students discover that this might not be the topic for them, and sometimes their own enthusiasm for a topic helps them identify it as one they would really like to do.

Once all group members (groups of three are usually an ideal size for this task) have completed their explanations, each one picks a topic from his or her list and begins a web with the help of the other group members. In webbing, the topic is written in the middle of the page within a circle, and students draw lines from this center to connect the topic to other circles that contain all the elements of their topic they can think of. These categories are divided again as students think of things that connect to the category. For instance, from the main topic "divorce," lines can be drawn and connected to circles which contain categories such as statistics, causes, effects on children, economic effects on family, where help is available. Each of these categories can have subtopics connected to lines drawn out from that circle.

Research Guidelines

If students have difficulty webbing their topic, it might mean the subject is too limited to pursue. Once students have developed a web and talked about their topic with members of their small group, they should be ready to decide on the topic. Once the topic is chosen, students can then be given instructions like the following:

> Your job is to prepare an exhaustive list of the resources in the library and the community that could be used to gain informa-

tion on your topic. Include such resources as community organizations, university departments, knowledgeable people, and places students could go on field trips to gain an understanding of the issue. From the library, you can find out what resources are available on the Internet, what Web pages may help with information on the topic, what fiction and nonfiction books address the topic, what CD-ROMs/laser disks, films, videos, music, or art might provide information on the topic. Your resource packet should be organized by type of resource and should include brief annotations (or explanations) of each resource, as well as complete bibliographic information. Your booklet should include a minimum of three resources from the community, ten from the library (books, magazines, filmstrips, etc.), five on the Internet, and any combination of five resources that include films, music, art, or CD-ROMs.

As you begin your quest to amass helpful resources, keep notes on all parts of your journey. This record of your research will be almost as helpful to next year's students as the resources themselves. Include in your record the "map" of your topic: how you started, what you looked up or went to first, what key words you used, what led to dead ends, and what resulted in obtaining good resources. This will be part of your packet.

When your packet is complete, make an attractive cover and fasten the whole thing together in some way.

Besides turning in your resource packet, you will also write a short paper explaining what you learned about research and what you learned about your topic simply by searching for resources on it.

Of course, teachers can set up any sort of minimum guidelines. It is also helpful to provide a sample of an annotation on each type of resource. Such sample annotations show students what kind of information a reader needs to make a decision about whether they would want to use the resource.

Keeping a Research Notebook

As students begin their research, have them keep a notebook on how they approached their topic, what false starts they had, what key words didn't work for their topic, and so forth. Because they don't have the pressure of completing a research paper, students should be more willing to record this kind of information, which is extremely helpful to younger students who get so discouraged when they look up a key word in the *Readers' Guide to Periodical Literature* and can't find information immediately. So the other significant part of this project is the record of the journey the researcher took, with all its twists and turns. What agency did a student call? What information did he or she hope to get? Why is this agency not one to consult for this particular research?

Research Fair

As a grand finale to the project, set up a "fair" in your room or in the library so that students from other classes can participate. If you hold the fair in your classroom, have one-third of the students at a time present their product. Simply arrange the chairs or desks in groups of three. The person explaining or showing the product remains in the group while the two "visitors" move to a different "station" every four or five minutes. To keep students focused, have them record their reaction to each topic on a sheet or form. When they have heard about all the topics, each student can then select the five that most interested him or her and explain why. After all students have heard from the first third of the class, the next third becomes the presenters, and then the final third.

After all presentations are done, students have seen enough examples to know what makes a research booklet effective. As a wrap-up to the project, students can write up what they thought was best about their own project and what they hope others gain from it. These evaluations can then be placed in the front of the booklet in a "Dear Reader" format.

Using Research Packets the Following Year

1. As part of a unit. A unit will introduce students to research and work to broaden their view of what resources are. In groups, students first write down everything they think of when they hear the word *research*. Next, they list all the sources they use to get information in their daily life. Then they list all the kinds of information they can get from radio, newspapers, TV, magazines, films, people, fiction books, nonfiction books, and the Internet. After groups share their responses with the whole class, they are now ready to peruse the research packets since they have just clarified what they think research is, their attitudes toward it, and what resources can be used.

Give one resource packet to each student. Create questions you want them to read for, such as which packet was most interesting and which kind of source they hadn't thought or heard about before. Students read all the packets in their group. After discussing the packets with each other, they report to the class which packet they found most interesting, which had the most diverse resources, which had the best topic, which had the most helpful explanations on the research procedures used, and so on. By working with packets of solid resources, students see more possibilities for the kinds of resources available on a specific topic.

2. To evaluate the effectiveness of the resources. Give each student a packet and have him or her evaluate the resources to decide which ones provide the best information. To do this, students will have to go to the library and read or view actual sources. Have them investigate about five sources for this study, rank the sources from high to low, and write up reasons for their rankings. Students can share their findings in small groups so that they will get a broader view of what makes a resource a good one.

3. As the basis of Academy Awards. Groups of five read packets and briefly discuss them before going on to the next batch. After reading all of them, groups nominate five packets and provide reasons for their choices. This will encourage students to create their own criteria for excellence. After students have developed categories such as best topic, most visually appealing, most diverse resources, and best in the field, have each group nominate one packet for each category. When all nominations are complete, the two with the most nominations are put on a ballot, the students vote, and then the awards are presented. Each group could then write a letter to a winner, telling him or her which attributes of the packet earned the award.

4. To do actual research. Since the search for resources has already been done for students, they can dig right in, locate the resources, and begin a research project.

APPROACHING RACE AND GENDER ISSUES IN THE CONTEXT OF THE LANGUAGE ARTS CLASSROOM

When we read works of literature with our students, we are comfortable framing discussions and activities in terms of the elements of literature. We have found ways to involve students that depend on their response to plot, setting, character, and theme. But knowing how to deal with the subtler elements of characterization such as gender and race portrayals has eluded many of us. Some of us feel we don't know enough to approach these issues. Others are uncomfortable raising issues of difference in class. Most often, however, we as teachers simply haven't found ways to comfortably raise these issues in the context of our teaching. Does it take creating an entire unit on only women or minorities? Does it mean we have to look for racial and gender implications in everything we do?

The intent of this section is to offer many possibilities for integrating race and gender issues into the fabric of the English language arts classroom so that teachers can find a way to begin dealing with these ever-present, extremely important aspects of life and literature. If these issues are never raised, if students are never encouraged to question the assumptions behind gender and race portrayals, the danger is that students will accept stereotyped portrayals of characters as the way people really are.

Raising the Issues and Beginning the Conversations

1. Sentence Starters. Ask students to write ten sentences beginning with "Being a female means . . ." or "Being a male means . . . ," depending on their gender. Then have students respond to those sentence starters or the following one in terms of the opposite sex: "The good thing about being a female is . . ."; "The good thing about being a male is . . . ." This will really get discussion going and quickly uncover the expectations each gender has for its own as well as for the opposite gender. These sentences can also be arranged into poems with two or more voices highlighting similarities or differences between the way males and females view themselves and each other.

Such a poem might look like this:

> Voice 1: Being female means being smart but not showing it.
> Voice 2: Being male means having a hard time showing emotions in public.
> Voice 1: Being female means never feeling "body image" security.
> Voice 2: Being male means hiding your appreciation of classical music.
> Voice 1: Being female means smiling in response to everything.
> Voice 2: Being male means that everyone assumes you know about cars and can fix them.

2. Character Descriptions. To encourage students to examine their assumptions about being male or female or being a member of a specific race, prepare several descriptions of characters excerpted from works of literature. Read the piece to the class, substituting a name such as *Chris* or *Terry* in place of the character's name and the pronouns referring to that character. After hearing the whole excerpt, the students must decide whether the character is a male or a female and what race they assume the character is, and give several reasons for their choices. Many of the students' stereotypes and conventional expectations can be revealed through this kind of assignment.

Brief examples include:

> "*Chris* wasn't used to carrying sadness around. *Chris* was used to seeing trouble and doing something about it." (This description from *Dicey's Song* (16–17) by Cynthia Voigt is of a white female.)

> "*Chris* took little interest in troublesome things, preferring to remain on good terms with everyone. Yet *Chris* was always sensitive to others." (This description from *Roll of Thunder, Hear My Cry* (21) by Mildred Taylor is of a black male.)

> "I don't like the idea of having a 'girlfriend/boyfriend.' I bet I never do. It's too much like having a dog." (This statement from *Midnight Hour Encores* (163) by Bruce Brooks was made by a white female.)

3. Personal Narratives. Another good way to make students aware of gender and/or racial issues is to have each student write a narrative based on a time he or she was treated a certain way simply because he or she was a male or a female or black or white or Latino (the list goes on). Before students are asked to write about their race, a high level of trust must be established in the class. In my experience at a racially mixed school, students were very willing to write about these racial experiences and share them with class members since it provided them with a vehicle for making other students aware of some of their concerns.

After writing these stories, students bring them to class and share them in small groups; students make a line in the margins next to the parts they think are especially powerful. Pieces of these stories, those indicated by the marginal lines, can be excerpted and used in a script that is read to the whole class. Through this kind of sharing, students are made aware that racism and sexism are far from dead.

4. Surveys. Before beginning a story or novel that may portray a character with an atypical gender role such as Charlotte in Avi's *The True Confessions of Charlotte Doyle*, make up a brief survey based on events or issues in the novel and pass it out to the class. Surveys such as these can help students become aware of their own attitudes. Survey statements can ask students to choose which gender is associated with such things as standing up to an authority figure, scrubbing floors, cooking meals, climbing high up on an unsteady rope ladder, knowing how to use a knife, dressing for practicality instead of appearance, criticizing others publicly, ignoring parental pressure, and making decisions about one's future.

After students respond with *male, female,* or *both,* have them write about the following questions: Which of the preceding categories do you believe a man or a woman should not be involved in? Why? Do you believe it is harder to be a male or a female in our society today? Explain. This kind of discussion can set the stage for the issues and themes that arise in the novel.

5. Collages. Ask students to create collages from pictures in magazine ads that show males and females engaged in various activities or members of different races engaged in activities. Around the edges of the collage have students list the verbs they think describe the actions in the pictures. On the back of the collage have students describe what the ads want the reader or potential customer to think or make connections to. How does this compare to how males, females, or members of different races are portrayed in the literature the students read?

6. Children's Books. Picture books are terrific for getting students to look at how males and females or people of different races are portrayed. Bring in lots of picture books from the library and have students analyze them in terms of who is the main character, who is shown doing what, how frequently people of color are depicted, and so on. Students can draw conclusions about whether these picture books contribute to or refute gender and racial stereotypes.

Questions to Consider in Discussions of Race and Gender in Literature

After some of the preceding activities have been completed and students know they will be looking at gender and race portrayals in literature, many of the following questions can be used to continue to sensitize our students to these issues:

1. List words used to describe male and female characters and characters of different ethnic backgrounds. Compare these words. Draw conclusions.

2. List what males and females and ethnic characters are shown doing in the story. Look at the verbs that describe what they are doing. Compare this information.

3. Who questions, confronts, interrupts, or initiates conversations? Discuss.

4. Compare the way female appearance is described with the way male appearance is described. What does this say about what we expect of males and of females?

5. What are minorities/majorities or males/females disapproved of for doing?

6. Compare minority/majority families. How are the fathers portrayed? The mothers? What's expected of each of them? What are they criticized for?

7. Discuss with members of your small group relationships shown in the literature. What characteristics are demonstrated as positive for a male in a relationship with a female and vice versa? Are the expectations the same for majority/minority members?

8. Do members of different races and/or genders gain status for different things (e.g., sports, competitiveness, nurturing, goodness)?

9. How does the author want you to view members of the races and genders portrayed? Does the author's own race or gender seem to affect character portrayal?

10. How would the character have changed if the author had assigned him or her a different race or gender?

11. How does the author characterize the genders and races? Look at the characters' speech, appearance, actions, and what others say about them.

12. How does the language in the story reinforce or refute racial or gender stereotypes?

13. What aspect of each character does the author and/or other characters pay the most attention to? Does this vary by race or gender?

14. Which characters seem to have the most interesting plans for the future? Does this vary by race or gender?

15. Compare the races and genders represented in the literature in terms of the following personality characteristics, which are frequently viewed as opposites in society: active/passive; selfless/selfish; rational/emotional; stable/unstable; courageous/afraid; risk taker/complier; aggressive/nonaggressive; challenging/obedient; low need for friendship/high need for friendship; competitive/nurturing. Discuss and draw conclusions.

16. Which of the character's experiences were related to the character's race or gender?

17. Which of the main character's experiences will you probably never have? Why?

Activities to Further Engage Students in Race/Gender Issues

The following activities can be undertaken while and after students read a story. This list should help extend students' responses to literature.

1. Become a Character. After reading a short story or novel, write as if you were one of the characters and talk about the way you were portrayed as a male or a female or as a member of a minority. For instance, if you were imagining yourself as Curley's wife in *Of Mice and Men*, you might write:

> I think John Steinbeck portrayed me very accurately. He really showed what a crummy life women had. Take me, for instance, I wasn't even given a name because the men in the story only wanted to see me as that *other*, that *woman*. I think Steinbeck did that to show his readers that women were viewed as objects, not people in their own right. He also showed how few options women like me had. I could get married or I could take my chances that something better might come along. Fat chance of that ever happening! I remember that guy who promised me I could be in pictures. I was so desperate for some kind of excitement in my life that I tried to believe him. Girls couldn't do nothin'. If you wanted to have a little fun you were seen as fast and not good enough to ever get married. So I made the big mistake of marrying Curley. What an insecure creep! No wonder I tried to get some attention from others. Yes, I did hang around the men a lot, but it was because I had absolutely nothing else to do. I was lonely, I didn't have a way to make women friends. If you tried to act the least bit friendly, those guys labeled you as a troublemaker and a tart. As if a woman don't want a little companionship.

2. Compare Characteristics. Make a list of the male characteristics shown in the novel that you see as admirable or not admirable. Make a list of the female characteristics shown in the novel that you see as admirable or not admirable. Make a list of the characteristics of people of color in the novel that you see as admirable or not admirable. Are males, females, and minorities depicted with a variety of personality characteristics? Discuss whether character portrayal is balanced. What conclusions can you draw? (These kinds of lists also make great fodder for discussions in small groups.)

3. Diagram the Relationships in the Story. Through drawing circles on a paper that represent characters, diagram the relationships shown in the story. Place the most important characters at the center of the page and connect the circles through a series of lines. A solid line with an arrow at the end can indicate that the character seeks a relationship with another character in the circle. A broken line could indicate that a relationship is present but not valued or desired. Lines composed of dots and dashes could indicate that one character has more power than another. (This activity works best if the teacher constructs a diagram from a different story as a model and explains what the diagrams should illustrate.)

4. Mimic Description. Locate a passage portraying a female, preferably at the point she is introduced into the story. Note how she is described. This often includes hairstyle, makeup, skin tone, shape of mouth, neatness of apparel, texture and fabric of clothing, style of clothing, and how she looks generally. Now find a place where a male is introduced into the story and add the kind of description to his introduction that is included in the female's description. If her mouth shape is described, describe his. If the color and style of her clothing is described, describe his. What effect does this have on the way you view this character? Can you draw conclusions about the effect characterization through physical description has on the way females are viewed?

5. Collect Passages. Find passages that describe males and females; that show who controls the conversations; that show any kind of criticism. Analyze your findings in terms of what things are expected of men and of women.

6. Rewrite Scenes. Choose a scene that didn't end satisfactorily or a scene that never occurred but that you would like to see happen. Write a script to change the scene or to create a new one so that gender or race issues are addressed.

7. Create a List of Rules. Choose a character who has very definite ideas about how males or females should behave or how people of different races should act. Create a list of rules that is implied by that character's actions, words, or descriptions. For instance, in Dickens's *Great Expectations,* how does Miss Havisham believe the "lower classes" behave? Create a list of rules of things she would like them to do to improve their behavior, such as speak and dress differently. In *Spite Fences* by Trudy Krisher, what rules would Maggie's family believe blacks should follow? For *The Shadowman's Way* by Paul Pitts, make up the list of rules that the Native Americans wish the whites would follow.

8. Give Advice to a Character. Examine characters in terms of how males and females act or are treated or how people of different races act or are treated. Write a letter of advice to that character, telling him or her how you think the character should react or change his or her behavior, and why.

9. Show the Wisdom of the Characters. To highlight the contributions of a character in a story or novel who perhaps transcends gender or racial labels, go through the story looking for what that character says that seems sound or perceptive. Compile these quotations into a booklet titled "The Wisdom of _____." Was it easier to find contributions for males, females, or minorities?

10. Meet a Character. Choose a character who represents a gender or race different from yours and write about what you would most like to ask the character or talk to that character about.

11. Keep a Character Journal. Select a character of a gender or race different from yours. In a double-entry format, keep a daily journal from the character's point of view of what happened and how he or she felt. On the other side of the page, write your personal reaction to the character's problems and experiences.

12. Imagine That a Character Visits Your School. Imagine that a character (especially one who represents a different race or social class or who has strong views on gender issues) has been lifted out of the story and dropped into your school. Write the scenario of what would happen if this character spent a day at your school. How would he or she act? How would students treat him or her? Which students might want to hang around this character? What issues might the character touch off in your school or what issues might the character want to raise?

13. Create an Alphabet Scheme. Create an alphabetical scheme based on how a character would describe his or her treatment at the hands of others or on the attributes this character would like to see in others. Melba Pattillo Beals in *Warriors Don't Cry* might describe her treatment at Central High School as: **A**ppalling when she was threatened by the crowds; **B**arbaric when her heels were repeatedly stepped on and bloodied as she walked through the halls; **C**ruel because she was treated as a nonhuman who had no feelings. If she was writing about the attributes she wished her schoolmates had, they might include: **C**ourage to be her friend and stop all the torment; **D**etermined to stop the prejudice in their own generation; **E**nterprising enough to find ways to support the nine black students in the building.

14. Rank Values. Rank characters on such values as acceptance (approval from others), achievement, companionship (friendship), honesty, justice, loyalty, morality, physical appearance, pleasure, power, recognition, self-respect, and wealth. Then compare values important to males or females and/or majority or minority members. Draw conclusions.

15. Generate Three Questions. After you've read a story or parts of a novel, bring to class three issues or questions you would like to discuss. Be sure to indicate on the paper if you are a male or female. The teacher will collect the questions and begin a whole-class discussion based on student questions. What differences, if any, do you see in the kinds of issues males and females want to discuss. Draw conclusions.

16. Find Character Quotations. After reading a novel, dig back into it to find ten quotations or sentences that reveal the character you've been assigned or have chosen and that show what the character is like. Explain what these quotations tell or show about your character. Compare quotations in terms of race and gender.

17. Reflect on Lessons in Life. In small groups, brainstorm a list of all the things readers can learn directly from the characters and their actions. These can be both negative and positive things. Then discuss which actions you wouldn't want to imitate and which you would like to emulate, and explain why. Then share these lists with the entire class to determine which gender or race is most often shown in positive ways.

18. Create Pamphlets. Create a pamphlet showing the things females are rewarded for in the literature you have read or the things males seem to be rewarded for. (This activity works only when students are aware of the difference in expectations for females and males and are more sensitive to sexism.) Do females or males receive approval for aggression? for being nurturing? (This pamphlet could be used in the classroom to raise awareness about issues of gender and to help students see the sexism around them. This could take the form of "Did you know . . . ?")

19. Write Dialogues. (While reading books or stories, stop at the parts where students react to what the characters do.) Write a dialogue first as a female and then as a male with the character whose actions you have reacted to most strongly. Compare the differences in these dialogues. (For example, in *The Crazy Horse Electric Game* by Chris Crutcher, Jenny asks Willie if he wants to go with her. Writing dialogues after this incident will usually reveal a vast difference in attitude between the sexes and will also reveal much of the gendered expectations students carry with them.)

20. Construct a Newspaper. After reading a novel that portrays a minority group or females, construct a newspaper from the point of view of a particular organization. For instance, after reading *Indio* by Sherry Garland, a newspaper titled *Native American News* could be constructed. After reading *The Grapes of Wrath* by John Steinbeck, the *Okie Outlook* could be written. In the pages of the newspapers, write editorials commenting on the overall portrayal of the group, feature articles on interviews with characters about conditions described in the novel or on how accurately they felt they were portrayed, and news stories on events in the novel.

Works Cited

Adler, C. S. *Youn Hee and Me.* San Diego: Harcourt, 1995.

Avi. *The True Confessions of Charlotte Doyle.* New York: Orchard, 1990.

Bauer, Marion Dane. *Face to Face.* New York: Clarion, 1991.

Beals, Melba Pattillo. *Warriors Don't Cry: A Searing Memoir of the Battle to Integrate Little Rock's Central High.* New York: Pocket, 1994.

Bloor, Edward. *Tangerine.* San Diego: Harcourt, 1997.

Brancato, Robin F. "Fourth of July." *Sixteen: Short Stories by Outstanding Writers for Young Adults.* Ed. Donald R. Gallo. New York: Dell, 1984.

Brooks, Bruce. *Midnight Hour Encores.* New York: Harper, 1986.

Bruchac, Joseph. *The Heart of a Chief.* New York: Dial, 1998.

Campbell, Joseph. *The Power of Myth.* New York: Doubleday, 1988.

Chambers, Aidan, ed. *A Haunt of Ghosts.* New York: Harper, 1987.

Crew, Linda. *Children of the River.* New York: Delacorte, 1989.

Crutcher, Chris. *The Crazy Horse Electric Game.* New York: Greenwillow, 1987.

Curtis, Christopher Paul. *The Watsons Go to Birmingham—1963.* New York: Delacorte, 1995.

Davis, Ossie. *Just Like Martin.* New York: Simon, 1992.

Dickens, Charles. *Great Expectations.* New York: Tor, 1998.

Fenner, Carol. *Yolonda's Genius.* New York: McElderry, 1995.

Fitzgerald, F. Scott. *The Great Gatsby.* New York: Scribner, 1995.

Gallo, Donald R., ed. *Short Circuits: Thirteen Shocking Stories by Outstanding Writers for Young Adults.* New York: Delacorte, 1992.

Garland, Sherry. *Indio.* San Diego: Harcourt, 1995.

Harte, Bret. "The Outcasts of Poker Flat." *Adventures in American Literature.* Ed. Francis Hodgins. San Diego: Harcourt, 1985. 360–67.

Hawthorne, Nathaniel. "The Minister's Black Veil." *Adventures in American Literature.* Ed. Francis Hodgins. San Diego: Harcourt, 1985. 220–29.

Jackson, Shirley. "Charles." *The Lottery and Other Stories.* New York: Noonday, 1982.

Koller, Jackie French. *The Falcon.* New York: Atheneum, 1998.

Krisher, Trudy. *Spite Fences.* New York: Delacorte, 1994.

Lasky, Kathryn. *Memoirs of a Bookbat.* San Diego: Harcourt, 1994.

Lawrence, Jerome, and Robert E. Lee. *The Night Thoreau Spent in Jail.* New York: Bantam, 1972.

Lee, Marie G. *Finding My Voice.* Boston: Houghton, 1992.

Masters, Edgar Lee. *Spoon River Anthology. Adventures in American Literature.* Ed. Francis Hodgins. San Diego: Harcourt, 1985. 436–39.

McCall, Nathan. *Makes Me Want to Holler: A Young Black Man in America.* New York: Random, 1994.

Meyer, Carolyn. *Drummers of Jericho.* San Diego: Harcourt, 1995.

Meyers, Walter Dean. *Malcolm X: By Any Means Necessary.* New York: Scholastic, 1993.

Nolan, Han. *A Face in Every Window.* San Diego: Harcourt, 1999.

Pitts, Paul. *The Shadowman's Way.* New York: Avon, 1992.

Prelutsky, Jack, ed. *The Headless Horseman Rides Tonight: More Poems to Trouble Your Sleep.* New York: Greenwillow, 1980.

———. *Nightmares: Poems to Trouble Your Sleep.* New York: Greenwillow, 1976.

Reiss, Kathryn. *The Glass House People.* San Diego: Harcourt, 1992.

Romano, Tom. *Clearing the Way: Working with Teenage Writers.* Portsmouth, NH: Heinemann, 1987.

Shoup, Barbara. *Wish You Were Here.* New York: Hyperion, 1994.

Spinelli, Jerry. *Maniac Magee.* Boston: Little, 1990.

———. *There's a Girl in My Hammerlock.* New York: Simon, 1991.

Steinbeck, John. *Grapes of Wrath.* New York: Penguin, 1992.

———. *Of Mice and Men.* New York: Penguin, 1993.

Taylor, Mildred D. *Roll of Thunder, Hear My Cry.* New York: Dial, 1976.

Strasser, Todd. "On the Bridge." *Visions: Nineteen Short Stories by Outstanding Writers for Young Adults.* Ed. Donald R. Gallo. New York: Delacorte, 1987.

Voigt, Cynthia. *Dicey's Song.* New York: Atheneum, 1982.

Woodson, Jacqueline. *If You Come Softly.* New York: Putnam's, 1998.

7 Resources for Your Teaching

Leila Christenbury

Leila gives suggestions for professional materials such as books, films, and periodicals which can help you in your teaching and provide both inspiration and practical help. The chapter ends with some quotations about teachers and teaching that you may find helpful as well.

The two things most teachers never have enough of are money and time. Time is a battle for most teachers. All of us struggle to keep up with our classes, our students, and our professional obligations, and most of us also feel serious about maintaining community ties. Often only in the time left over is there space for our personal life and our family. Because most of us want to make a contribution in a number of competing areas, we rarely have enough time to read and to prepare well for our classes.

Money is also tight for most teachers. None of us entered the profession for its vast financial rewards, and for almost all of us there are car and house payments, family expenses, college loans, personal debts, and professional dues. Our nine-and-a-half-month yearly income often needs to be supplemented with summer work—for most of us, there is never quite enough money to do everything we want to do.

Thus, between lack of money and time, we have plenty of reasons to forgo purchases of books and journals related to teaching. They pinch an already tight budget, and we also have little time to do them justice. Yet besides this book, many invaluable materials are available to help you in your daily teaching and to give you ideas and encouragement. So, despite the limitations of money and time, I urge you to think about buying or subscribing to at least some of the following, all of which are briefly annotated. If you simply cannot afford the cost, ask your school librarian, department chair, or team coordinator to help fund the purchase. Your PTA organization may have a book fund for teacher materials, and you may also find resources in the community. Having a resource library is very helpful in getting ideas for teaching, and the effort you make to secure some of these materials will have long-term benefits. Other teachers will also profit from your recommendations, and they will be grateful for the treasure trove of ideas. It may not be ideal, but you *can* sandwich in a bit of reading every week—and a few minutes with these resources will help you energize your teaching and will provide ideas and inspiration. The following list is by no means inclusive, but many of these resources can form the core of a beginning professional library.

General Texts on Secondary English Teaching

Christenbury, Leila. *Making the Journey: Being and Becoming a Teacher of English Language Arts.* 2nd ed. Portsmouth, NH: Heinemann, 2000.

> Filled with teacher stories and anecdotes, this book combines a personal history of teaching with teaching ideas and strategies. *Making the Journey* covers language, literature, writing, and computers and also includes a chapter on questioning strategies and beginning your life in the classroom.

Milner, Joseph O'Beirne, and Lucy Floyd Morcock Milner. *Bridging English.* 2nd ed. Upper Saddle River, NJ: Merrill, 1999.

> This is a 500-plus page mini-encyclopedia of teaching English. The authors are smart and well informed, and they give their readers a ton of information on all the important subjects regarding the English classroom. Charts, boxes, lists, and generous appendices make this book comprehensive and valuable.

Tchudi, Stephen, and Diana Mitchell. *Exploring and Teaching the English Language Arts.* 4th ed. New York: Longman, 1999.

> This book is long on both theoretical background and common sense, providing great advice and many specifics on a huge range of topics. How to craft a unit, integrate the curriculum, and create a classroom community are just some of the issues addressed. Most teachers have used Tchudi and Mitchell's work for years.

General Texts on Middle School English Teaching

Atwell, Nancie. *In the Middle: New Understandings about Writing, Reading, and Learning.* 2nd ed. Portsmouth, NH: Boynton/Cook, 1998.

> If there's one book you should have in your library, this is it. Teacher Nancie Atwell thoroughly explains her classroom philosophy—why and how she teaches the way she does—

and, even more to the point for you, provides examples, charts, forms, and lists. Atwell's reading/writing workshop and her use of minilessons have made a huge impact on both secondary and middle-level language arts classrooms. If you don't know this book already, you'll find it appealing and extremely useful.

Rief, Linda. *Seeking Diversity: Language Arts with Adolescents.* Portsmouth, NH: Heinemann, 1992.

I love this book and the spirit behind it. Like Nancie Atwell, Linda Rief invites her readers into her classroom to see how she organizes for the teaching of reading and writing. Rief's understanding of the middle schooler, her sense of care for her students as individuals, and her sure-handed presentation of how she organizes her class make this book practical and also inspiring.

Two other excellent books are Mary Mercer Krogness's *Just Teach Me, Mrs. K.: Talking, Reading, and Writing with Resistant Adolescent Learners* (Portsmouth, NH: Heinemann, 1995) and Janet Allen and Kyle Gonzalez's delightfully titled *There's Room for Me Here: Literacy Workshop in the Middle School* (York, ME: Stenhouse, 1998). Both books, written by veteran teachers, are practical, well thought out, and interesting.

Literature

Teaching Strategies

Daniels, Harvey. *Literature Circles: Voice and Choice in the Student-Centered Classroom.* York, ME: Stenhouse, 1994.

Using independent reading and cooperative learning, Daniels shows you how to integrate literature circles into your classroom. Illustrated by the stories of 22 classroom teachers, this practical book provides strategies and examples to help teachers offer students varied roles in reading groups.

Langer, Judith A. *Envisioning Literature: Literary Understanding and Literature Instruction.* New York: Teachers College P, 1995.

This book is a bit more theoretical than many of those suggested in this chapter, but don't let that scare you off. It is well informed, well written, and thoroughly grounded in best practice. Langer takes the reader into classrooms and illustrates her points with student/teacher dialogue and experiences, providing information on literary thought, the nature of literary experience, and how to reach students for whom reading is a foreign (and even unpleasant) experience. Langer's central focus, as the title implies, is *envisionment*, "text-worlds in the mind," which are individual and a product of culture and experience.

Using the Classics

Davis, James, and Ronald E. Salomone, eds. *Teaching Shakespeare Today: Practical Approaches and Productive Strategies.* Urbana, IL: NCTE, 1993.

> Thirty-two essays on teaching Shakespeare fill this book with practical tips for the classroom. Approaching the plays, performing them, dealing with "difficult situations" in Shakespeare, and looking at frequently and infrequently taught plays makes this a useful handbook for the novice or even veteran Shakespeare teacher.

Edgar, Christopher, and Ron Padgett, eds. *Classics in the Classroom: Using Great Literature to Teach Writing.* New York: Teachers & Writers Collaborative, 1999.

> This book is based on students' creative responses to some of the most central classics texts, including Greek myths, *The Epic of Gilgamesh, Beowulf,* and the works of Ovid, Homer, Chaucer, Sophocles, and Catullus, among others. Generously illustrated with student work, this book is intriguing in its range of literature and encouraging in its firm belief that the classics can inspire students.

Rygiel, Mary Ann. *Shakespeare among Schoolchildren: Approaches for the Secondary Classroom.* Urbana, IL: NCTE, 1992.

> Four plays—*Romeo and Juliet, Julius Caesar, Hamlet,* and *Macbeth*—form the centerpiece of this useful book, which gives teachers ideas for covering the plays and their language, sources, and plots.

Salomone, Ronald E., and James E. Davis, eds. *Teaching Shakespeare into the Twenty-first Century.* Athens: Ohio UP, 1997.

> The language of Shakespeare, performing the plays, and the literary theory surrounding Shakespeare's work are all topics of this book. Almost three dozen chapters offer the classroom teacher numerous approaches to *Macbeth, Othello, Julius Caesar, Hamlet, A Midsummer Night's Dream, Much Ado about Nothing,* and Shakespeare's sonnets, among other texts.

See also Ruth Townsend and Marcia Lubell's *Rediscovering the Classics: The Project Approach* under the Unit Ideas section (below).

Young Adult Literature

Brown, Jean E., and Elaine C. Stephens, eds. *United in Diversity: Using Multicultural Young Adult Literature in the Classroom.* Urbana, IL: NCTE, 1998.

> The authors present teachers with ideas for working with almost 200 multicultural pieces of young adult literature and also list resources which can be helpful for keeping up with this ever-expanding field.

Bushman, John H., and Kay Parks Bushman. *Using Young Adult Literature in the English Classroom.* 2nd ed. Upper Saddle River, NJ: Merrill, 1997.

> This is a friendly, accessible book which gives a quick look at almost everything needed regarding the teaching and reading of young adult literature. The authors, well acquainted with the field and with young people, provide background on censorship and the history of young adult literature and offer suggestions on organizing for the classroom, using reader response, and getting students to write as they read. Connecting young adult literature to the classics is addressed in its own chapter.

Donelson, Kenneth L., and Alleen Pace Nilsen. *Literature for Today's Young Adult Literature.* 5th ed. New York: Longman, 1997.

> For some, this is *the* one book you need on this topic. The authors (former co-editors of *English Journal*) are the premier experts in the field, and their comprehensive text stands as the last word on the history of young adult literature, the genres (romance, science fiction, historical fiction, autobiography, horror, etc.), and many other topics. Updated extensively with every edition, this text gives reliable assessments of very current and classic young adult literature and offers ideas for teaching in the classroom. This is a classic text with continuing appeal.

Kaywell, Joan, ed. *Adolescent Literature as a Complement to the Classics.* Vol. 1 (1993), Vol. 2 (1995), Vol. 3 (1997), Vol. 4 (2000). Norwood, MA: Christopher-Gordon.

> If using young adult literature is a problem in your school because others assume it takes time away from the reading and study of the classics, this series is for you. Each volume features different classic texts—from *Great Expectations* to *The Great Gatsby* to *Don Quixote*—and links each one, through theme or character or plot, to appropriate young adult novels. Specifics reign in this series, and you will find these volumes a useful, helpful set of books.

Monseau, Virginia R., and Gary M. Salvner, eds. *Reading Their World: The Young Adult Novel in the Classroom.* Portsmouth, NH: Boynton/Cook, 1992.

> The 13 chapters in this text provide teachers a wealth of background on reading, writing, and teaching the young adult novel. Three young adult authors share their ideas, and the other contributors—teachers of young adult literature—offer information and strategies on censorship, cultural diversity, gender issues, and the place of the young adult novel in the traditional classroom.

Poetry

Dunning, Stephen, and William Stafford. *Getting the Knack: 20 Poetry Writing Exercises.* Urbana, IL: NCTE, 1992.

> The authors, two teacher poets, are experts in the field, and the 20 exercises they present are classroom tested and classroom ready. Filled with poetry from the greats as well as from students, this book gives specific direction to teachers who are interested in having their students write poetry but are not sure where—or how—to start.

Tsujimoto, Joseph I. *Teaching Poetry Writing to Adolescents.* Urbana, IL: NCTE, 1988.

> The author presents a framework for poetry in the classroom, including making, organizing, and presenting assignments. He also gives specific, practical advice on 18 different kinds of poetry, from the transformation and animal poem to the paradox poem, from the bitterness poem to the end poem, among others. Directions for teachers and examples from students in Tsujimoto's classroom are provided for all of the poetry lessons.

Booklists

Phelan, Patricia, ed. *High Interest—Easy Reading: An Annotated Booklist for Middle School and Senior High School.* 7th ed. Urbana, IL: NCTE, 1996.

> Nineteen categories of books contain about 300 annotations for readers who need a bit of a nudge to get them to open—and enjoy—a book. Books included are those published from 1993 and 1994.

Samuels, Barbara G., and G. Kylene Beers, eds. *Your Reading: An Annotated Booklist for Middle School and Junior High.* Urbana, IL: NCTE, 1996.

The editors have reviewed thousands of books and offer 1,200 annotations on recent works which may appeal to middle school student readers. Nonfiction is included as well as young adult books.

Stover, Lois T., and Stephanie F. Zenker, eds. *Books for You: An Annotated Booklist for Senior High*. 13th ed. Urbana, IL: NCTE, 1997.

This reference work comprises 1,400 titles, all of which are cataloged by subject area (e.g., humor and satire, self-help, science fiction) and all of which are briefly annotated. If you have students who will only read *one* kind of work, this is a fine resource.

Censorship of Literature

Rationales for Challenged Books. CD-ROM. Urbana, IL: NCTE, 1998.

This CD offers 200 rationales for using the 170 books and films included on the disk and can help teachers choose well when making their book selections. The rationales give teachers invaluable information, including reviews, plot summary, quality assessments, and ways to use the material in the classroom. If you want to introduce material in your classroom which is not currently on a sanctioned or approved list, you may want to consult this source.

Reading

Keene, Ellin Oliver, and Susan Zimmerman. *Mosaic of Thought: Teaching Comprehension in a Reader's Workshop*. Portsmouth, NH: Heinemann, 1997.

Using their own reading processes as a foundation, the authors discuss what happens—and does not happen—with the students they teach and the many teachers they observed in the Denver, Colorado, schools. A helpful appendix offers a chart of reading models, a schedule for reader's workshop, and a series of reading strategies for students.

Weaver, Constance, ed. *Practicing What We Know: Informed Reading Instruction*. Urbana, IL: NCTE, 1998.

This collection of 33 essays covers the waterfront in reading, including phonics, word skills, and miscue analysis, and gives classroom teachers, not just reading specialists, strategies and ideas for improving student reading.

Wilhelm, Jeffrey. *"You Gotta BE the Book": Teaching Engaged and Reflective Reading with Adolescents*. New York: Teachers College P/NCTE, 1997.

While this popular and well-regarded book contains much reading theory, it also provides practical advice for dealing with reluctant readers. Wilhelm offers suggestions for using creative approaches to reading, including drama and media. An appendix gives teachers guidance on what readers do and what questions teachers can ask, and it suggests possible activities.

Writing

Edgar, Christopher, and Ron Padgett, eds. *Classics in the Classroom: Using Great Literature to Teach Writing.* New York: Teachers & Writers Collaborative, 1999.

This unusual book contains ideas for "imaginative approaches to the classics" which can stimulate student writing. Among the classics presented are Homer's *Odyssey*, Sophocles' *Oedipus Rex*, Ovid's *Art of Love*, Dante's *Inferno*, Ellison's *Invisible Man*, and Whitman's "Song of Myself."

Kirby, Dan, and Tom Liner, with Ruth Vinz. *Inside Out: Developmental Strategies for Teaching Writing.* 2nd ed. Portsmouth, NH: Boynton/Cook, 1988.

The authors would be the first to tell you that there is nothing revolutionary about their book or their approach. What makes this text such a delight, though, is the breezy, friendly advice it gives and the vision the writers paint of a classroom which is friendly to writing and friendly to students. Most readers never tire of the strategies and the way in which they are presented. If you are a bit puzzled about writing in your classroom, *Inside/Out* will give you ideas and confidence.

Romano, Tom. *Writing with Passion: Life Stories, Multiple Genres.* Portsmouth, NH: Boynton/Cook, 1995.

Within the framework of telling his personal stories, Romano presents a multiplicity of ways to invite students to write and to work on their writing. Centering on student choice and interest, Romano convincingly shows how students can find success in the multigenre research paper, in experiments of voice and alternate style, and through reading poetry and prose. Written in a lively, compelling style, this book practices what it preaches.

Spandel, Vicki and Richard Stiggins. *Creating Writers: Linking Writing Assessment and Instruction.* 2nd ed. New York: Longman, 1997.

This is one of the most practical books I have encountered, and I trust the authors implicitly. If you are interested in issues of assessing writing, the authors provide excellent strategies for holistic scoring, primary-trait scoring, and especially multiple-trait scoring. How to use the assessment, how to troubleshoot problems, and how to communicate scores to students—and parents—are all part of this excellent book.

Villanueva, Victor, Jr., ed. *Cross-Talk in Comp Theory: A Reader.* Urbana, IL: NCTE, 1997.

At almost 800 pages, this is a superior compendium of the major articles which have shaped the last 30 years of composition theory. All the greats in writing are represented here: Janet Emig, Mina Shaughnessy, Mike Rose, and Linda Flower, among others. The topics too are excellent, encompassing the theory, practice, and research regarding writing and the writing process.

Language

Thomas, Lee, and Stephen Tchudi. *The English Language: An Owner's Manual.* 5th ed. Boston: Allyn, 1999.

The authors present invaluable background on language play and the nature of language, language's role in society, and language's history. Grammar, multiple grammars, and dialect are also explored. If you missed basic background in language, this book will provide much needed background in a readable, easily understandable style.

Grammar and Usage

Kolln, Martha, and Robert Funk. *Understanding English Grammar.* 5th ed. Boston: Allyn, 1998.

For those of us who have forgotten (or, face it, never learned) the fine points of grammar, this 14-chapter book provides virtually all you need to know about sentence patterns, verbs, nouns, pronouns, and modifiers. A section on rhetorical grammar is especially useful, and each chapter offers suggestions for classroom applications.

Weaver, Constance. *Teaching Grammar in Context.* Portsmouth, NH: Boynton/Cook, 1996.

This book is a dream for the classroom teacher, filled with enough theory to give it a foundation yet packed with practical strategies, suggestions, and ideas. If the subject of grammar and usage—and teaching it to your students—mystifies or even scares you, try this book.

Assessment

Claggett, Fran. *A Measure of Success: From Assignment to Assessment in English Language Arts*. Portsmouth, NH: Boynton/Cook, 1996.

> With a real sensitivity to some of the current testing pressures under which teachers labor at the school, district, and state levels, Claggett reviews the measuring of student work in both reading and writing, offering theoretical frameworks and practical ways to implement and score measures of assessment. Generously illustrated with student work, Claggett discusses individual assignments, projects, and portfolios.

See also Vicki Spandel and Richard Stiggins's *Creating Writers: Linking Writing Assessment and Instruction* under the section on Writing (above).

Computers

Crump, Eric, and Nick Carbone. *Writing Online: A Student's Guide to the Internet and World Wide Web*. 2nd ed. Boston: Houghton, 1998.

> This book is clear, no-nonsense, basic, and up-to-the-minute. Yes, it is billed as a student text, but teachers will find it most usable too. Issues of Netiquette and plagiarism, and practical advice on online resources, e-mail, listservs, graphic browsers, and even how to create a Web page, are all included.

Jody, Marilyn, and Marianne Saccardi. *Using Computers to Teach Literature: A Teacher's Guide*. 2nd ed. Urbana, IL: NCTE, 1998.

> The authors show how books and computers can interact successfully and provide strategies and advice for interested teachers. While geared more to middle school classrooms and younger students, *Using Computers* offers Web sites, advice on using electronic books, and suggestion for how to create a classroom community with computers.

Film

Constanzo, William V. *Reading the Movies: Twelve Great Films on Video and How to Teach Them*. Urbana, IL: NCTE, 1992.

> This is a fantastic resource with the art of film, the language and technology of film, the history and theory of film, and film in the English class all detailed in the first section. Following that background is an exploration of a number of classic films, including *Citizen Kane, On the Waterfront, Rebel without a Cause, The Graduate*, and *Do the Right Thing*. If you want to use one of these great films in your teaching, Constanzo's book is a must.

Teacher Research

Hubbard, Ruth Shagoury, and Brenda Miller Power. *Living the Questions: A Guide for Teacher-Researchers*. York, ME: Stenhouse, 1999.

> The book starts with the charming comment, "May your garden of questions always bloom," and the comment reflects the spirit of investigation behind this useful, helpful book. Topics for beginning—and veteran—teacher-researchers include why one should research, how to frame a research question, how to deal with data, and how and when to join a research community. The place of students in research is also explored in this practical, friendly book.

Teacher Stories

Power, Brenda Miller, and Ruth Shagoury Hubbard, eds. *Oops: What We Learn When Our Teaching Fails*. York, ME: Stenhouse, 1996.

> Stories of teacher failure are most often never told, but this book breaks the mold and features a wide variety of personal accounts of situations in which teachers tried but just didn't make it. Field trip buses unordered, lessons that go awry, and students who are difficult are all part of *Oops*. There are few books like this one, and it may just cheer you up—or at least show you that you are not alone.

Unit Ideas

Johannessen, Larry R. *Illumination Rounds: Teaching the Literature of the Vietnam War*. Urbana, IL: NCTE, 1992.

> Part of NCTE's Theory & Research into Practice series (TRIP), this invaluable book makes a case for teaching the literature of the Vietnam war, cites critical studies of literature and film, and provides lesson plan ideas, resources, and practical strategies. If you are interested in incorporating material about Vietnam in your classroom, this book is one-stop shopping.

Townsend, Ruth, and Marcia Lubell. *Rediscovering the Classics: The Project Approach*. Norwood, MA: Christopher-Gordon, 1999.

> The authors offer seven student-directed projects that center on seven classic texts and invite students to see the works in a new light. Thus the project unit on *Macbeth* involves the theme of "sex, violence, and just desserts"; *The Scarlet Letter* focuses on "sin and guilt, the American way." The project on *Hamlet* is organized around the idea of "everything you ever wanted

to know about the meaning of life." Examples of activities and sample student work, criteria sheets, and lists of related works are also provided for each project.

Workman, Brooke. *Teaching the Sixties: An In-depth, Interactive, Interdisciplinary Approach.* Urbana, IL: NCTE, 1992.

The 90 lessons in this book offer teachers background, handouts, and detailed daily plans. All of the lessons address the turbulent decade of the 1960s, and provide suggestions for warm-ups, assignments, and projects.

Journals Worth Your Time

English Journal

Continuously published since 1912 (that's not a typo, by the way; this magazine is one of the oldest academic journals in the country), *EJ* is a comprehensive magazine for English teachers. Regardless of the current editor's personal or professional quirks (I was editor for five years, and as editor I had plenty of both), *EJ* gives practical advice, theoretical background, and tons of specifics in terms of books, ideas, and practices. Most editors "theme" the issues so that each *EJ* concentrates on one topic (such as media literacy or humor or multicultural literature), but there are also standing columns on subjects such as teaching ideas, book reviews, and young adult literature. The contributors are teachers, and that always lends weight to the comments and advice. This journal is a must for you; get your own subscription or regularly read the one in your school library. Published six times a year (every other month) by the National Council of Teachers of English; write NCTE at www.ncte.org or 1111 W. Kenyon Road, Urbana, IL 61801-1096 for a subscription.

Voices from the Middle

The new kid on the block in journals—it was first published in the early 1990s—*Voices from the Middle* appears quarterly. Brief, breezy, and concise, the journal offers themed articles, clip-and-file book reviews for both teachers and students, and columns which address concerns of the middle school teacher. If you don't have much time and want to stay in touch professionally, *Voices from the Middle* may be the ideal journal for you. Published by the National Council of Teachers of English; write NCTE at www.ncte.org or 1111 W. Kenyon Road, Urbana, IL 61801-1096 for a subscription.

Organizations You Need to Know About

American Library Association
Publisher of *Booklist* and professional organization for librarians and those interested in censorship issues. Contact: ALA, 50 E. Huron Street, Chicago, IL 60611 or www.ala.org.

Association for Supervision and Curriculum Development
Publisher of *Educational Leadership* and professional organization for educators involved in administration and curriculum. Contact: ASCD, 1250 N. Pitt Street, Alexandria, VA 22314 or www.ascd.org.

International Reading Association
Publisher of *Journal of Reading* and *Signal* and major professional organization for all those interested in the teaching of reading. Contact: IRA, 800 Barksdale Road, Box 8139, Newark, DE 19714-8139 or www. reading.org.

National Council of Teachers of English
Publisher of *In the Middle, English Journal,* many booklists, and books for teachers of English language arts (K–university) and major professional organization for teachers of English. Contact: NCTE at www.ncte.org or 1111 W. Kenyon Road, Urbana, IL 61801-1096 or call 1-800-NCTE.

Phi Delta Kappa
Publisher of *The Kappan* and professional honor society for teachers at all levels. Contact: PDK, 8th and Union, P.O. Box 789, Bloomington, IN 47402.

Twenty Quotations for Teachers

When the pupil is ready, the teacher will appear.
                              Eastern proverb

Do what you can, with what you have, where you are.
                              Theodore Roosevelt

*Give a man a fish, and you feed him for a day. Teach a man to fish,
and you feed him for a lifetime.*
                              Chinese proverb

*Be patient toward all that is unresolved in your heart and try to love the
questions themselves like locked rooms and like books that are written in a
very foreign tongue. Do not now seek the answers, which cannot be given
you because you would not be able to live them. And the point is, to live
everything. Live the questions now.*
                              Rainer Maria Rilke

A child's interest is the basis of all learning.
                              John Dewey

I hear and I forget.
I see and I remember.
I do and I understand.
    Chinese proverb

There is no frigate like a book.
                              Emily Dickinson

*To acquire the habit of reading is to construct for yourself
a refuge from almost all the miseries of life.*

W. Somerset Maugham

Noise is one of the essential parts of civilization.

Anonymous

*All practical teachers know that education is a patient process of the mastery
of details, minute by minute, hour by hour, day by day.*

Alfred North Whitehead

A teacher affects eternity; he can never tell where his influence stops.

Henry Adams

We teach who we are.

John Gardner

*I have often reflected upon the new vistas that reading opened to me. I knew
right there in prison that reading had changed forever the course of my life.
As I see it today, the ability to read woke inside me some long dormant
craving to be mentally alive.*

Malcolm X

To teach is to learn twice.

Joseph Jourbert

I touch the future. I teach.

Christa MacAuliffe

Not to know is bad; not to wish to know is worse.

African proverb

Imagination is more important than knowledge.

Alfred Einstein

Education is what remains when we have forgotten all that we have been taught.

George Savile

Make the work interesting and the discipline will take care of itself.

E. B. White

Until I feared to lose it, I never loved to read. One does not love breathing.

Harper Lee

Epilogue

Diana Mitchell

earning about teaching didn't happen for me all at once. I got the basics down quickly because I was in a team-teaching situation, but honing my abilities to motivate and involve students took time. It took time mainly for me to sort out what I believed in, what was important about teaching English language arts, and what it was I was supposed to be doing.

I figured out that I had to be a learner in the class too, not someone who had all the prepackaged answers. I had to build on what the students brought with them to class, not disparage them for not knowing what I knew. I also understood that my interest and enthusiasm in the classroom were essential. I had to be committed and involved in the learning. When I reflected on the importance of English language arts, I learned to think in terms of long-term goals because that helped me keep things in perspective. I knew I wanted my students to love reading and to be confident writers, speakers, and researchers. I wanted them to know that reading and writing and speaking could empower them to make the kind of impact on others that they wanted to make. I wanted them to become passionate lifelong learners. Keeping these far-reaching goals in mind helped me measure the importance of what I was doing in class so that I didn't get bogged down in unimportant tasks. Then I figured out that I was trying to help students make connections to life through their reading and writing, as well as help them see how their classwork connected to other classwork. This was a class about life using reading, writing, speaking, viewing, and researching as the means to figure out life's questions. I also knew my job was to help students grow in the language arts by providing models of writing and reading, time for group and individual work, time for feedback and reflection, and lots of opportunities to both read and write. Once I began to understand the essence of both teaching and the language arts, teaching began to get easier.

But like me, you won't do everything perfectly all at once. In spite of this, students will respond to your enthusiasm and your caring and your efforts at involving them in the work of the class.

In those early years of my teaching, I often wished I were past the first five years because common wisdom held that it took five years to really learn to teach. I found out when I attended a ten-year class re-union that this "wisdom" wasn't accurate. I was then in my thirteenth year of teaching, and the reunion was held for students I'd had the first and second year of my teaching career. I didn't even know if students would remember me, and I was amazed and humbled by their responses. Several spouses of my former students told me that their spouses talked about me and my class and what an impact it had on them because I constantly exhorted them to think and to challenge information (I taught them from 1965 to 1967, the beginning of U.S. involvement in Vietnam). I had felt I was fumbling around, not quite knowing for sure what I was doing, but my students saw who I was and what I believed in and re-sponded to the passion I showed for my subject and to my invitations to them to become involved in dialogue and discussion. So although you won't figure out all the parts and pieces of teaching in one fell swoop, it will come to you gradually if you work and watch students and listen to what they tell you both verbally and nonverbally.

I hope that the ideas, suggestions, and activities in this book will be helpful to you. But please remember, your goal is not to be like me— or any other teacher you have read about. You are in the process of cre-ating an entirely new, never-before-seen language arts teacher. You are in the process of becoming the best teacher you can be as you combine the art and craft of teaching in a way unique to you and your personal-ity. And I hope that some of these teaching ideas will ease you into this demanding—but exciting and rewarding—career.

Leila Christenbury

When I first began teaching, I was not, I think, a very good person. As a rule, I thought I was smarter than most and, as a rule, I did not have much patience with people or even, despite my education, much tolerance for opposing viewpoints. Some of these personal characteristics were part of being young and simultaneously both insecure and arrogant. Some of these characteristics were the product of years of being encouraged and even rewarded to be concerned about myself, my grades, my life, my career, my needs, and the endlessly fascinating me.

Going into the classroom at twenty-three years of age changed many of those characteristics. For the first time in my life, and on a sus-tained basis, I had to engage with, respond to, and meet the needs of countless others. The fact that they were shorter and younger than I didn't change the nature of their needs, and the fact that I was being paid didn't blunt the compelling aspect of the work. The people with whom I shared the classroom became, in essence, a real part of my world and my life, and I began to work as hard as I ever had to live up to their expectations. In direct and indirect ways, they eroded my well-developed egocentricity and asked me to open my mind, be kind, be funny, be smart, be attentive, and be patient. They also showed me, in highly unexpected moments, that they themselves were often terribly intelligent and creative. My students also demonstrated that they needed from me challenge and inspiration. And so the bulk of my life has been, in essence, in their service, and, along the way, I think I have had a chance to become somewhat of a better person.

These people, these students, have shaped my life and led me through the years to consider how and what I teach. Because of them, I continue to work on my teaching and to seek out teaching ideas and activities which will provoke, inform, inspire, and meet my students wherever they might be.

Through books such as this one, through the work of other teachers and your own experiences in the classroom, I wish for you a similar experience. Our time in the classroom can be transformative in profound ways, and as we share the hours with our students, we make our own unique configurations of the art and craft of teaching—art and craft that sparks, for both teacher and student, genuine learning.

Index

Authors

Diana Mitchell is retired from Sexton High School in Lansing, Michigan, and is adjunct professor of English education at Michigan State University and co-director of the Red Cedar Writing Project. Co-author of *Exploring and Teaching the English Language Arts*, Mitchell has published numerous articles in professional journals on teaching, gender issues, and young adult literature. A former president of the Assembly on Literature for Adolescents of NCTE, she has edited her state language arts journal and, from 1994 to 1998, the Teaching Ideas column for *English Journal*.

Leila Christenbury is professor of English education at Virginia Commonwealth University in Richmond, where she teaches secondary English methods, young adult literature, and a seminar for student teachers. A former high school English teacher and director of the Capital Writing Project (Richmond), she is the author of *Making the Journey: Being and Becoming a Teacher of English Language Arts*. She has served as editor of *English Journal* and co-editor of *The ALAN Review* and is currently president-elect of the National Council of Teachers of English.

ॐ

This book was set in Palatino and Helvetica by Electronic Imaging.
Typefaces used on the cover include Elli, Mason Sans Super, and Adobe Garamond.
This book was printed on 50-lb. Offset paper by Versa Press.